This b

RF

Great Hollywood Westerns

TED SENNETT

ABRADALE PRESS

HARRY N. ABRAMS, INC., *Publishers*, NEW YORK

AFI PRESS

For my family,

with boundless love

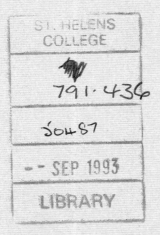
Project Director: Margaret L. Kaplan
Editor: Lory Frankel
Designer: Dirk Luykx, with Jean Smolar
Photo Editor: John K. Crowley

PAGES 2–3   Silverado *(Columbia, 1985)*; PAGES 4–5   Cheyenne Autumn *(Warner Bros., 1964)*; PAGES 6–7   A Man Called Horse *(National General, 1970)*; PAGES 8–9   *John Wayne in* The Horse Soldiers *(United Artists, 1959)*; PAGES 1, 10–11   The Cowboys *(Warner Bros., 1972)*; PAGES 12–13   The Professionals *(Columbia, 1966)*.

Library of Congress Cataloging-in-Publication Data
Sennett, Ted.
Great Hollywood westerns / by Ted Sennett.
p.   cm.
Includes bibliographical references and index.
ISBN 0-8109-8120-3
1. Western films—United States—History and criticism.
I. Title.
[PN1995.9.W4S44   1992]
791.43'6278—dc20   92-9268
CIP

Contents

Introduction 15

1 **The Silent Years** 23   2 **Wagons West** 39   3 **Settling the Land** 59

4 **Men Alone** 91   5 **Men Together** 143   6 **Savage or Saint?** 177

7 **The Distaff Side** 201   8 **Off the Beaten Trail** 223

9 **Decline and Fall** 235

Acknowledgments 262   **Bibliography** 262   **Index** 263   **Credits** 271

Introduction

OVER THE DECADES of movie history, the images remain indelible: a lone rider, moving slowly against a background of vast, open plains and towering mountains . . . a dust-laden town where snarling gunslingers, trail-weary cowboys, and demure, bonneted housewives mingle under the scorching sun . . . a swarm of Indians on the warpath, fiercely attacking a circle of wagons . . . families standing proudly beside their makeshift cabins in the wilderness, struggling against overwhelming odds to build a home that can endure for generations. From the nickelodeon to the present, these images of the West have been projected in the mind's eye of every moviegoer.

The Western, in fact, may well be the oldest film genre. As early as 1872, an English photographer named Eadweard Muybridge, living in the United States, showed the first horse in motion. Asked to demonstrate whether at any moment a trotting horse lifts all four legs off the ground, he created a technique that clearly depicted the horse's silhouette moving against a graph-paper screen. When Thomas Edison combined Muybridge's invention with other techniques, he came up with a kinetoscope viewer that filmed anything that moved. Undeterred by his New Jersey location, he chose many Western subjects, giving them such titles as *Sioux Indian Ghost Dance* and *Cripple Creek Bar-Room*. Not long afterward Edwin S. Porter, an engineer employed by Edison, entered the annals of film history with the first narrative film, *The Great Train Robbery*, which, in primitive form, launched some of the Western themes that have persisted over the years. From these beginnings, the Western ultimately matured into the durable films of John Ford and Howard Hawks.

In a sense, the Western was an extension of the extremely popular dime novels that flourished in the mid-to-late nineteenth century. First sold in 1860 by Irwin Beadle and Co., these books related exciting, fast-moving tales of real and fictional characters whose adventures in war or on the frontier never came to an end. Novels by Ned Buntline and Prentiss Ingraham turned the life of "Buffalo Bill" Cody into a series of heroic exploits on the plains. The melodramatic style of outlaw Jesse James and his brothers lent itself to exaggeration in dime-novel literature, and the deadly James boys became the heroes of ballads and tales. Gunfighters who had existed for years on both sides of the law found themselves the star attractions of avidly read magazines and books. The truth was ugly, so why print the truth?

This idealized vision of an experience that had been grueling at its best and almost intolerable at its worst filtered into the early Western movies, which gradually hardened this vision into myth. In reality, settling and conquering the wilderness had involved the constant threat of illness, starvation, and marauding Indians. A bone-numbing weariness and a mind-numbing isolation sapped the spirit and the will to survive. Justice was harsh, and death was often sudden. Yet the Western movie, while hardly ignoring the hardships and terrors of the Old West, gave us something else.

Against vistas of awesome majesty and splendor, the Western created a world of moral certitude, where the "good guys," stoically brave, dependable, honest, and true, triumphed over the venal, coldly vicious "bad guys," where persevering pioneer families planted their roots beside the vast cattle empires. In the cinematic West, gunfighters clashed on the streets of Tombstone, stagecoaches roared through Monument Valley, and men like Jesse James, "Wild Bill" Hickok, and Wyatt Earp, whose true roles in Western history have always been open to question, evolved into heroes and trailblazers whose deeds and exploits became grist for the Western mill. After a while, the rituals of the Western movie became fixed in time; viewers could rest assured that they would see the shoot-outs, the Indian attacks, the bar-room brawls, and even, on occasion, the exchanged vows of love and devotion in the prairie moonlight.

Along with the rituals and the familiar characters, the Western film forged its own set of attitudes. At least until the sixties, when revisionist views in an age of dissent and skepticism began to change the character of the genre, the traditional Western had offered certain truisms, repeated over time by Western filmmakers to the point that their audiences came to expect them: Strength and resilience resided in the family unit . . . nurturing the land was an almost mystical experience, and protecting it deserved the most that anyone could give . . . duty in defense of one's land and country remained a sacred obligation, and honor dictated that such duty never be shirked. These beliefs and attributes had long been considered proudly American, and, injected into the Western film, they formed a dream of America as it saw itself and as it wanted to be seen by the world. Small wonder that the genre enjoyed such huge popularity for so many years.

Respect and admiration for tradition also implied a resistance to change and a deeply entrenched belief in maintaining the status quo, and the Western, perhaps of all the film

The Searchers *(Warner Bros., 1956). Riders move against the awesome vastness of the Western wilderness. Many Western films emphasized human isolation and loneliness in the face of this expanse.*

PAGE 14   True Grit *(Paramount, 1969). A panoramic scene: the genre often celebrated the majestic beauty and grandeur of America's Western lands.*

genres, was the most insistent on preserving attitudes that could be called either conservative or reactionary, depending on one's point of view. Until social upheavals of the postwar years prompted changes in many points of view (not only in Westerns), the Western film could hardly be considered enlightened. While lynching was deplored, summary justice at the end of a rifle was not, and the biblical injunction of "an eye for an eye" was openly condoned. The Indians, on the whole, were depicted as barbaric savages with no claims on the land. Women were helpless, subservient creatures, useful as wives, mothers, and schoolmarms, but little else. Over all, the traditional or conservative Western implied that evil at the worst, temptation at the least, resided in the "civilization" that continually threatened to encroach on Western lands.

The traditional or conservative Western could also be counted on to take a hawklike attitude toward the resolution of any conflict. Over and over, Westerns from the twenties to the fifties implied that aggression in defense of one's home and family was not only a justified response, but that evading the responsibility to defend them at any cost was degrading and cowardly. A preordained fatalism ("A man's gotta do what a man's gotta do") fused with a firm rejection of isolationism ("There are some things a man can't run away from") to create the belligerent, gun-totin', sharp-shootin' heroes and varmints of countless Western movies. If these movies fell somewhat short of all-out militarism (and even John Ford, for all his love of military ritual, was not really militaristic), they still managed to rattle a few swords. Small wonder that General and later President Eisenhower enjoyed reading Western novels or that Colonel Potter of the television series "M*A*S*H" frequently noted that his favorite writer was Zane Grey.

When the time was ripe to reverse or alter many of the prevalent attitudes in Westerns, Hollywood, in its usual fashion, veered somewhat too far to the other side of the spectrum. Faced with rising concerns about social problems, a brace of films, starting with *Broken Arrow* in 1950, tried to rectify the screen's largely biased treatment of Indians by turning shrieking Indian savages into deeply wronged and

She Wore a Yellow Ribbon *(RKO, 1949). Trooper Tyree (Ben Johnson) rides the range in John Ford's stirring film. A former rodeo champion, Johnson contributed his strong yet easygoing presence to a number of Ford's Westerns.*

PRECEDING PAGES   Buffalo Bill *(Fox, 1944). Indians launch a massive attack in William Wellman's colorful but largely fictitious movie about the celebrated Western figure.*

noble saints. Confronted with women who had been an integral part of the wartime work force, producers began to make Westerns in which shy, demure, acquiescent maidens gave way to tough women who cracked the whip. After many years of coping with problems no weightier than taming a town or routing a villain, the Western acquired a moral conscience, at least in the examples of *High Noon* and its clones. By the sixties, the traditional Western had been largely usurped by a different breed, which purported to show the Old West "as it really was": dirty, mean-spirited, and dangerous. The "spaghetti" Westerns that enjoyed popularity from the mid-sixties to the early seventies took this view several steps further into a bleak and violent world that made the traditional West look like Disneyland. Through the seventies and eighties, the Western film surfaced now and again, with an occasional nod to the past, but by now, it has become an endangered species. The headiest days of the genre may have passed.

Most books on the Western have been content to offer a chronological history of the Western, but I have chosen instead to examine the principal trends and approaches that have emerged in the genre from the silent days to recent years. Rather than tracing the careers of John Ford and John Wayne, I have looked at the changing ways in which the genre has, for example, treated Indians and women and how it has handled such major themes as the settling and the decline of the Old West. I hope that the effort will prove to be enlightening.

If Westerns are no longer being actively produced, many of the most durable movies are still available for viewing on television and videocassette recorders. Besides their individual merit as films, they reaffirm the grandeur of the American landscape and the urgent need to preserve it. They also remind us, however much the reminder is colored with myth, that in a time not so very long ago, men and women dared to wrest a home out of the wilderness against apparently insurmountable odds. On these bases alone, Western films will continue to be viewed with pride and pleasure.

Tumbleweeds *(United Artists, 1925). In his final film, William S. Hart (second from right) starred as ranch boss Don Carver. Fourteen years later, he reissued the film with a moving prologue in which he expounded on the pleasures of making Westerns ("Oh, the thrill of it all!") and bid farewell to his fans.*

The Silent Years

"The rush of the wind that cuts your face. . . . the pounding hooves of the pursuing posse. Out there in front, a fallen tree trunk that spawns a yawning chasm, with a noble animal under you that takes it in the same low, ground-eating gallop. . . . Oh, the thrill of it all!"

—William S. Hart, in his spoken farewell to his audience in the 1939 reissue of *Tumbleweeds* (United Artists, 1925)

THE WESTERN EXPERIENCE—the experience in which America's vast Western lands evolved from a wilderness into a nation—can only be described in contradictions: As an ordeal in which suffering remained as real and pervasive as the sun and sky—and a rousing adventure in which freedom and independence were the rewards. As a crushing of the human spirit, weighed down by the burdens inflicted by man and nature—and as a triumph of the human spirit, in which the survivors not only realized the fruits of their labors but also provided an indestructible legacy for the generations that followed. On the bones and the hearts of its founders, the American West persevered and flourished.

It also endured a nonstop assault by men who were determined to seize whatever the land could offer. Oases of timber were cut down to make room for new settlements. The earth was torn up to discover every glint of yellow dust that might turn out to be gold. The prairie echoed to the sound of gunfire as buffaloes were shot into extinction. Above all, the land from Ohio to California was covered with graves dug roughly out of the unyielding soil: the graves of countless men, women, and children who were unable to survive the rigors of the trip westward.

Still, hopes endured, and despite continual rivalry for the land that erupted into periodic warfare between cattlemen and homesteaders, despite the law of the gun that often sup-

planted the law of reason, a Western civilization began to emerge that could boast some of the vigor, tenacity, and pride that later developed into the movie myth of the Old West. Ramshackle cow towns began to grow into cities. Slowly but inevitably, laws were enacted to curb the greedy pillaging that had taken place for decades and to give everyone a fair share of the dream. Newspapers of the day recorded achievements, however small: the raising of a church, the opening of an ambitious new business, the arrival of new families. The sense of exhilaration that had driven the first pioneers into the wilderness continued to give the West its very own cachet.

By the last years of the nineteenth century, however, the heady days of the Old West were finally coming to an end. The frontier had been conquered by people with a vision and people with a lust for power and gold—the settlers, the ranchers, the trappers, the prospectors, and many others who forged trails through an unexplored domain. Often their vision and their ambitions had been achieved at the expense of the original settlers, the Indians, who were beaten into submission through a long and brutal series of wars. Yet as the new century approached, memories of disease and starvation, of unimaginable hardships and unendurable events were relegated to the past, to be replaced by a romanticization that saw only bravery, endurance, and the promise of a bountiful future.

As the Old West faded, many writers, artists, and entrepreneurs joined to promote a rose-colored vision of times
gone by. Certainly one of the strongest influences on the
country's perception of Western history emerged with the
influx of dime novels. Starting as early as 1860, while the Old
West still thrived, publishers churned out novels that glamor-
ized and idealized the American frontier as a place where
tough, resolute men battled nefarious villains for land, power,
or the love of a beautiful woman. Pulp Westerns featuring
such characters as Deadwood Dick and Hurricane Nell
enjoyed wide popularity. Many of them drew on living
heroes for their inspiration: William F. Cody turned into
"Buffalo Bill," and James Butler Hickok became "Wild Bill"
Hickok, central figures in exploits that almost invariably contained chases and shoot-outs. Cody became a national hero
and ultimately the centerpiece of a hugely successful Wild
West show, which featured displays of daredevil riding and
crack shooting. Audiences enthused over Annie Oakley's
skill with a rifle or Sitting Bull's mere presence as the last of
the great Indian chiefs. Soon, Wild West shows were touring
America and Europe, spotlighting figures lifted from the
pages of the dime novels: Cherokee Ed, Bronco Ben, Pawnee
Bill, and Lone Star May.

Many writers of a somewhat more literary bent also
contributed to America's romantic view of the Old West. In
1902, a Philadelphia lawyer named Owen Wister won fame
with his novel *The Virginian*, concerning a slow-talking but
fast-drawing Western loner who defeats the dastardly Trampas. A series of novels poured from the prolific pen of Zane
Grey, creating Western images and characters that would be
repeated in countless movies across the decades. Grey's melodramatic tales of hard-riding heroes and villains—*Riders of
the Purple Sage* attracted the most attention—made up in
swift action for what they lacked in credibility. Artists also
played crucial roles in mythologizing the West; such figures
as Charles Russell and Frederic Remington sought to preserve the essence of the West in their paintings and sketches
of the rugged terrain, the tenacious people, the horses, and
the buffaloes.

Few writers of the time were willing to reject the myth
for the truth. One was Mark Twain (pen name for Samuel L.
Clemens), who had attracted attention with the publication
of *Innocents Abroad* (1869), a humorous, biting narrative
of his journey from Europe to the Holy Land. In *Roughing
It* (1872), Twain described the trip he had taken with his
brother from Missouri to Nevada Territory when his brother
was appointed secretary of the Territory. Rather than an idealized view, Twain offered a clear-eyed, frequently harsh, and
always unsentimental account of a once nearly uninhabited
land in the throes of transition. Wickedly funny anecdotes

and tall stories mingled with unflinching accounts of summary justice, vicious bigotry, and grinding hardships. In
place of an uplifting narrative of pioneer courage, Twain presented this vividly real account of his stagecoach journey
through the desert:

> The poetry was all in the anticipation—there is none in
> the reality. Imagine a vast, waveless ocean stricken dead
> and turned to ashes; imagine this solemn waste tufted
> with ash-dusted sage bushes; imagine the lifeless silence
> and solitude that belong to such a place; imagine a
> coach, creeping like a bug through the midst of this
> shoreless level, and sending up tumbled volumes of
> dust, as if it were a bug that went by steam; imagine this
> aching monotony of toiling and plowing kept up hour
> after hour, and the shore still as far away as ever, appar-
> ently; imagine team, driver, coach, and passengers so
> deeply coated with ashes that they are all one colorless
> color; imagine ash drifts roosting above mustaches and
> eyebrows like snow accumulations on boughs and
> bushes. This is the reality of it. . . . a thirsty, sweltering,
> longing, hateful reality!

Clearly, Twain's unblinkered view of the Old West was
infinitely less preferable to avid readers than the adventure-
some fantasies of Zane Grey, and when Grey's novels and
similar books soared in popularity, the burgeoning interest in
the Old West was not lost on those responsible for the infancy
of motion pictures. In his New Jersey laboratory, Thomas
Edison created a machine called the kinetoscope, which
allowed a single viewer to watch a brief flickering movie.
The idea caught on, and rows of machines, grouped in
penny arcades, blossomed across the country. When Edison invented a projector that permitted a group of people to
watch the same movie, he looked for subjects to photograph.
With little hesitation he chose the colorful West, photographing Indian dances, a bucking bronco, and a group of Western
dandies lounging in a bar.

It was inevitable that the film pioneers after Edison,
planting their roots in the soil of California, would turn to the
body of literature and myth concerning the West for their first
endeavors. For one thing, many of the cowboys and even
some of the notorious outlaws who had actually ridden the
plains were still available to tell their stories and to add a realistic note in front of the cameras. For another, horses and
cattle could be mustered nearby to bring authenticity to even
the slightest tale. Figures known to the public, such as "Buffalo Bill" Cody, could be called upon to make an appearance
on film. Like Edison's primitive efforts, many of the first movies made in California depicted Western scenes, crudely
staged and with little pretense of reality.

The Great Train Robbery *(The Edison Company, 1903). This landmark Western film featured a startling last frame in which the gunslinger (George Barnes) fired twice directly into the camera and then vanished behind the smoke.*

However, by the early years of the new century, the novelty of brief moving films was starting to fade. Audiences were growing weary of the same scenes, and the ramshackle movie theaters had gained notorious reputations as firetraps or gathering places for sinful activities. It took a man named Edwin S. Porter, a director and cameraman working for Edison, to move motion pictures to a new and more sophisticated level. After creating a 425-foot-long movie called *The Life of an American Fireman* in 1902, Porter decided to make a nearly reel-long film with a Western setting that would contain an actual story concerning a train robbery and the pursuit and capture of the criminals. The resulting movie, *The Great Train Robbery* (1903), turned out to be a landmark in film annals. For the first time, cinematic techniques were used to tell a story—Porter's shrewdly edited images advanced the narrative frame by frame, generating an excitement that no movie before it had approached.

In the opening shot, Porter used superimposition to show an arriving train as viewed through the window of a railroad telegraph office. After bandits enter and tie up the telegraph operator, the film moves with ease from the exterior locale to an interior set of the train's express car, a feat remarkable for a time when single sets and single time spans were the norm. For the scene in which the bandits rush into the car and do battle with the drivers, Porter used skillful stop-motion photography, substituting dummies for the actors to film the characters being thrown from the moving train. He even added a startlingly realistic touch—when passengers rush from the train to escape the robbers, one of them is shot down in cold blood. Although primitive in execution, these scenes carry a degree of credibility and suggest that Porter was deliberately trying to avoid glamorizing the outlaws.

Once the robbery is committed and the bandits flee into the woods, Porter generates a bit of suspense by having the telegraph operator's little daughter discover her father's plight. He then adds a touch of authentic flavor by cutting to a lively dance hall in town, where Westerners force a tenderfoot to dance by shooting at his heels. In the film's final section, the bandits are chased and caught in a series of primitive action scenes. By the time a gunslinger (George Barnes), at the movie's end, fires twice into the camera and disappears behind the billowing smoke, film history had clearly been made. The movie, hugely popular with audiences, prompted many unabashed imitations. Porter himself remained an influential force in films through the first decade of the century.

With the success of *The Great Train Robbery*, Edison continued to turn out brief Western films, including one called *The Little Train Robbery* (1905), in which a gang of children hold up a miniature train and are captured by policemen in rowboats. Another, entitled *Rescued from an Eagle's Nest* (1907), featured an aspiring young actor named D. W. Griffith as the father of a baby abducted by a patently fake eagle. Other companies started producing Western films, turning away from New Jersey settings to the more natural background of California. Gradually, the soon-to-be-familiar ingredients began to appear in primitive form; *A Race for Millions* (1906), for example, included a car racing a train, a showdown in the deserted main street, and a sneering, mustached, hard-drinking villain.

In 1908 a major figure in the development of the Western arrived on the scene in the unlikely person of a photographer's model and actor named Max Aronson. A beefy man with no ranch or rodeo experience, Aronson had played featured roles in Westerns, including one of the bandits in *The Great Train Robbery*, before making a short film called *Bron-*

cho Billy and the Baby, adapted from a story by Peter B. Kyne. The plot concerned a sentimental badman who surrenders his freedom to help a critically ill child (a plot that was to appear more than once in the future). The movie pleased the public to the extent that Aronson adopted the name of Gilbert ("Broncho Billy") Anderson and wrote, directed, and starred in nearly four hundred popular one- and two-reel Westerns, each with its own plot drawn from pulp magazines and dime novels. As the rugged "Billy," whose situation and even occupation could change from movie to movie, this stocky and unhandsome actor became, in fact, the first identifiable hero of Western movies and the first actor to be given screen credit. Filmed mostly against California locations, his "Broncho Billy" Westerns used many of the plot lines that became basic to the genre, and Anderson, despite (or, perhaps, because of) his endearing awkwardness, enjoyed a huge following. Anderson continued to make films after his popularity waned, but he ultimately drifted into oblivion. His only recognition came with a special Oscar in 1957 for "his contributions to the development of motion pictures as entertainment." He died in 1971, aged eighty-eight.

About the same time that "Broncho Billy" was attracting audiences, directors new to film were turning to the Western for their maiden efforts. Coming to California after years as an actor, writer, and manager in the theater, Cecil B. DeMille launched his film career by coproducing and codirecting (with Oscar Apfel) a well-received six-reel movie called *The Squaw Man* (1914), based on a popular stage play. Dustin Farnum starred as a disgraced English earl whose adventures on the Western frontier bring him a squaw and a half-breed son. Eventually his name is cleared and he inherits an earldom, but not before he accidentally (and conveniently) shoots his wife. Often cited erroneously as the first important Hollywood production, *The Squaw Man* nevertheless helped to establish Hollywood as the heart of the nation's film industry.

DeMille also directed the first film adaptation of *The Virginian* (1914), the perennial Owen Wister story, with Dustin Farnum as the uncompromising lawman whose code of honor is so severe that he is not above hanging his best

The Deserter (New York Motion Pictures, 1912). Indians prepare for an attack in Thomas Ince's Western. To heighten the realism of his movies, Ince hired an entire Wild West show made up of cowboys, trick riders, Indians, horses, buffalo, and cattle.

friend. The movie featured the classic encounter between the Virginian and the villainous Trampas; when Trampas flings a curse at the Virginian, the lawman replies, "If you want to call me that, smile." Another recurrent Western tale, Rex Beach's *The Spoilers*, also had its first film version around this time, starring Dustin Farnum's burly brother William. Its final fistic battle in a saloon became the eagerly awaited highlight of four subsequent remakes.

In addition to DeMille, other major directors-to-be chose the Western for their initial efforts. In 1908, during his first month behind the camera at Biograph Studios, D. W. Griffith made three movies with Western settings: *The Fight for Freedom*, *The Redman and the Child*, and *The Greaser's Gauntlet*. As he began to work more frequently in California than in New Jersey, he chose increasingly to use Western locales for his backgrounds; many of his films made around 1912 feature such actresses as Blanche Sweet and Mary Pickford in dramatic tales of love and death in the desert. *Fighting Blood*, *The Wanderer*, and *The Goddess of Sagebrush Gulch* are among the movies that revealed Griffith's maturing cinematic skill and his penchant for stories of sweeping action. His many Westerns for Biograph peaked with *The Battle at Elderbush Gulch* (1913), a tightly made two-reel film in which future Griffith stars Lillian Gish and Mae Marsh appear as a young mother and a child caught up in savage Indian warfare. The simple story of settlers rescued from the Indians not only boasted good photography and expert editing but also demonstrated that Griffith was beginning to develop his cinematic language, using close-ups and panoramic shots for dramatic emphasis.

The highly influential producer-director Thomas Ince also found his cinematic roots in the Western. Like Griffith, Ince had come from the theater, but not long after his arrival in California in 1911, he knew he had found his niche in the burgeoning film industry. He began producing and directing Western films that depended for their success on carefully structured shooting scripts and economical production methods. Working ceaselessly, he strove to create Western films that resembled documentaries in their scrupulous attention to detail. To ensure this quality, and to give the public a fair share of lavish Western action, Ince bought an entire Wild West show and stocked his studio in Venice, built on nearly twenty thousand acres of land, with horses, buffaloes, Western props, and authentic Indians and cowboys who were exceptionally skilled in shooting and riding. The studio, eventually known as Inceville, became a breeding ground for movie cowboys, including Tom Mix and Buck Jones.

In the early years, Ince directed or codirected all of his films, giving them much of Griffith's sweep while offering subtler characterizations as well as action sequences built more on solid planning than on instinct. Even more than Griffith, Ince stressed the moral issues in his stories; his movies were filled with hellfire ministers, weak or bad men who find redemption, and wicked women who give up their sinful ways. Very often, the cost of salvation is high; Ince's heroes and heroines tend to die tragic deaths. For all their moral zeal, however, Ince's Westerns included their share of spectacular action. In such films as *Custer's Last Fight* (1912) and *The Deserter* (1912), he depicted historical events in a way that clearly presages the films of John Ford in their panoramic battle scenes and careful attention to authentic detail. *The Deserter*, in particular, contained a number of remarkable sequences (a fierce Indian attack, a military funeral) in its tale of an army lieutenant (Charles Ray) who deserts when thwarted in love, then sacrifices his life in the heroic rescue of a besieged wagon train. After his posthumous pardon, a title reads, "A soldier, a hero, a *man* marched in the last grand review before the Eternal Commander."

For a time Ince's moral intensity and his approach to filmmaking were embodied in the extraordinary presence of William Surrey Hart, the first major Western star and the first indelible influence on the Western genre. With his rumpled, bulky Western costume, his long, bony face, and an austere countenance suited to express rage or righteous fervor, Hart rode into Ince's films in 1914, bringing with him a reverence for Western traditions—he was friendly with many of the legendary Western figures—and an eagerness to communicate the simple, timeless poetry he felt was reflected in the landscape of the Old West. No conventional Western hero in the later style of the handsome cowboy astride his equally handsome horse, Hart starred for over a decade in a series of moralistic melodramas that pleased audiences with their familiar (later, overly familiar) pattern of sin and reformation.

A stage actor for twenty years before entering films at age forty-four—he played Messala in the original company of *Ben Hur* in 1899—Hart joined his former roommate and acting colleague Thomas Ince at the California studios of the New York Motion Picture Company, which Ince headed. Starting as a villain in his first two-reelers, Hart graduated to a five-reeler entitled *The Bargain* (1914), which he coauthored. It was so successful that Ince rushed him into another movie, *On the Night Stage* (1914), in which he again attracted attention as a badman, this one named "Texas." Hart had returned to New York, expecting to resume his career as a stage actor, but Ince, realizing that he had the makings of a star, summoned him back and offered him a contract as a director-actor.

Starting with two-reelers, Hart soon established the format he would follow with little variation for the rest of his career, casting himself (under his own direction) as the good-

Hell's Hinges (Triangle, 1916). Outlaw Blaze Tracey (William S. Hart) finds himself attracted to demure Faith Henley (Clara Williams), whose brother (Jack Standing) is a minister. Hart himself directed the film, revealing a surprising aptitude for handling large-scale scenes, evident in the rousing climax.

bad man, whether bandit, gambler, gunfighter, or sheriff, whose nobler instincts finally triumphed, sometimes through the devotion of a good woman. Some of the titles—*The Sheriff's Streak of Yellow* (1915), *The Conversion of Frosty Blake* (1915), *Keno Bates—Liar* (1915)—betrayed his intensely moral stance; all of these two-reelers revealed his concern with realistic detail, even in the most melodramatic of stories. There is nothing glamorous in his settings: his Western streets are thick with dust, and his Western buildings are tumbledown shacks. In *Keno Bates—Liar*, a typical entry, Hart plays the soft-spoken owner of a gambling hall who shoots a fleeing bandit, then lies to the bandit's sister, whom he has come to love, about her brother's evil ways and his own role in the killing. When the girl learns the truth, she forgives Keno, and "the sun of love has dissolved the clouds of misunderstanding."

When Hart moved with Ince to the newly formed Triangle Company in 1915, he starred in and directed or codirected some of his most memorable films. (Ince had joined D. W. Griffith and Mack Sennett as the third corner of the triangle.) Full-length features that allowed Hart to flesh out the basic plot lines, these films reiterated his fundamental concern with honor, sacrifice, and redemption while assuring a reasonable amount of fast-moving Western action. *The Aryan* (1916) cast him as a bitter man who finds peace of mind when he saves a beleaguered farm community from bad men, while *Wolf Lowry* (1917) found him playing a hardened rancher who sacrifices his happiness for the woman he loves. Frequently, Hart played nihilistic outlaws who melt before the heroine's gaze; love reforms him in *The Return of Draw Egan* (1916) and *The Devil's Double* (1916), and in *The Gun Fighter* (1917), he even gives up his life to ensure the heroine's safety.

During his Triangle period, Hart did his best work in *Hell's Hinges* (1916). He played Blaze Tracey, a gunfighter introduced in a title as "a man-killer whose philosophy of life is summed up in the creed 'Shoot first and do your disputin' afterward.'" As portrayed by Hart, Blaze appears to be burn-

ing with his own white hot flame, but one look at the minister's sister, Faith, and the fierce tiger becomes a love-smitten kitten. "When I look at you," he tells her, "I feel I've been ridin' the wrong trail." Unfortunately, Faith resides in the town of Hell's Hinges, which evil men have turned into "a gun-fighting, man-killing, devil's den of iniquity that scorched even the sun-parched soil on which it stood."

When Faith's weakling brother is seduced by the local tart at the behest of the villainous "Silk" Miller, Blaze sets out to destroy the sinners of Hell's Hinges, even at the cost of destroying the town. ("I'm shootin' straight tonight and I'm plumb willin' to kill!") Aided by cameraman Joseph August, Hart as star and director (with Clifford Smith) invested the climactic sequences with a ferocity and a verisimilitude astonishing for this time. The wild melee between the good and bad citizens of the town singes the screen, and the view of Blaze Tracey amid the flames, his face smoldering with

the blind rage of retribution, remains one of the memorable images of the early silent years. It lingers even after the flowery title tells us of peace and enthuses about the "baby dawn" that "wreathes the gray horns of the mountains with ribbons of rose and gold."

In 1917, Hart left Triangle to follow Ince to Artcraft Productions, a distribution company for Famous Players-Lasky (soon to become Paramount Pictures). Here, after a bitter falling out with Ince, he produced and starred in a new series of Westerns, many under the direction of Lambert Hillyer, that synthesized his concerns. Over the next eight years, whether playing an outlaw or a lawman, Hart could be counted on to turn away from the path of hedonism and corruption to ride the trail to decency and self-respect. Occasionally, Hart played surprising variations on his theme: in *Branding Broadway* (1918), he was a tough gunman looking for adventure in New York City, and in *The Money Corral*

(1919), he portrayed a cowpuncher who cleans up the Chicago underworld. Most of the time, however, Hart kept his franchise on the wide open spaces in such movies as *Selfish Yates* (1918), *Breed of Men* (1919), and *The Toll Gate* (1920). In the latter film, directed by Lambert Hillyer, he played Black Deering, a betrayed outlaw who falls in love with his betrayer's wife. Near the end, when she learns of his innocence, she tells him, "They may call you Black Deering, but by God, you're white!"

By the time he made *Tumbleweeds* (1925), his last, longest (eight reels), and most ambitious production, Hart's style was falling out of favor with moviegoers, who preferred the simpler heroics of Tom Mix. Filmed for United Artists at a then-large budget of $312,000, *Tumbleweeds* represented not only Hart's swan song in films but also his personal valedictory to the West he had always loved. Under King Baggot's direction, Hart played Don Carver, rugged boss of the Box K Ranch, who in 1889 defies the homesteaders in their plan to settle the Cherokee Land Strip, then changes his mind when he falls in love with a homesteader's daughter. A highlight of the film, beautifully photographed by Joseph August, was the land rush sequence, in which a sea of homesteaders sweep across the prairie in their wagons, even impressing the "tumbleweeds"—the cowpunchers and cattlemen—who oppose

them. The scene, which later inspired an equally impressive sequence in Wesley Ruggles's epic Western *Cimarron* (1931), deployed three hundred wagons, over a thousand horses, and nearly a thousand men.

Realizing that *Tumbleweeds* marked his last work, just as the coming of the settlers marked the end of the great cattle ranches, Hart included a scene early in the film in which he removes his hat, gazes at the cattle herds moving across the plains, and says, "Boys, it's the last of the West." Fourteen years later, when *Tumbleweeds* was reissued, Hart added a synchronized sound track and a spoken prologue filmed on his California ranch, in which, in a sonorous voice, he said farewell to his audience. "I loved the art of making motion pictures," he exclaimed. "It is as the breath of life to me. . . ." He closed by saying, "The boys up ahead are calling. They're waiting for you and me to help drive this last great roundup into—eternity. Adios, amigos, God bless you all, each and every one." Hart died in June 1946, warmly remembered by those who had ridden with him along the Western trails.

With the fading of Hart, the mantle of Western movie stardom was taken up by an entirely different performer named Tom Mix. Unlike Hart, Mix did not aspire to realism in the Western, nor did he adopt the austere Hart persona. Mix was much more concerned with showmanship, offering

OPPOSITE   White Oak *(William S. Hart Company, 1921).*
Gambler Oak Miller (William S. Hart) throttles the villainous
Mark Granger (Alexander Gaden). Among his other crimes,
Granger has betrayed Oak's beloved sister.

Tumbleweeds *(United Artists, 1925). In his final film,*
William S. Hart played Don Carver, the hard-bitten, cool-
headed range boss who believes that homesteaders are "the
orneriest critters" on earth—until he falls in love with one of
them. The film's highlight was the spectacular land rush
sequence.

his loyal audiences an abundance of hard-riding action and
a flamboyantly dressed cowboy who could rout the villains
in the space of an hour. A Western hero with an appropriate
background—he had been a soldier in the Spanish-American
War, a championship rodeo rider, and a law-enforcement
officer—Mix began performing in one-reel Westerns around
1909 and in subsequent years made scores of simple, mostly
routine movies in which he was often the star, writer, and
director. In 1917, when Hart's supremacy was starting to
erode, Mix signed with Fox studios and became the screen's
most popular Western star.

Mix's films had no pretensions and offered little that was
new or original in the way of plot, characterization, or atmosphere; they were made simply to display Mix's riding and
roping talents or the cleverness and ingenuity of his horse,
Tony. Most of them contained fights and chases, sometimes
with large dollops of raucous comedy, and many of them
were filmed against beautiful Western backgrounds. Such
typical films as *Just Tony* (1922), *North of Hudson Bay*

The Last Trail *(Fox, 1927). Tony the Wonder Horse stands by patiently as cowboy star Tom Mix romances Carmelita Geraghty. In the film, Mix is described as having "the fastest horse, guns and smile in the West."*

OPPOSITE   The Untamed *(Fox, 1920). Tom Mix is ready to take on the villains. Mix's fast-moving, unpretentious Westerns contrasted vividly with William S. Hart's realistic and austere movies.*

(1923, one of two Mix movies directed by John Ford), *The Lone Star Ranger* (1923), and *Riders of the Purple Sage* (1925) revealed Mix to be more of a personality than an actor, but his boundless energy, charm, and vitality kept him an appealing Western performer until the sound years, when he floundered badly. His last movie, made in 1935, was a cheaply made serial called *The Miracle Rider*. He was killed in an automobile accident in 1940.

At the peak of his popularity, Mix enjoyed the adulation of legions of fans. He was not, however, the only Western star of the silent years. Mix's closest rival was Fred Thomson, an ordained minister turned movie star whose films echoed Mix's in their emphasis on dazzling stunts and fast action. Dressed in costumes more suitable to a rodeo than a range, Thomson rode his horse, Silver King, through a number of smoothly made Westerns in which he performed most of the stunts without a double. Many of his films, such as *Thundering Hoofs* (1924) and *The Bandit's Baby* (1925), blended sentiment and humor along with the hard-riding action. Unfortunately, his career ended with his untimely death in 1928. Hoot Gibson, a rodeo champion from Nebraska, also mixed comedy and action in a series of Westerns that brought him fame in the twenties. Gibson seldom wore a gun—he borrowed one from a friend when it was needed—but he managed very well with his fists in such Westerns as *The*

Hard-Boiled (*Lipton Productions, 1926*). *Tom Mix, seen here with Tony the Wonder Horse, was a skilled horseman and flamboyant showman who retained his popularity for many years.*

The American cowboy, photographed by J. C. H. Grabill in 1887. Unlike the elaborately attired cowboy star Tom Mix, the cowboy usually wore simple, practical, roughly made clothing, although many cowboys prided themselves on adding individualistic touches.

Sawdust Trail (1924), *The Taming of the West* (1925), and *The Flaming Frontier* (1926), which featured Dustin Farnum as Custer.

One silent Western star, Ken Maynard, found favor with movies that discarded plot lines for virtually nonstop action. An extremely skilled horseman who performed his own tricks and stunts, Maynard often filmed his fast-moving action scenes against actual backgrounds, using many more horses, wagons, and extras than the usual low-budget Western. Such movies as *The Demon Rider* (1925), *Señor Daredevil* (1926), and *The Red Raiders* (1927) usually ended with Maynard astride his amazingly well-trained horse, Tarzan, racing to rout the villains. He made a smooth transition to sound, even introducing song into Westerns, but his popularity declined by the late thirties. Ultimately, his alcoholism plunged him into poverty and obscurity.

Although few of the Westerns starring these movie cowboys pretended to be anything more than fanciful fiction, one Western actor, Tim McCoy, starred in a series of well-turned Westerns at MGM that used aspects of American history as their springboard. Brief and, for the most part, competently made, these movies were used by the studio as second features to supplement its major product and as training ground for up-and-coming directors. Striking a handsome and rugged figure in his cowboy costume, McCoy emphasized story over action, even taking the time to document such historical events as the plot by the Canadian French to conquer the Ohio Territory in pre-Revolutionary days (*Winners of the Wilderness*, 1926). Such movies as *War Paint* (1926), *The Frontiersman* (1927), and *Spoilers of the West* (1927) drew appreciative fans. He continued to make well-attended movies into the thirties, and after a few years with the circus and his own Wild West show, he returned to films in 1940, teaming with Buck Jones for a series of low-budget Westerns. Another durable Western star whose career spanned the silent and sound eras, Jones, in the twenties, appeared in a number of Westerns that, despite their meager budgets, managed to combine realistic backgrounds, reasonable stories, and hard-riding action with an extra serving of folksy humor. Astride his horse, Silver, Jones cut a lighthearted figure.

Of the many silent Western stars, perhaps the one closest to William S. Hart in spirit and style was Harry Carey. Like Hart a mature-looking man, Carey also veered toward the kind of plots Hart favored, often playing bad men with good instincts. (His 1926 movie *Satan Town* drew directly on Hart's *Hell's Hinges*.) Under John Ford's direction, he made twenty-six Westerns—*Straight Shooting* (1917) and *Hell Bent* (1918) survive—appearing frequently as a wily, good-natured character named Cheyenne Harry. Occasionally he collaborated with Ford in writing, producing, and directing. Later in the twenties, he starred in a group of well-made little Westerns that drew on his genial personality. He developed into a solidly reliable character actor in the sound era, often featured as a down-to-earth codger with a wryly humorous approach to life. After his death in 1947, Ford dedicated his 1948 film *Three Godfathers* to Carey, calling him "Bright Star of the early western sky."

With the exception of Hart's well-mounted morality plays, most of the silent movies starring the popular cowboys were extremely modest efforts. By 1923, however, the producers at Paramount, convinced of the genre's ongoing popularity, decided to increase the budget and produce the first epic-size Western drama. Director James Cruze, previously known for his lightweight films with Wallace Reid and Fatty Arbuckle, was assigned to the large-scale (ten-reel) production of *The Covered Wagon*. Basically the story of the pioneer experience—the courage, resilience, and terrible hardships of men and women as they struggle to create a new home in the wilderness—the film adapted Emerson Hough's best-

The Covered Wagon (Famous Players-Lasky/Paramount, 1923). The wagon train moves through the unknown wilderness. James Cruze's epic-size Western emphasized the rituals and travails that were to become central features of the genre: a funeral, a wedding, a river crossing, an Indian attack, and others. In actuality, the wagon trains experienced far worse adversities than the screen ever depicted, including raging illnesses and terrible starvation—neither of these photogenic.

The Iron Horse *(Fox, 1924). George O'Brien and Madge Bellamy starred as young lovers in John Ford's lavishly detailed account of the building of the great railroads that brought civilization to the West. The film used two towns built especially for it and deployed some five thousand extras.*

selling 1921 novel into a stirring and (for its time) impressive achievement. *The Covered Wagon* demonstrated to filmmakers, perhaps for the first time, the power and the scope of the Western landscape and the mythic quality of the Old West.

The plot of *The Covered Wagon* follows a well-worn path: against a background of the two-thousand-mile covered-wagon trek from Kansas to Oregon, two men—one decent but misunderstood, the other dastardly—compete for the heroine's love. Cruze was less concerned with the story than with depicting the events and the rituals in the lives of the pioneers, from the first cry of "Westward ho!" as they begin their journey to the triumphant moment when they rush from their wagons to kneel in a prayer of thanksgiving. With the indispensable aid of Karl Brown's camera, Cruze offered sequences that would be repeated countless times in the years ahead: a burial and a birth on the plains; a treacherous river crossing, with horses, cattle, and wagons reaching the bank in a mighty surge; a buffalo hunt; a wedding; and, inevitably, a savage Indian attack. Cruze staged this last scene with sharp attention to detail; the view of a distraught mother huddled against a wagon wheel with her children conveys a vivid sense of numbing terror. The movie virtually created the characters who would become indelible figures in Western movie lore: the spunky heroine, the decent, wronged hero, the cantankerous scout.

A year after the release of *The Covered Wagon*, John Ford topped his already prolific output of Western films with *The Iron Horse* (1924), a massive frontier drama about the building of the transcontinental railroad. The building of the railroads across the Western plains would become a recurrent theme in Westerns; here, Ford gave it an epic sweep that paid full tribute to America's pioneering past. Filmed almost entirely in the Nevada desert, *The Iron Horse* contains some of the elements that could be found in Ford's later Westerns: the feeling for outdoor spectacle, the delight in re-creating

(and also idealizing) the day-to-day lives and enduring rituals of the West-bound settlers, and the boisterous Irish humor of the railroad workers.

In addition to showing the brutal conditions under which the railroad gangs worked, particularly the rigors of winter and the repeated Indian attacks, *The Iron Horse* includes scenes of documentary-like realism that would not be matched for years. The sequences in which one town (North Platte) is demolished and another (Cheyenne) is built as the new headquarters for the railroad teem with vivid details, as does the re-creation of the historic moment on May 10, 1869, in which the Union Pacific and Central Pacific railroads met in a "wedding of the rails." Although the film is saddled with a conventional plot line—young Davy Brandon's search for his father's killer and his dream of a transcontinental railroad—Ford's increasingly assured directorial style brought a vigor and excitement to the key scenes. (Ford later claimed that the film was ruined when studio executives insisted on his adding more close-ups of the heroine.) *The Iron Horse* won praise and audience approval, yet Ford followed it with only one other silent Western until sound: *Three Bad Men* (1926), a sentimental tale concerning three chivalrous outlaws who join in the gold rush of 1877 and finally sacrifice their lives for an orphan girl. Ford waited thirteen years to return to the genre with *Stagecoach* in 1939.

Despite its fading popularity, the Western continued to serve as a staple genre until the coming of sound. Many directors who would later achieve prominence learned their craft filming Westerns. Henry King, already an established director, guided young Gary Cooper in his first important role in *The Winning of Barbara Worth* (1926), an epic film about the settling of the West. A year earlier, a young assistant director named William Wyler, who had been marking time at Universal since coming to America in 1921, had started making brief but tidy two-reel Westerns called Mustangs, and then longer (five-reel) films called Blue Streak Westerns. Eventually, he graduated to feature-length films such as *Straight Shootin'* (1927) and *Thunder Riders* (1928) before moving to loftier projects. Many other rising directors, including William Wellman, Richard Thorpe, and George Marshall, added Westerns to their movie mix of comedies, dramas, and romances.

By the early sound years, the major themes, attitudes, and concerns of the Western movie had already been established. In the decades that followed, they would be refined and altered, sometimes drastically, to conform with the times in which the films were made. The changes that took place in the genre—and the reasons they occurred—constitute the balance of this book.

Northwest Passage (*MGM, 1940*). *Major Robert Rogers (Spencer Tracy, center) leads his Rangers into dangerous territory. Director King Vidor took his cast and crew into the wilds of Idaho, around Lake Payette, which resembled the Canadian terrain of two hundred years earlier.*

Wagons West

AMONG THE STORIES of America's founding, the saga of the settling of the Western territories looms epically large. Recounted over the years in songs, legends, diaries, and countless films, it continues to fascinate us with vivid tales of tenacity and courage. Movies, on the whole, have shown us only scrubbed images of the almost unbearable hardships faced by many thousands of men, women, and children as they crossed two thousand miles of a strange and hostile land.

What were the dreams that lured these people westward? Many of those who had been rejected or dismissed by conventional society dreamed of finding their own place: an untrammeled area of land on which to build their own farm or home. The word *property* itself took on a new meaning and luster. For some, the Western land beckoned with no boundaries at all but only the golden promise of vast plains and a limitless sky. These became the trappers, the mountain men, the saddle tramps who embraced their isolation without fear or regret. Others pursued the dream of untold wealth in the form of gold wrested from the stubborn earth. (This dream died hard: men would sometimes stand all day in freezingly cold water to pan a few pitiful fragments of gold.) Still others, like the Mormons, dreamed of freedom from religious persecution. Whatever the dream, the pioneers endured blazing heat, disease, hunger, and assaults by outlaws and Indians. Many died along the way.

Out of hope and determination, the survivors forged the great Western trails. Starting in the late 1830s, thousands of disgruntled Missouri and Iowa farmers packed all their worldly possessions and headed their wagons and prairie schooners across the Oregon Trail to the lush, green fields of the Willamette Valley. Despite its many dangers, the Santa Fe Trail lured traders, who could find substantial profits for their goods in the bustling towns of New Mexico Territory. After the Civil War, traders drove hundreds of thousands of longhorns over the Chisholm Trail from Texas to the Kansas railyards.

The westward expansion brought with it an extraordinary variety of people, all confronting their own visions of the future. There were the cattlemen, working to supply food to the pioneers while shaping their own sprawling empires. There were the families eking meager livings from the soil or toiling in makeshift shops in ramshackle towns. There were the prospectors and the gamblers, the cowboys and the outlaws, the schoolmarms and the dance-hall girls. In the churning cauldron of the West, one could find the treacherous and the righteous, men scheming for power and men grateful for small blessings. Such an astonishing cast of characters, playing roles in so expansive a drama, could hardly be neglected by the film industry, and the story of the settling of the West has remained a staple theme from the days of *The Covered Wagon* to the present.

The early Western experience, covering the period in the eighteenth and early nineteenth centuries in which men first confronted the unknown West, has generally received short shrift in films. The explorers who sought to blaze new trails through the seemingly impenetrable wilderness have only occasionally found favor with moviemakers. One notable film, King Vidor's *Northwest Passage* (1940), adapted part of Kenneth Roberts's popular novel concerning the expedition of Rogers' Rangers into Canada in 1759 to rout an

Indian tribe that had been raiding the colonists during the French and Indian Wars. The movie traced the perilous, often gory adventures of the Rangers, led by Major Robert Rogers (Spencer Tracy), as they accomplished their mission, then set forth on their hazardous return journey. The vivid hues of Technicolor photography enhanced a fast-paced adventure story that benefited from being partially filmed on location in Oregon. The company spent twelve grueling weeks in the wilderness, under extremely difficult conditions. By the time they were ordered to curtail the production, only half of the screenplay had been filmed. Curiously, the movie ends with Rogers preparing for a new journey—his search for the Northwest Passage—which was originally intended to be the more important section of the film. Still, *Northwest*

Northwest Passage (MGM, 1940). In one of this film's spectacular scenes, Rogers' Rangers attack the village of the Abernaki Indians. The screenplay used only a portion of the Kenneth Roberts novel; the rest of the story, which was to deal with Rogers's search for the Northwest Passage, was abandoned, and the production ended, when Tracy refused to work any longer with director King Vidor.

In this historical photograph, riders move through Canyon de Chelly in northeast Arizona. Today, this area contains the ruins of several hundred prehistoric Indian villages.

Passage managed some memorable moments, none more so than the one in which a crazed ranger insists on retaining the severed head of an Indian victim.

The lives of the "mountain men" who wandered the trails of the vast Northwest Territory during the first decades of the nineteenth century were dramatized in William Wellman's *Across the Wide Missouri* (1951). Set against beautifully photographed backgrounds, the film told a rambling but rather flavorful story of a rugged trapper named Flint Mitchell (Clark Gable), who ventures into the uncharted wilderness of Colorado in 1829, where he encounters precious beavers and unfriendly Indians. The harshness and brutality all around him culminate in the death of his Indian wife (Maria Elena Marques)—interracial marriages

OPPOSITE   Across the Wide Missouri *(MGM, 1951). Clark Gable played two-fisted trapper Flint Mitchell (*BELOW*), whose marriage to a Blackfoot maiden (Maria Elena Marques;* ABOVE*) ends tragically.*

The Big Sky (Winchester, 1952). Kirk Douglas starred as carefree Kentucky trapper Jim Deakins, who travels up the Missouri River to new territory. A. B. Guthrie, Jr.'s novel formed the basis of a boisterous but not always successful movie under Howard Hawks's indulgent direction.

usually end in disaster—and he devotes the rest of his life to raising their child, who, as an adult, narrates his father's story. Alarmed by the leisurely pace that allowed characters some breathing space—Adolphe Menjou had a particularly good time as an eccentric old French-Canadian trapper—the studio cut the film to seventy-six minutes and released it without fanfare.

Adventurous fur traders also figured importantly in Howard Hawks's 1952 adaptation of A. B. Guthrie, Jr.'s novel *The Big Sky* (1952), with a pungent but sprawling screenplay by Dudley Nichols. Kirk Douglas starred as Jim Deakins, a restless Kentuckian who, in 1830, joins his young companion Boone Caudill (Dewey Martin) in an eventful journey up the Missouri River to unexplored territory. Part of the story concerned the men's triangular relationship with an Indian princess (Elizabeth Threatt), but, as usual, Hawks's most persuasive scenes involved the lusty communal lives of the men, as they brawl in taverns, drink heavily, and finally go about the important business of traveling two thousand miles on a riverboat to trade for valuable beaver pelts with the hostile Blackfoot Indians. Russell Harlan's brilliant black-and-white photography captured the majesty and grandeur of the natural surroundings. (Much of the film was shot in Grand Teton National Park.)

The tribulations of the first pioneers in the years before the massive westward journey were depicted in two 1939 films: William A. Seiter's lively but minor *Allegheny Uprising*, with John Wayne as a battling frontiersman, and John Ford's adaptation of Walter D. Edmonds's novel *Drums along the Mohawk*. The latter focused on young Gil Martin (Henry Fonda) and his wife, Lana (Claudette Colbert), as they try to build a life in the wilderness of upstate New York at the time of the Revolutionary War. Following many terrible setbacks, they finally succeed, but only after Lana, a properly bred Albany girl, discovers her own inner strengths and resources.

Although not a Western in the strictest sense, *Drums along the Mohawk* contains themes that would emerge repeatedly in Ford's later Western films. The need to hold one's ground, to defend the sacred land ("This is our home and our land, and I say it's worth fighting for!") would find its echo in Ford's cavalry films. The shared experiences of a community and standing together against adversity are emphasized in *Wagonmaster* and other Ford films, including the non-Western *How Green Was My Valley*. Ford displayed his ability to stage effective action scenes—the long sequence in which Gil flees from pursuing Indians has a visceral excitement. As he moves steadily through the night, the landscape around Gil changes from darkly ominous to brightly lit, signifying his journey from danger to safety. Henry Fonda gave a strong, sensitive performance as Gil, particularly in the scene

Drums along the Mohawk *(Fox, 1939). John Ford's lively film—his first in Technicolor—centered on the brave settlers of Mohawk Valley (from left: Ward Bond, Henry Fonda, and Claudette Colbert) who forged a home in the wilderness at the time of America's Revolutionary War (*ABOVE*). Among other things, they endured numerous Indian raids (*OPPOSITE*). In the film's climactic sequence, Lana Martin (Claudette Colbert) defends the pioneer women and children against an approaching onslaught (*LEFT*).*

in which, wounded and exhausted, he must describe the battle with the Indians. The actor moves us with his quiet intensity as he talks about having to put a soldier out of his misery. He ends on a stirring note: "We won! We licked them! We showed them they couldn't take this valley!"

If these early settlers failed to occupy a prominent place in the annals of the Western film, their successors—the people who moved beyond the trailblazers to claim the vast lands of the American West—have filled countless screens with their presence. Their true stories of survival against staggering odds have an innate drama about them. Many came alone on horseback, but most shared a communal adventure, moving in their wagon trains across the vast and inhospitable plains. Assembled at such Missouri towns as Independence, Saint Joseph, or Kansas City (then called Westport), the wagons largely brought together disgruntled farmers hoping to make a new start in the Promised Land. These pioneers placed all their worldly possessions in the wagons—pots and

pans, furniture, guns and ammunition, and even cows and chickens, as well as such staple foods as flour, sugar, bacon, and beans. Some of the wagons were sturdy Conestogas, built to survive the rough and treacherous roads. Many others were box wagons fitted with curved ribs over which canvas was stretched to form a cover against the sun and rain.

The hardships endured by the wagon trains have been recorded in diaries and other first-hand accounts. Death was a common occurrence, not only for livestock but for many of the men, women, and children afflicted with various ailments, especially cholera. Blizzards often engulfed the wagons, leaving frozen bodies in their wake. Some children fell off wagons, to be crushed to death by the wheels. Frequently, food and water were available in desperately small quantities, making the pioneers even more susceptible to disease. And always there was the threat of an Indian attack. Survival required extraordinary powers of endurance.

Emphasizing both firmness of purpose and vulnerability—men, women, and children as isolated figures in a

The Big Trail (Fox, 1930). Raoul Walsh's large-scale Western starred young John Wayne (right), in his first major role, along with Ian Keith and Marguerite Churchill (ABOVE). OPPOSITE Pioneers set out on the long journey westward. In his autobiography, Each Man in His Time *(New York, 1974), Walsh related the hazards of on-location shooting: "The trails that existed were primitive enough to be realistic and the toppled wagons and broken wheels that showed on the film were not fakes or purposely contrived" (page 242).*

pitiless land—images of the wagon train have dominated Western films from the beginning. Most notably, James Cruze's *The Covered Wagon* (1923) established for all time the indelible view of the wagon train snaking its way across the Western prairie. Other films followed in the sound era, making the view at least an integral part of the story, while softening the true impact of the pioneer experience. In the cinematic West, wagons were often larger and more imposing than those that actually crossed the plains, clothing was cleaner and tidier than the rough-hewn attire of the pioneers (at their worst, the starched pinafores and well-cut trousers suggest What the Well-Dressed Pioneer Will Wear), and the only dire threat to the wagon train was an Indian attack, although in actuality there were not as many attacks as the movies would have us believe.

Still, an occasional film has succeeded in recording a reasonable facsimile of the experience. Raoul Walsh's early

sound film *The Big Trail* (1930) followed a wagon train from the time of its assembly through its many tribulations to the ultimate arrival at its destination. A standard revenge plot was linked to the Western journey—a man searches for his father's murderer—but the movie derived most of its interest from the large-scale depiction of the first trek along the rugged Oregon trail.

Filmed in a wide-screen process called Grandeur, sequences of the wagons crossing the rivers or being dismantled so that the pioneers can make their way across the mountains had a documentary-like quality that far surpassed the awkward scenes advancing the story. Other obligatory scenes, including a buffalo hunt and an Indian attack, were also given an authentic look by Walsh and his photographers, Lucien Andriot and Arthur Edeson. During the shooting of one crucial scene, in which the pioneers ford a river during a fierce rainstorm, the cast nearly drowned in the raging water.

An authentic photograph of the Oklahoma land rush, taken on September 16, 1893. A month earlier, a proclamation had been issued that on this day, the lands of the Cherokee would be opened for settlement. According to witnesses, at noon on September 16, one hundred carbines fired into the dry air, and thirty thousand men and women began their dash across the country.

The lead was played by young John Wayne, starring in his only major film before *Stagecoach*. He was recommended to Walsh by John Ford, who "liked the looks of this new kid with the funny walk—like he owned the world." Surprisingly, despite its epic size, *The Big Trail* failed at the box office, while only a year later, another epic Western, *Cimarron* (1931), became a big hit and won an Academy Award for its over-the-years story of Oklahoma's emergence into statehood as seen through the eyes of a pioneer family. The unquestionable highlight of Wesley Ruggles's adaptation of Edna Ferber's novel was the opening land rush sequence, which rivaled the one in *Tumbleweeds* in scope and excitement.

Views of the twisting wagon trains acquired a mythic permanence in many subsequent Westerns of the thirties and forties, occasionally dominating a film for much of its running time. Henry Hathaway's *Brigham Young* (1940) primarily concerned the long, arduous trek of the Mormons, one of the most obstinate and persecuted of groups, across the desert. Led by Brigham Young (Dean Jagger), the Mormons, or at least the Mormons of this long and ponderous movie, perse-

vered despite adversities placed in their path by both man (religious bigots) and nature (a swarm of locusts attacks their farmland). The sequence in which the founding leader, Joseph Smith (Vincent Price), is murdered in prison by an angry mob is well handled. For the sake of adding some drama to the story, Lamar Trotti's screenplay took considerable liberties with the truth, injecting a mild love story between the film's nominal leads, Tyrone Power and Linda Darnell. In an attempt to make the movie seem more like a

Cimarron *(RKO, 1931). This Cherokee Strip land rush sequence was the indisputable highlight of Wesley Ruggles's epic Western. The only Western ever to win an Academy Award for Best Picture, the film told the story of Oklahoma's emergence into statehood through the lives of pioneer Yancey Cravat (Richard Dix) and his wife, Sabra (Irene Dunne).*

Brigham Young *(Fox, 1940). Mormon leader Joseph Smith (Vincent Price, front) is brought to trial by a hostile community for his religious beliefs. Behind him are some of his followers, played by John Carradine, Tyrone Power, Linda Darnell, and Moroni Olson. After Smith's death, his leadership is assumed by Brigham Young, who brings the Mormons to their promised land in Utah.*

conventional Western than a biography with a Western setting, the studio added the word *Frontiersman* to the title, to little avail.

The Mormons also figured importantly in *Wagonmaster* (1950), an underrated John Ford Western that made the wagon train experience the heart and the sinews of its basically simple story. While many other movies had used the wagon trains as a symbol of pioneer hardiness and determination, Ford's film went one step further, adding a touch of poetry to the symbol with its repeated views of the wagons against the awesome background of the Western sky. Drawing on a screenplay by his son Patrick and Frank Nugent, Ford gave the film an uncommon luster with the glowing black-and-white photography of Bert Glennon, as well as adding resonance with the use of traditional Western folk songs and hymns.

At a measured but never sluggish pace, *Wagonmaster* depicts the journey of the Mormons to their promised land in the wilderness, led by their elder Wiggs (Ward Bond) and a staunch wagonmaster named Travis Blue (Ben Johnson). Along the way they encounter a band of stranded medicine-show performers, who join the train; some friendly Indians; and, especially, the evil Cleggs—father and sons—who nearly wreck the journey with their vicious, greedy ways. The Cleggs eventually take over the wagon train, but in a shoot-out with Travis and others, they are killed. (In a gesture typical of many Westerns, Travis flings his gun away after shooting the elder Clegg—registering distaste and even revulsion for a necessary but violent action.) The jubilant Mormons finally arrive at their valley, ready to begin a new life.

Perhaps more than in any of his larger Western films,

OPPOSITE   Brigham Young *(Fox, 1940). The Mormons journey to their promised land. Although its view of the Mormon leader and his followers was hardly accurate, the film offered some well-executed sequences.*

Wagonmaster *(RKO, 1950). Mormon Adam Perkins (Russell Simpson, second from left) has a moment of contention (RIGHT) with wagon master Travis Blue (Ben Johnson). Looking on are Sister Ledyard (Jane Darwell) and Mr. Peachtree (Francis Ford). John Ford's brother Francis played small roles in many of his films.* BELOW   *The Mormons move across the harsh, forbidding wilderness to their promised land. In his biography of director John Ford (Lorrimer, 1984), Andrew Sinclair wrote aptly that this film was "a tribute to the abiding values of courage and endurance, loyalty, and faith in troubled times" (page 155).*

Ford here conveyed the essence of the pioneer experience in a series of lyrical images. Despite bursts of violence, we remember the moments of quietude and hope: the Mormons and the cowboys warily trading words in the center of a hot, dusty town; the Mormon men, women, and children delighting in their discovery of water; or the joy with which Sister Ledyard (Jane Darwell) raises her ram's horn to the sky to call the group to a meeting. One sequence in which the Mormon pilgrims dance to a tune called "Chuckaswanna Swing" has the feeling for community that Ford often celebrated in his films. Later in the movie, they join in a dance with the Indi-

PRECEDING PAGES How the West Was Won *(MGM, 1963). A cattle stampede, one of the familiar occurrences in Hollywood's Westerns.*

Bend of the River *(Universal, 1952). Cowboy Glyn McLyntock (James Stewart) accompanies farm girl Laura Baile (Julia Adams) on the trek westward. This film was one of a series of rugged, crisply made Westerns directed by Anthony Mann in the fifties.*

ans, and it is an inspired moment of simple pleasure as the disparate groups circle around the fire. When the Mormons reach the valley, they stand together and sing, their faces glowing with happiness and relief. Like many of Ford's characters, they have challenged adversity and won.

The wagon train experience figured prominently in other fifties Westerns. *Bend of the River* (1952), one of the group of superior Westerns directed by Anthony Mann, focused on Glyn McLyntock (James Stewart), a tough cowboy with a checkered past, who leads a group of pioneer farmers to Oregon. He must contend not only with the ubiquitous Indians but also with his former friend Emerson Cole (Arthur Kennedy), who joins with miners in an attempt to seize the farmers' precious supplies. Glyn's worst problem, however, is his own past history: years before, with Cole, he had been one of the notorious "border raiders," and his neck bears the scars of a near hanging. Now he is using the journey westward as his own painful journey to a new identity. In the strong climactic scene, Glyn fights with Cole in a bubbling stream, ending with Cole's drowning and Glyn's final redemption. As Glyn, James Stewart added several layers to his usual amiable, down-home persona, giving the character a fierceness and gritty determination far removed from his Tom Destry of thirteen years earlier.

How the West Was Won (MGM, 1963). In an early sequence of this massive film, the Prescotts (Karl Malden, Carroll Baker, Agnes Moorehead, Debbie Reynolds) struggle to stay afloat on the turbulent river. A few moments later, the parents are drowned, leaving the daughters to find their own way in the strange new world.

While *Bend of the River* concentrated on the interaction of one man with the westward-bound pioneers, many other Westerns were concerned, at least in part, with the events that swirled around the pioneer families in their wagons. Most often the families were depicted with rosy hues: the stern but loving paterfamilias, clutching the reins as he and his family move through the desert; the self-effacing wife and mother, keeping a firm resolve in check for all emergencies; the flaxen-haired children, half afraid and half elated by the pros-

pect of adventure. These idealized families bear little true resemblance to the West's pioneer families in daily conflict with scorching heat, hunger, dwindling resources, and hostile neighbors.

One such family, the Prescotts, prevailed in MGM's sprawling epic *How the West Was Won* (1963). The first film to use the wide-screen Cinerama process for a dramatic narrative, the movie employed three directors—Henry Hathaway, John Ford, and George Marshall—to chronicle the adventures of the family, headed by father Zebulon (Karl Malden) and mother Rebecca (Agnes Moorehead). When the parents are drowned in the raging waters of a river (a typical Cinerama sequence), the story focuses on their daughters, Lily (Debbie Reynolds) and Eve (Carroll Baker), as they move from the pioneering 1830s to the post–Civil War era. James R. Webb's cliché-ridden screenplay, narrated by Spencer Tracy, focused on Lily's evolution from rustic maiden to Nob

*How the West Was Won (MGM, 1963). Buffalo hunter
Jethro Stuart (Henry Fonda) meets with the Indians in a scene
from the Cinerama epic concerning three generations of pioneers.*

Hill matron and her marriage to Cleve van Valen (Gregory
Peck), a gambler who becomes a railroad tycoon; a more
demure Eve marries a folksy trapper named Linus Rawlings
(James Stewart). As the years pass, Eve's son Zeb (George
Peppard) assumes the family mantle, serving with honor in
the Civil War and then becoming a righteous family man and
Indian fighter who ultimately sympathizes with the plight of
the Indians.

Crowded with incident, *How the West Was Won*
seemed determined to include virtually every item in the
Western canon, from the dauntless trek into the untamed
wilderness to the struggle of cattlemen against invading
homesteaders, from a fierce battle between Union and Confederate soldiers to a ferocious Indian attack on the railroads.
Unfortunately, very little of the standard material is handled
with any freshness or originality, and the dialogue has the
staleness of day-old bread ("I'm a sinful man, deep, dark,
sinful . . ." "I like spirit in a woman.") Throughout the film,
logic and credibility are sacrificed to permit a number of
spectacular Cinerama effects, such as a buffalo stampede.
Characters burst into song so frequently that at times the
film appears to be a revival of *Annie Get Your Gun*.

Of the various episodes, only John Ford's section on the
Civil War succeeds. Eve's farewell to son Zeb as he goes off
to war and the prayer to her dead father that Zeb be spared
have the touching, honest sentiment that Ford handled so
expertly, and he also staged the 1862 Battle of Shiloh with
his customary skill; he conveyed all the brutality and horror
that sickens General Grant (Henry Morgan) and makes him
threaten to resign his command. This section has the crisp-
ness and assurance that the movie's other rambling sequences
lack.

Many films have recorded the trek westward: the extraordinary journey against impossible odds in search of a
dream. By now the wagon train remains an image even in
the minds of filmgoers who may not have seen a Western for
years or have forgotten its power to stir us with its simple
eloquence. It is true that the wagon train of movie memory
reveals little of the pain, the sorrow, and the terror that the
actual pioneers experienced. But as part of a Western legend,
it cannot be easily dismissed or forgotten.

Western Union *(Fox, 1941). The men involved in the build-ing of America's first telegraph line hold a meeting. Fritz Lang, the film's Austrian-born director, loved the American West and carried out considerable research on the period before starting the production.*

Settling the Land

"Take 'em to Missouri, Matt!"

—John Wayne to Montgomery Clift in *Red River* (United Artists/Monterey, 1948)

BY THE MIDDLE OF THE CENTURY, most of the West had been explored and much of it had been exploited. The fur traders had virtually destroyed the beaver population. New farms were springing up in almost every territory, and small ramshackle communities began appearing where there had once been only wilderness. Indians resisted the encroachment on their land in ways that were often violent, but little could stand in the way of the country's expansion. Then, on January 19, 1849, John Augustus Sutter, a wealthy German immigrant who had come to America in 1834, discovered gold at his sawmill. Despite all efforts to keep his discovery a secret, the news spread quickly. Gold fever became rampant, and the "forty-niners" began the rush that would change the nation forever.

By the time the fever subsided, every Western territory had felt its effects. Although California was the mecca, it was a long and difficult journey to the coast, and who was to say that gold couldn't be found elsewhere? Rough mining communities turned up everywhere, crowded with miners, gamblers, prostitutes, and speculators looking for easy riches and/or a good time. As respectability took over, these towns grew into communities complete with the fixtures familiar to every Western fan: the hotel, the post office, the sheriff's office, the saloon, and the shops, joined inevitably by the church and the schoolhouse. Soon cowboys walked the dusty streets along with bonneted housewives, while grizzled prospectors mingled in the saloons with the dance-hall girls. Law and order was a concept observed only intermittently—a sheriff could become a statistic or an incautious gambler

could become a corpse with a single well-aimed bullet. The West may have been largely won by 1850, but it was far from tamed, and this "untamed" West was transformed into movie myth. The myth created an iconography for the frontier town that remains virtually unchangeable—who could not recognize the towns of *Destry Rides Again* and *Silverado*, movies made nearly five decades apart?

The settling of the West hardly stopped after the burgeoning of the mining towns into thriving communities. The people building new lives in the territories from Ohio to California presented expanding needs to be met. One of the most basic of these needs was the ability to communicate with each other through the mails; letters that were delivered sporadically, if at all, became the lifeblood of the settlers, especially those in the distant California mining communities who had to get letters of credit to the banks. It soon became increasingly necessary to transport goods and people, as well as the mail, as swiftly as possible from East to West or one Western town to another. Yet neither communication nor transportation was easy in the West. Finding quicker ways to cross the plains was a precarious and often hazardous undertaking, a job that had to be done if the West were to thrive and become civilized.

Inevitably, the drama inherent in this struggle to civilize the West through faster means of communication and transportation found favor with filmmakers of Westerns over the years. The story suggests a favorite movie theme—ultimate triumph against insurmountable odds—and if these films merely used the historical facts as a jumping-off place for fiction, at least they give a sense of what was accomplished by brave and resolute men. Frank Lloyd's *Wells Fargo* (1937), for example, offered a mostly fanciful account of the founding of the first express company by two enterprising businessmen named Henry Wells and William Fargo. Still, it provided a reasonable idea of how the ubiquitous Wells Fargo wagon, carrying everything from gold to corsets, had traveled, not without incident, across the Western territory for many years. The rambling narrative dealt with the adventures of the company's principal advance man and messenger, Ramsay MacKay (Joel McCrea), as he makes his first Wells Fargo trip from Tipton, Missouri, to San Francisco, as well as his over-the-years relationship with his wife, Justine (Frances

Dee, McCrea's wife in real life). McCrea's low-key style, reminiscent of William S. Hart, suited the role well, and Frank Lloyd punctuated the story with action scenes that displayed the film's larger-than-usual budget.

Another way of transporting mail across the country was the Pony Express, which lasted for more than a year starting in April 1860. Teams of riders, usually small men or young boys, traveled to 190 way stations on a nearly two-thousand-mile run from Saint Joseph, Missouri, to Sacramento, California. They were allowed to carry only two revolvers, even though parts of their route crossed hostile Indian territory. The Pony Express figured in a number of Westerns, giving its name to James Cruze's 1925 follow-up to *The Covered*

Wagon and to Jerry Hopper's 1953 movie starring Charlton Heston. Heston played Buffalo Bill, who actually rode for the Pony Express when he was merely fifteen.

Even more vital than the express wagons and Pony Express were the telegraph lines that eventually extended from the East Coast to the Western plains and mountains. The awesome effort to build these lines and the fierce resistance of Indians to the "singing wires" became the focus of Fritz Lang's film *Western Union* (1941). The central story concerned Vance Shaw (Randolph Scott), a former outlaw who joins visionary Edward Creighton (Dean Jagger) and his team in the formidable task of laying telegraph lines across the Western terrain. Opposition to the venture comes from Vance's nasty brother Jack (Barton MacLane) and his band of outlaws as well as from Indian tribes who resent the wires disrupting their land. Vance must also contend with a pompous Eastern dude named Richard Blake (Robert Young), who vies with him for the affection of Creighton's sister Sue (Virginia Gilmore). The Western Union lines are completed, Richard proves his bravery, and Vance sacrifices his life to the effort.

Apart from its spectacular scenes (the launching of the trip westward, the burning of the camp by Jack and his men), the movie merits discussion as the work of Fritz Lang, the Vienna-born director who had made his reputation in German films with the futuristic melodrama *Metropolis* (1927) and the psychological thriller *M* (1931). A refugee from Nazi Germany living in America since 1935, Lang had directed four films that reflected his ironic and fatalistic view of society. He brought this view to *Western Union*, which, for all its familiar trappings, offered yet another Langian hero in Vance Shaw. Like Eddie Taylor in Lang's *You Only Live Once* (1937), Vance is unable to escape his tragic destiny, although in his search for redemption from an outlaw past, he subjects himself deliberately to the most trying ordeals. (At one point, tied up by the villains to prevent him from warning the camp, Vance painfully burns the ropes away.) In the midst of all the brightly colored Western scenery and the traditional Western concerns of the story, he is the one dark figure among the many sympathetic characters, a haunted man who seems fated to ultimate destruction.

Wells Fargo (Paramount, 1937). Joel McCrea (center, holding a shotgun) starred as Ramsay MacKay, troubleshooter for Wells Fargo, the West's first express company. Like Randolph Scott, McCrea adopted an acting style heavily influenced by William S. Hart: austere, taciturn, and uncluttered.

While the Wells Fargo wagons brought much-needed goods to the Westerners, and Western Union sent news and messages whistling through its telegraph wires, nothing until the coming of the railroads surpassed the stagecoach as the means of bringing people closer together. Starting in 1858, stagecoaches covered a distance of over 2,700 miles in twenty days, carrying passengers and mail. Traveling over rough and almost impassable roads, the coaches stopped periodically at "swing stations," where the horses were exchanged for fresh ones, and at "home stations," where the horses were corralled and unpalatable food was served to the weary passengers. Aboard the coach, travelers who attempted to sleep were jostled awake by the swerving of the vehicle. No food or drink was allowed between home stations, although passengers were permitted to bring their own snacks and whiskey. Twenty days later, if the trip had not been interrupted by sudden illness or an onslaught of Indians, the rain-soaked, dust-laden, hungry, and usually exhausted travelers emerged at their destination.

The stagecoach was highly visible in many silent and early sound Westerns, usually triggering the start of an outlaw or Indian attack on the open plains or the arrival of central characters in town. No film did more to ensure its durability as a fixture of the Western film than John Ford's landmark *Stagecoach* (1939). Ford's first Western after a thirteen-year hiatus, it won admiring reviews on its release for its straightforward story of a group of beleaguered stagecoach passengers on a journey through Apache territory in New Mexico of the 1880s. Reviewers praised Dudley Nichols's spare screenplay (from a story by Ernest Haycox), the striking black-and-white photography of Bert Glennon (most notably the few important scenes filmed in Monument Valley), and, especially, Ford's expert direction.

In due time, however, *Stagecoach* took on a special significance beyond its initial release, winning an honored place as the Western film that redefined and revitalized the genre. Nothing in its story or presentation was especially new; by this time the characters were a familiar, almost obligatory part of the Western myth: the revenge-minded cowboy, the prostitute with a heart of gold, the crusty but sympathetic sheriff, the dandyish gambler, and the others who rode the stagecoach to Lordsburg. Nor did its themes of redemption and revenge offer any special freshness. What Ford managed to do, by way of his collaborators and his own instinctive respect for the material, was to give the characters and their plight an emotional resonance that turned them into believable flesh-and-blood figures, with their own set of strengths and weaknesses. In addition, *Stagecoach* crystallized the conventions of the Western movie in a way that influenced filmmakers for years to come; such scenes as the Indian attack on

the stagecoach, the cavalry rescue, and the climactic shoot-out on a dusty, deserted street became the standards to be emulated and imitated. (A dismal 1966 remake only served to emphasize the virtues of the original.)

For Ford, and for his leading player, John Wayne, *Stagecoach* had particular relevance. Ford had used the Western terrain many times before, yet this was the first movie to fully capture and express his deep-rooted reverence for the American landscape—the vast plains and towering mountains never looked so majestic, and the people who moved across them never appeared so vulnerable. Although most of the film was shot on sound stages with rear-screen projection, the scenes filmed in Monument Valley made the deepest impression. The valley, a stretch of desert land approximately two thousand square miles astride the Utah-Arizona border, became not only Ford's most famous physical setting but also his moral landscape, whose giant boulders represented the durability and resilience of American values.

With *Stagecoach*, John Wayne, an actor in scores of minor Westerns, became the star who embodied these values in his attitude and demeanor. His Ringo Kid, an outlaw on the run, takes on a kind of nobility during the course of the film and affirms a code of behavior that would inform many subsequent Fordian and other Western heroes. ("There are some things a man can't run away from.") He also finds love and promise for the future with the scorned prostitute Dallas (Claire Trevor), whose maternal instincts are awakened by the birth of a baby to the officer's wife, Mrs. Mallory. (One of the film's memorable shots has the Kid gazing at Dallas as she nestles the newborn infant in her arms.)

In the rush to meet the growing need for faster means of transportation and communication, nothing exceeded the impact of the railroads. Before the Civil War, some short railroads had operated in limited areas, but the war revived the long-standing dream of an intercontinental railroad. By

Stagecoach (*Walter Wanger/United Artists, 1939*). *The stage-coach passengers leave the home station to embark on the next leg of their journey* (OPPOSITE). *From left: John Carradine, Andy Devine, George Bancroft (with rifle), Chris-Pin Martin (who runs the station), Louise Platt, Donald Meek, Claire Trevor, John Wayne, and Berton Churchill. One the set of the film* (RIGHT), *George Bancroft, who played Sheriff Curley Wilcox, talks with Charles Eldridge, a former Indian scout who actually took part in the campaigns against Geronimo and his marauding Apaches. Riding on the stagecoach are John Wayne ("the Ringo Kid") and Andy Devine ("Buck").* BELOW *The stagecoach roars through John Ford's beloved Monument Valley. In his landmark Western, John Ford took many familiar elements of the genre and distilled them in a way that influenced many later filmmakers.*

WALTER WANGER production • directed by JOHN FORD

h CLAIRE TREVOR • JOHN WAYNE • Andy Devine • John Carradine

mas Mitchell • Louise Platt • George Bancroft • Donald Meek

ton Churchill • Tim Holt   Released thru United Artists

A poster for Stagecoach *(Walter Wanger/United Artists, 1939).*

OVERLEAF   Union Pacific *(Paramount, 1939). To make the film, director Cecil B. DeMille received the cooperation of the Union Pacific Railroad, which made available the old records and papers pertaining to the railroad's construction. The railroad also gave him vintage trains and experienced crews to run them.*

1861, the dream began to be realized, although for a number of years it was sullied by greed and self-interest. Two companies, the Central Pacific (starting in California) and the Union Pacific (beginning in the East) were given the contracts, the grants, and the financing for its construction, but in their bitter rivalry to accumulate more money from the government, they simply ignored the need to meet at some point; while laying many miles of track, they actually passed each other. Both railroads also employed the cheapest labor available, the Central Pacific using Chinese coolies and the Union Pacific hiring an equal number of Irishmen. Soon ramshackle rail towns, dirty and corrupt, sprang up along the train routes. Ultimately, after years of waste, Congress ordered the two lines, which were clearly more concerned with building the railroads than operating them, to meet at a specific location. Finally, on May 10, 1869, at a point near Ogden, Utah, the two companies joined to drive in the last spike that would complete the cross-country railroad.

In *The Iron Horse*, John Ford had made this incident the climax of his movie, and in 1939 Cecil B. DeMille freely adapted the story of the first intercontinental railroad for his long, sprawling epic *Union Pacific*. In DeMille's characteristically hyperbolic style, the film turned history into fiction. The plot pitted Union Pacific troubleshooter Jeff Butler (Joel McCrea) against the forces of the competitive Central Pacific, represented by Sid Campeau (Brian Donlevy) and his brash partner-in-crime, Dick Allen (Robert Preston). Once friends, Jeff and Dick had become sworn enemies, rivals not only for railroad supremacy but also for the hand of Mollie Monahan (Barbara Stanwyck), the engineer's strong-minded daughter. After much furious contention and several major setbacks, the Union Pacific succeeds in linking the East and West coasts ("This great nation is united with a wedding ring of iron"). Campeau and Dick are both killed, leaving Jeff and Mollie to begin life together.

Red River (United Artists-Monterey, 1948). The bitter conflict between Tom Dunson (John Wayne) and his surrogate son, Matt (Montgomery Clift), forms the core of Howard Hawks's sweeping Western film (LEFT). Despite their very different acting styles, Wayne and Clift played well together. OPPOSITE Cowboys drive their cattle along the Chisholm Trail. Howard Hawks's expert direction, a well-wrought screenplay by Borden Chase and Charles Schnee, and Russell Harlan's fine black-and-white photography combined to produce an exemplary Western film.

In DeMille's familiar fashion, with directorial assistance from James Hogan and Arthur Rossen when DeMille fell ill, *Union Pacific* hurtles from one action scene to another, bearing a heavy cargo of florid, fustian dialogue. Too many seriously intended scenes come perilously close to parody—one especially solemn moment, in which the Indian-besieged Jeff and Mollie prepare to die, barely manages to avoid embarrassment by a hair. (Jeff is about to shoot Mollie as she prays, when they are rescued at the last moment.) Still, DeMille stages a number of spectacular scenes in the excessive (132-minute) running time, including not one but two well-handled train wrecks, the requisite Indian attack, a train robbery, and any number of fistfights.

With its imposing size and a whistle suggesting adventure around the bend, the old-style railroad train has always played a crucial role in Western films, sometimes serving as the impetus for a lively comic chase—the Marx Brothers in *Go West* (1940) comes to mind—or as the setting for a colorful musical number, such as "On the Atchison, Topeka and the Santa Fe" in *The Harvey Girls* (1946). Often, contention over the building of the railroad becomes the central concern of the story, as in Edwin L. Marin's *Canadian Pacific* (1949), in which Randolph Scott's line surveyor clashes with trapper

Victor Jory and his men over the building of the Canadian Pacific Railroad. A competition similar to that between the Union Pacific and the Central Pacific serves as the focus of Byron Haskin's *The Denver and Rio Grande* (1952), which had Edmond O'Brien, Sterling Hayden, and others caught up in the struggle to be the first to cross the Rocky Mountains. Trains, of course, also figure prominently in Westerns ranging from *The Great Train Robbery* to *The Train Robbers* (1973), and they play important roles in *High Noon* (1952) and its many imitators, including *Last Train from Gun Hill* (1959).

At the same time that the railroads triggered Western expansion, they also gave new impetus and urgency to a traditional institution: the cattle drive. Over the years, ranchers had grown rich and powerful providing essential beef to the pioneers, especially after Abilene, Kansas, became a convenient stockyard and shipping port. In the process, they had amassed vast expanses of land as their private domain. If they could forge new trails to the railroad depots in Kansas and Missouri, they could take advantage of almost limitless and profitable markets in the East.

Endless, arduous, and often dangerous cattle drives had long been part of the Western scene. One of the most spectacular had taken place from the Western states to New York City in 1853. By the mid-1860s, with the cattle industry booming, they had become indispensable to a ranch's growth and prosperity. Except for a three-year slump in the 1870s, the cattle boom continued until 1886, when the worst storms in Western history sounded the death knell for the industry.

Many Western films used the cattle drive as the focal point for both personal and epic drama, but few have done so with the conviction and sweep of Howard Hawks's *Red River* (1948). Widely regarded as one of the great Westerns,

the film fuses the story of a complex man whose pride and arrogance nearly bring about his destruction with the historically based story of the opening of the Chisholm Trail in 1866, in which two hundred thousand head of cattle crossed the Red River on a trek to Sedalia, Missouri.

The central character, Tom Dunson (John Wayne), is a man obsessed. Early in the film, when we see him looking out over the land he covets (a great shot by cinematographer Russell Harlan), we understand his dream of a cattle empire over which he holds sole dominion. Unfortunately, this empire-builder insists on total and unquestioning allegiance, whatever the risk to his men's safety or even the cost in lives. His adopted son, Matt (Montgomery Clift), moving into manhood, opposes him over whether to drive the cattle to Missouri or Kansas, which triggers a deeper conflict that spins Tom out of control and turns him into a driven, unforgiving man. When Matt succeeds in wresting his leadership from him, he becomes a darkly vengeful figure, bent on kill-

ing Matt for humiliating him and rendering him powerless. At the end, Tom and Matt are reconciled by Tess (Joanne Dru), the spirited girl who loves Matt.

In Borden Chase's well-wrought screenplay, the father-son conflict coexists within the larger framework of the cattle drive and the forging of a trail that will bring essential new markets for the beef. Chase suggests, in fact, that Tom Dunson, for all his failings, is the kind of tough, driven, professional man the West needed. When he tells his men, "There'll be no quittin' along the way," his face tells us that he means it. He pushes his men relentlessly on the drive, and when one of them inadvertently starts a stampede, Tom wants to whip him in front of the others. In the first hint of rebellion, Matt stops him, and Groot (Walter Brennan), Tom's faithful old friend, tells him, "You was wrong, Mr. Dunson." Finally, when three defectors are caught and one is shot (the others are sentenced to hang), we come to recognize the tyranny that lies at the heart of Tom's obsession. Matt recognizes

it as well—he shoots the gun out of Tom's hand and takes charge of the drive. The lines are drawn for the bitter struggle between them.

At this point the movie softens somewhat with the entrance of Tess Millay, who is rescued from an Indian attack. She is needed as a mediator between Matt, whom she loves, and Tom, whom she understands. In an important scene with Tom, Tess urges him to change his mind about killing Matt, but Tom is unable to relent. ("I thought I had a son. But I haven't, and I want one.") We sense, however, one glimmer of new awareness. Tom can recognize the painful similarity between Tess and Fen (Coleen Gray), the girl he had left fourteen years earlier. Also longing for peace and stability (the continual longing of women in Western films), Fen had pleaded to go with Tom. He had refused, and she was killed in an Indian raid.

Tess becomes the catalyst for the film's controversial ending. As Tom and Matt finally confront each other, and Tom begins to shoot around an immobile Matt, Tess fires a gun into the air and begins to scold them into reconciliation. The scene has frequently been criticized as disappointingly flat, and in fact it is hard to reconcile Tess's schoolmarm attitude with the rest of the film. What is wrong is not the reconciliation itself—we can accept that Tom, for all his threats, has come to realize that his need for his son is stronger than

his battered pride—but the almost comically bantering way in which Tess brings the two men together. ("I'm mad—good and mad!")

Apart from the ending, which Hawks always defended, *Red River* qualifies as a first-rate achievement, even more so when one realizes that this was Hawks's first Western (unless one includes films in which he was involved but not credited). Hawks carried off several large-scale sequences with aplomb, particularly the river crossing of cattle and men, which has enormous sweep and scope. Also vividly presented is the start of the cattle drive, rightly seen from Tom's viewpoint, in which the cries of the men and the lowing of the cattle blend with the song on the soundtrack to create a palpable excitement. Russell Harlan's camera makes the cattle stampede both thrilling and terrifying.

Red River also contains one of John Wayne's best performances. Although the complexities of his character are all evident in the screenplay, Wayne gives Tom some extra shading that brings a new dimension to the kind of character the actor had played many times before: the single-minded man who refuses to surrender to weakness or to acknowledge his vulnerability. Hawks said of Wayne: "They don't think of him as being an actor, but Christ, he's a damn good actor. He does everything, and he makes you believe it" (McBride, *Hawks on Hawks*, p. 114). As Matt, Montgomery Clift never looks entirely at home on the range—the actor's Method approach to a character was evident even in this star-making role. Yet he works with Wayne, an instinctive actor, better than anyone might have expected.

In the annals of Western films, ranchers like Tom Dunson who protect their domains (often against the homesteaders, in a favorite Western conflict) are frequently ruthless men who are not afraid to seize control when the opportunity arises. They strive to reign over vast areas of land, to carve their own empires out of the wilderness. The land is sacrosanct, and they oppose any encroachment on it with guns and manpower, even when the encroachment comes from within their own families. They illustrate a favorite Hollywood dictum that power corrupts. The Western genre includes many films in which a self-made and domineering rancher, unable or unwilling to give up even a foot of his hard-won land to anyone, sends his domain (and often himself) crashing to ruin. In no other film genre, except possibly the gangster film, can we find so many formidable men who, out of stubborn pride and ambition, refuse to yield, or who will readily sacrifice their families to a vision of power.

One of these celluloid cattle barons is Senator Mc-Canles (Lionel Barrymore), head of the embattled McCanles clan, in David O. Selznick's grandiose production of *Duel in the Sun* (1947). Lord and master of the vast ranch called Spanish Bit, McCanles rules with an iron hand, cowing the wife (Lillian Gish), whose long-ago indiscretion has haunted their marriage, and watching over his two sons, swaggering, lecherous Lewt (Gregory Peck, ludicrously miscast) and

decent, honorable Jesse (Joseph Cotten). Into this potentially explosive household comes a tempestuous half-breed, Pearl Chavez (Jennifer Jones), whose father (Herbert Marshall) has been hanged for killing his half-breed wife and her lover. Pearl becomes intimately involved with Lewt, irresistibly drawn to his rough and brutish ways. Also inflaming the situation is the angry opposition of Senator McCanles to the infringement of the railroads on Spanish Bit. The film's much publicized climax had Pearl and Lewt ending their passionate love-hate affair in a long and bloody mountaintop encounter in which they shoot each other and die in each other's arms.

For producer David O. Selznick, *Duel in the Sun* represented a herculean effort to duplicate his historic success with *Gone with the Wind*. He took charge of every aspect of the film, writing the screenplay, making certain that Jennifer Jones, his protégée and wife-to-be, received maximum attention, and bombarding King Vidor, the director of record, as well as others who figured in the production, with constant memorandums. Although he received sole credit after arbitration, Vidor had left the production following a long contretemps with Selznick, and several important scenes were

directed by Josef von Sternberg. The film was an audacious and extravagant gamble for Selznick, yet no amount of expense or effort could disguise the basically meretricious nature of the enterprise.

Virtually every scene of *Duel in the Sun* brims with high-powered emotion that teeters dangerously on the edge of parody. From its portentous opening, in which the unmistakable voice of Orson Welles intones that we are about to see a story of "wild young lovers who found heaven and hell in the shadow of the rocks," to the notorious climax in which the blood-smeared lovers, fatally wounded, crawl across those rocks to expire together, the movie never allows a moment to pass without heavy emphasis or a patch of florid dialogue. "I'm just trash, like my Ma!" Pearl cries, as she flashes her teeth and narrows her eyes to express her wanton nature. "Pearl Chavez is my girl!" Lewt exclaims, adding, "and she'll always be my girl!" in case we missed the point. "Oh, my sons! My sons!" Senator McCanles wails, all too biblically. By the time the sun blazes down on the dead lovers, the movie has exhausted not only its store of Western clichés but the patience of its audience.

In truth, *Duel in the Sun* contains sequences of superbly staged action, most notably in the massing of the cowboys and wranglers of Spanish Bit to offer armed resistance to the railroads. To Dimitri Tiomkin's thumping music, the swarm of riders moves across the landscape, filling the screen with an exciting sense of assembled power and purpose. Some of the intimate scenes (but not the overbaked scenes of heated passion between Pearl and Lewt) allow for distinctive if somewhat excessively histrionic performances by veteran actors. When Senator McCanles finally confronts his dying wife, Laura Belle, with the past event—Laura Belle's indiscretion with Pearl's father—that wrecked their married lives, we cannot help but admire the seasoned expertise of Barrymore and Gish.

Another iron-fisted cattle baron who faces dissension in his own family appeared in Anthony Mann's 1950 Western *The Furies*. In a film that mixed a sprinkling of psychological motivation and a patina of Freudian frosting into its dense melodramatic plot, Walter Huston (in his last role) played T. C. Jeffords, a cattle king who controls a vast stretch of New Mexico Territory called the Furies. (Intimations of Greek tragedy in the ranch's—and film's—titles are not accidental.) Jeffords must contend with his strong-willed daughter, Vance (Barbara Stanwyck), who both admires and opposes her father. Their stormy love-hate relationship erupts with the appearance of Rip Darrow (Wendell Corey), an ambitious gambler who covets some of the land that Jeffords stole from his father. Jeffords's treachery against some squatters—and Vance's fluctuating passion for Rip—combine to turn Vance and her father into mortal enemies. A scheming widow named Flo Burnett (Judith Anderson) contributes to the turbulence, which ends in Jeffords's death. Presumably, Vance and Rip will settle down to run the Furies.

A hard-breathing drama, *The Furies* lacks the cohesive style and pictorial expansiveness of Anthony Mann's other Westerns of the period. It gains interest only from its depiction of Vance Jeffords's ferociously possessive feeling for her father, which compromises her relationships with all other men. (She cajoles and badgers him more like a wife than a daughter.) When she learns that T. C. and Flo Burnett are to be married, her rage becomes almost homicidal—she flings a pair of scissors at Flo, disfiguring her face. Her discovery that Jeffords has hanged Juan Herrera (Gilbert Roland), leader of the squatters and a former lover, becomes fuel to fire her hatred; her all-consuming love turns into a deep-seated loathing. "You're in love with hate!" Rip tells her. As played by Stanwyck in her most intense style, Vance Jeffords is truly an avenging fury, reconciled to her father only shortly before his death at the hand of Herrera's mother (Blanche Yurka).

Interestingly, both *Duel in the Sun* and *The Furies* are based on novels by novelist-screenwriter Niven Busch, who favored the theme of interfamilial relationships in Western settings. His screenplay for the Western *Pursued* (1947) is also heavy with psychological underpinnings concerning parents and children.

In conventional terms, Vance's behavior in *The Furies*, and even her name, suggest the bold, aggressive attitude of a son rather than a daughter. And, indeed, a frequent Western theme was to place a powerful father, usually a rancher, in contention with his sons and heirs, who sought to usurp the

OPPOSITE   *Duel in the Sun (Selznick International, 1947). Despite her strenuous efforts, Jennifer Jones as the tempestuous and ill-fated Pearl Chavez—all flashing teeth and flashing eyes—never fully convinced.*

The Furies (Paramount, 1950). *Vance Jeffords (Barbara Stanwyck) reacts to the news of her father's engagement to Flo Burnett (Walter Huston and Judith Anderson, reflected in the mirror) by hurling a pair of scissors at Flo. Charles Schnee's screenplay hinted at Vance's unnatural attachment to her father.*

power for their own ends. Spencer Tracy, for example, starred as a rancher with filial problems in Edward Dmytryk's 1954 Western *Broken Lance*. Bringing his rugged, persuasive presence to the role of Matt Devereaux, Tracy wrangles with his sons by a first marriage, who bitterly resent the son he sired with his second, Indian wife (Katy Jurado). The crosscurrents of hatred ultimately bring about Devereaux's death, as well as open warfare in which Joe (Robert Wagner), the half-breed son, is pitted against his scheming half-brothers for control of the cattle empire. After a violent battle, Joe not only triumphs but also wins the hand of the governor's daughter (Jean Peters).

Expansively filmed in the wide-screen CinemaScope process, *Broken Lance* rises above its conventional plot line (derived, incidentally, from an earlier non-Western drama entitled *House of Strangers*) through the central performance of Spencer Tracy as the formidable Devereaux patriarch. His lined face framed by white hair, Tracy inhabits the role in his customary fashion, creating the fully rounded character of a man whose ruthlessness stems from an unwavering determination to keep his beloved land from the mining interests. When Matt testifies at a court hearing occasioned by the copper company's claim against his ranch, Tracy

Broken Lance *(Fox, 1954). Powerful rancher Matt Devereaux (Spencer Tracy) rides the range. In one of his few Westerns, Tracy brought his rugged presence and air of authority to the role of a man obsessed with his land.*

A cowboy rides the range on the Z.T. Ranch in Wyoming in 1921. Even until comparatively recent times, the American cowboy had a hard life that called for stoic endurance.

distills his many years of acting into a dynamic expression of anger and pride. In the film's climactic and most electrifying scene, Matt finally confronts his oldest son, Ben (Richard Widmark), who spews forth a torrent of bitter accusations. Tracy's face as the venom envelops him reflects a mixture of pain and contempt.

William Wyler's large-scale Western *The Big Country* (1958) also concerned a rancher and his family in violent conflict, this time not so much with each other as with another, less favored family. In a star-heavy cast, Charles Bickford played rancher Henry Terrill, who is embroiled in a murderous feud for control of vital water rights with the scruffy Hannasseys, headed by old Rufus Hannassey (Burl Ives). Gregory Peck appeared as Eastern dandy Jim McKay, who travels to the Southwest to marry Terrill's vain, frivolous daughter, Pat (Carroll Baker), and in so doing becomes involved in the feud. Adding fuel to the fire are Julie Maragon (Jean Simmons), a schoolteacher who owns the ranch on which the contested water runs, and Steve Leech (Charlton Heston), the lecherous foreman of Terrill's ranch, who has an eye for Pat. Bursts of gunfire, shifting loyalties, and dangerous confrontations lead to a final encounter of the two "selfish, ruthless, vicious old men," as Jim calls them. In the end, he rides off with Julie, with whom he has fallen in love.

Under Wyler's deft direction, *The Big Country* weaves some familiar threads into an epic-size canvas: the "Westernizing" of an effete Eastern dude; families locked into a repeating cycle of attack and retaliation that neither can escape; sons and daughters unable to come to terms with their overbearing fathers. A number of screenwriters, including novelist Jessamyn West, dispensed the clichés as if they were newly minted. Wyler kept the action churning (especially in a lengthy brawl between Jim and Leech), and Franz Planer's photography captured the awesome setting in all its splendor. Yet for all its size and production values, the film's only memorable moments arrive near the end. In a climactic duel between Jim and Rufus Hannassey's son Buck (Chuck Connors), Buck jumps the signal to fire and wounds Jim. Contemptuous of such treacherous behavior, Rufus spits at his son, and when Buck moves to kill him, Rufus shoots him. Rufus's grief as he cradles his dying son in his arms conveys a

The Big Country *(United Artists, 1958). Rancher's daughter Pat Terrill (Carroll Baker) breakfasts with her intended, Easterner Jim McKay (Gregory Peck), in William Wyler's large-scale Western. At the end, McKay leaves the frivolous Pat for the independent, mature schoolteacher Julie Maragon (Jean Simmons).*

The Big Country *(United Artists, 1958). Gregory Peck starred as Eastern dandy Jim McKay (ABOVE) in William Wyler's elaborate Western drama revolving around two feuding families. At one point (OPPOSITE, ABOVE), McKay engages in fisticuffs with Buck Hannassey (Chuck Connors). In the violent climax (BELOW), rancher Rufus Hannassey (Burl Ives), about to expire, gazes at the body of his archenemy, Henry Terrill (Charles Bickford), whom he has just killed. Wyler's pictorially splendid but dramatically diffuse film had as its subtext the senseless futility of warfare.*

true sense of hopelessness and loss. When Rufus Hannassey and Henry Terrill face each other against the austere land-scape, the film has finally achieved some of the tragic sense that remained elusive throughout the previous two hours.

Family tensions sparked by racism gave an unusual coloration to John Huston's uneven but often forceful Western drama *The Unforgiven* (1960). Ben Maddow's screen-play, based on a novel by Alan LeMay, concerned the Zachary family of settlers in Texas of the 1850s: the frail but steel-willed mother (Lillian Gish), her three sons, Ben (Burt Lancaster), Cash (Audie Murphy), and Andy (Doug McClure), and her daughter, Rachel (Audrey Hepburn, much too sophisticated in diction and bearing for the role). When it emerges that Rachel is not a Zachary but an Indian girl rescued from a tribal massacre, the family erupts into con-flict, mainly between patriarchal Ben, who secretly loves Rachel, and Indian-hating Cash. When the Kiowa Indians attempt to claim Rachel as their own, the stage is set for a ferocious Indian attack. The ordeal ends with death for some, and the promise (however ambiguous) of a future for Ben and Rachel.

clan by age and right, it is Mattilda Zachary who dominates the events, by her actions: she harbors the secret of Rachel's Indian heritage, and when a demented old man (Joseph Wiseman) attempts to reveal the truth, she hesitates not a moment to have him hanged ("It's finished! And high time!"). When the Indians attack, Mattilda places her piano in front of the besieged ranch and plays it as a kind of "magic" that will keep the Kiowas at bay. Mortally wounded in the attack, she assumes the blame for all that has happened. Here, Gish embodies not the fading flower of *Duel in the Sun* but a strong presence in the household.

As the West continued to expand and thrive through the last decades of the century, the dangers involved in settling the uncharted wilderness increased rather than lessened. For pioneers facing the daily threat of Indian attack or assaults by marauding Mexican renegades and bandits, the presence of military forces became a comfort and a source of reassurance. Even before communities were established or ranchers claimed the land, military outposts sprang up in remote parts of the West, manned by soldiers with a rough-and-ready approach to their perilous assignment. As the influx of settlers increased over the years, disputes over ownership of the land, often erupting into warfare, made the forts even more essential as bulwarks of defense. In such places as Fort Laramie, Fort Kearney, or Fort Defiance, weary pioneers could find protecting troops and often essential services, such as a blacksmith shop or a post office.

For director John Ford, the life-style of the soldiers who manned these outposts, and their sense of honor, duty, and pride, held enduring interest and appeal, and he found one of his most inspiring sources of film material in the role of the military in conquering the West. He was especially stirred by the cavalry, clearly relishing the image of cavalrymen astride their noble horses, marching off on their mission with a song. His reverence for the military may have led him to questionable conclusions, but it also resulted in an unofficial trilogy of films in which he expressed his feelings without apology or equivocation.

Fort Apache (1948), the first and most problematic of Ford's cavalry Westerns, draws on the massacre of General

Although the story turns conventional somewhere at midpoint, *The Unforgiven* touches with some conviction on a subject that surfaced occasionally in Westerns: the virulent bigotry that flourished among the pioneers and settlers of the West. The blistering hatred of the Indians that Ethan Edwards brought to his search for his kidnapped nieces in *The Searchers* (1956) or the fury that leads to the lynching of Marty Purcell's Indianized brother in *Two Rode Together* (1961) suggests some of the pervading racism of the time. In *The Unforgiven*, Huston gives dramatic point to racist attitudes in Cash Zachary's hysterical harangues against his "sister" (Audie Murphy's best performance) and in a powerful scene in which a grieving pioneer mother recoils from Rachel ("Don't touch me!").

Apart from its concern with bigotry on the plains, *The Unforgiven* sheds unusual light on the matriarchal role in the pioneer family. In the frequent absence of men, many women took control of the family. Although Ben Zachary heads the

Fort Apache *(RKO, 1948). The men of Fort Apache (including, at the center, Henry Fonda, John Wayne, and Ward Bond) await an Indian attack. Many of John Ford's Westerns pay tribute to America's professional soldiers.*

Custer and his men at Little Bighorn. The Custer-like central figure, Colonel Owen Thursday (Henry Fonda), is a stern, implacable martinet whose rabid hatred for Indians and stubborn refusal to compromise ultimately hurtle him and his troops into a fatal encounter with Cochise and his Apaches. Thursday's vigorous opposition comes from Captain Kirby York (John Wayne). A seasoned, levelheaded army veteran who understands the rage of the Apache against treacherous

Fort Apache (RKO, 1948). The Apaches gather for an attack on the cavalry patrol. However questionable its point of view about the need to hold fast to our legends of the West, even if they are false, John Ford's Western demonstrates the director's consummate skill at staging massive action sequences.

whites, he makes a last-ditch effort to prevent war. Frank Nugent's screenplay weaves other elements into the story, especially a tepid romance between Thursday's daughter (Shirley Temple) and a young lieutenant (John Agar), but York's conflict with Thursday constitutes the film's core. After Thursday and his men are wiped out, York, out of respect for the regular army and its traditions, eulogizes the colonel by saying, "No man died more gallantly or won more honor for his regiment!"

Ford's love for the rituals of military life permeates the film's leisurely first reel. While the plot lines are being developed, especially Thursday's clashes with York over the dealings with Apaches, Ford concentrates on life at Fort Apache: the rowdy antics of Sergeant Mulcahy (Victor McLaglen), the training routines, and the stirring Grand March at the regimental dance. Although the movie lacks the vibrancy and beauty of Ford's Technicolor Westerns, Archie Stout's black-and-white photography heightens the director's evident pleasure in re-creating a vanished period in American history.

Once the lines of conflict are drawn, the pace quickens as Ford sets the battle scenes in motion. From the first imposing view of Apaches before their attack on a cavalry patrol to the final, fearsome ambush of Thursday and his troops, the film sweeps us into the action, compensating in large measure for the sluggishness that preceded it.

Despite its Fordian virtues, *Fort Apache* raises serious questions about its point of view. Until Thursday chooses to sacrifice his life in payment for leading his men into an ambush, he is characterized as a rigid, vainglorious, and near psychotic man. In the closing scene, however, as York proceeds to turn Thursday into a heroic legend, we are asked to make an abrupt reversal: to accept the ideas that his disastrous behavior should be discounted in our need to believe in heroes and that his actions should be buried under a blanket of praise "for the regiment." In refusing to censure a military miscalculation that cost many lives, the film would also absolve all other military blunderers, both past and present. Despite Ford's continued defense of his point of view (in later years, he told Peter Bogdanovich in *John Ford*, page 86, "It's good for the country to have heroes to live up to"), *Fort Apache* compels us to ask, "What price the legend?"

Fort Apache *(RKO, 1948). John Wayne as Captain Kirby York and Henry Fonda as Colonel Owen Thursday arrive ultimately at opposing points of view in John Ford's military Western. This is a rare color still from the black-and-white film.*

OPPOSITE She Wore a Yellow Ribbon *(RKO, 1949). The principals gather at the regimental dance (from left: Harry Carey, Jr., Joanne Dru, John Agar, John Wayne, Victor McLaglen, Mildred Natwick, and George O'Brien). John Ford enjoyed portraying the rituals of life on the Western frontier.*

Frank Nugent and Laurence Stallings, Winton C. Hoch's Academy Award–winning photography, and a memorable performance by John Wayne.

The movie centers on Wayne as Captain Nathan Brittles, a tough and seasoned officer on the verge of enforced retirement. Revered by his men at an army post in the remote Southwest, he longs to lead them in one last grand gesture, but when his final mission ends in disaster, he appears to be leaving under melancholy circumstances. However, when his efforts fail to avert a war with hostile Indians, he leads the troops unofficially in a sweeping battle. At the last minute, Brittles is made Chief of Scouts with the rank of lieutenant colonel. Except for the tiresome romantic triangle involving two troopers (John Agar and Harry Carey, Jr.) and the girl (Joanne Dru) they both love, the movie concentrates on Brittles as Ford's definitive man of valor and honor. As written and played, he is miles removed from Henry Fonda's icy martinet in *Fort Apache*; he visits his wife's grave regularly, speaking to her with an unassuming directness and warmth ("Maybe I'll push on West"), and he is not above shedding a tear when his troops present him with a watch inscribed "Lest we forget." And, unlike Thursday, he shows concern and respect for the Indians. Playing a role older than his actual age, Wayne invested the character with a matchless strength and authority.

Although *She Wore a Yellow Ribbon* lacks the complexity of Ford's greatest Western, *The Searchers*, on repeated viewings it continues to impress with its scope and beauty. Monument Valley never looked more breathtaking than

Ford followed *Fort Apache* with another cavalry Western, *She Wore a Yellow Ribbon* (1949), one of his finest films and one that richly embodied his principal themes and attitudes. Whereas *Fort Apache* had been clouded by a debatable point of view, *She Wore a Yellow Ribbon* leaves no doubt of its overriding intention of paying tribute to the United States Cavalry in the days when the West was being settled. The film, drenched in reverence for the gallant cavalrymen, fairly glows with affection for their rituals and rites of passage. Coupled with Ford's usual sentimentality and a generous dose of his familiar rowdy humor, this obeisance to the military could quickly become intolerable. Ford's surefooted direction makes it work, helped by a leathery screenplay by

bathed in Winton Hoch's Technicolor hues, and once again Ford staged the major action scenes, especially the climactic battle with the Indians, with the skill of an assured veteran. (Although the Indians are depicted as anonymous screaming savages, Ford has Brittles meet with a sympathetic old Indian in a desperate last effort to avert war, an element repeated from *Fort Apache*.) *She Wore a Yellow Ribbon* can also serve as an anthology of Fordian sequences: a makeshift operation on a wounded man, conducted in the midst of an awesome thunderstorm; the funeral of a beloved officer; the stirring march of the troops to the title song; and Brittles's moving farewell to his troops ("I've always been proud of you!"). At the film's end, a voice intones, "The dog-faced soldiers . . .

the regulars . . . the fifty-cents-a-day professionals, riding the outposts of a nation. . . . Wherever they rode, and whatever they fought for, that place became the United States." In that moment, however insistent the sentiment, Ford's pride becomes ours.

Rio Grande (1950), the third part of Ford's loose cavalry trilogy, failed to match either the dynamic force of *Fort Apache* or the pictorial splendor of *She Wore a Yellow Ribbon*. Superficially, Ford brought back some of the elements of the latter film: John Wayne as a crusty officer, this time a colonel named Yorke; boisterous comedy in the burly form of Victor McLaglen, repeating his *Ribbon* role of Sergeant Quincannon, and the sturdy presence of such actors as Ben

Rio Grande *(Republic, 1950). Much of John Ford's Western concerned the troubled marriage of Colonel Kirby Yorke (John Wayne) and his wife, Kathleen (Maureen O'Hara;* ABOVE*). In contrast with the usual steadfast military wives in Ford's Westerns, Kathleen loathes everything that the army stands for. Colonel Yorke leads his men in an attack (*RIGHT*) in the third part of John Ford's trilogy about the United States Cavalry (*Fort Apache *and* She Wore a Yellow Ribbon *are the other two). This film marked a falling off from Ford's earlier and sturdier Westerns.*

Johnson and Harry Carey, Jr. Yet *Rio Grande* has a dispirited, perfunctory air that no amount of music—the Sons of the Pioneers sing a number of bouncy tunes—could easily dispel. The central conflicts involved Yorke with his young son, Jeff (Claude Jarman, Jr.), a raw but eager recruit in his father's cavalry unit, and with his estranged wife, Kathleen (Maureen O'Hara), who, unlike most military wives, detests the army and all it represents. In a climactic Indian battle, Jeff proves his mettle, while Yorke and Kathleen are reconciled. Although Bert Glennon's black-and-white photography caught the rugged beauty of the terrain, and Ford staged the big scenes with his usual finesse, *Rio Grande* adds up to less of a summary of past endeavors than an intimation of the less vigorous Western work to come.

The Horse Soldiers *(United Artists, 1959). Colonel Marlowe (John Wayne) leads the troops in John Ford's Civil War Western. Ford's pictorial sense never deserted him, even when, as in this case, the story was less than persuasive.*

While Ford's cavalry trilogy basically concerned the staunch military defense of the Western frontier, many of the Westerns that followed in the fifties used the Civil War and the clashes and tensions it precipitated as focal point of the action. Robert Wise's taut film *Two Flags West* (1950) threw Yankee soldiers and Confederate prisoners together at a remote Western fort commanded by a Northern colonel (Jeff Chandler) with a pathological hatred of Indians and rebels. Ultimately, a noble Southern officer (Joseph Cotten) leads his men in defending the fort against an Indian attack. John Sturges's *Escape from Fort Bravo* (1953) had a similar plot line: conflict at a wilderness outpost where Northern soldiers, headed by an authoritarian officer (William Holden), guard Confederate prisoners. Here, the officer clashes with his Confederate counterpart (John Forsythe), not only over their opposing loyalties but also over the woman (Eleanor Parker) they both love. All difficulties are resolved in a well-staged Indian attack on the fort.

The Horse Soldiers (1959), John Ford's first Western after *The Searchers*, also involved conflict in a military situation, this one, however, between two officers on the same side of the battle. John Wayne and William Holden played argumentative leaders of a Union cavalry patrol, on a mission to destroy the railway lines being used to bring supplies to Confederate troops. Wayne's Colonel Marlowe, a hard-line, realistic authoritarian, and Holden's Major Kendall, a liberal-minded, fiercely compassionate man, argue repeatedly during their perilous mission. Complicating matters is Hannah (Constance Towers), a Southern belle who is scheming to sabotage their plans but who falls in love with Marlowe instead. Despite a rather muddled screenplay, based on a true incident, *The Horse Soldiers* manages a fair quotient of sequences that demonstrate Ford's mastery of the genre and his love for military ritual. A particular highlight is the battle scene in which Confederate soldiers pour from a train to engage the Union troops, while their colonel, seen in reflection through a window, watches them with pride. (We later see this colonel wounded and staggering with the Confederate flag.)

Major Dundee (Columbia, 1965). Charlton Heston played the title role of a Union officer who leads Confederate prisoners on a raid against the Apaches. Years later, in his book The Actor's Life *(Dutton, 1978), Heston wrote, "I think we all wanted to make a different film. Columbia wanted a cowboy and Indian story. I wanted a film that dealt with the basic issue of the Civil War, and Sam [Peckinpah] wanted the film he later got to make. . . . It was called* The Wild Bunch*" (page 208).*

OPPOSITE *The Horse Soldiers (United Artists, 1959). Colonel Marlowe (John Wayne), Southern belle Hannah (Constance Towers), and surgeon Major Kendall (William Holden) confer over Hannah's maid, Lukey (Althea Gibson), who is dying of wounds incurred in the battle. Except for a segment of* How the West Was Won *(1963), this was John Ford's only sound film to deal with the Civil War.*

Two sixties military Westerns, both set in the same year of the Civil War, 1864, continued the fifties pattern of pitting two strong men against each other in a clash of wills. Sam Peckinpah's *Major Dundee* (1965) echoed *Two Flags West* in its focus on a Union officer (Charlton Heston) who must lead a scruffy group of Confederate prisoners (Heston calls them "thieves, renegades, and deserters") deep into Mexico on a punitive raid against the Apaches. Richard Harris played the Irish-born Confederate cashiered officer who opposes and finally assists him, ultimately sacrificing his life. The conflict between their opposing codes of behavior constitutes the heart of the film. *Major Dundee* could claim many virtues: a screenplay by Peckinpah, Harry Julian Fink, and Oscar Saul that created a genuinely complex character in Heston's troubled Major Dundee, a physical production of impressive scope that combined both panoramic Fordian imagery with Peckinpah's own penchant for gritty, realistic detail, and a climactic battle scene that ranks among the best ever filmed. Unfortunately, the studio's mutilation of the film—two key scenes were deleted after much wrangling and ill will—resulted in critical disapproval and audience confusion. A much inferior film, Edward Dmytryk's Civil War drama *Alvarez Kelly* (1966), also had Union and Confederate forces in conflict, here over badly needed cattle. Based on actual events, the film pitted Kelly (William Holden), an uncommitted Irish-Mexican war profiteer, against Colonel Tom Rossiter (Richard Widmark), a Confederate officer who forces

Kelly to stampede cattle meant for Union troops into Confederate territory. Rossiter's vengeful hatred of Kelly stems from Kelly's having assisted Rossiter's fiancée, a crafty Southern belle, to elope with another man. The movie suffered from Dmytryk's rather desultory direction and indifferent performances by the leading players.

The journey westward had been one of America's great adventures, and in transmuting its hardships and rewards into epic images, films have given us a permanent vision of the experience. If the vision has been clouded by fantasy, it has also stirred our imaginations with stories of courage and endurance. The pioneers forged a home in the wilderness out of unimaginable suffering. The movies forged a filmic heritage out of dreams.

Men Alone

"All gunfighters are lonely. They live in fear. They die alone, without a woman or a dime or a friend."

—Burt Lancaster in *Gunfight at the O.K. Corral* (Paramount, 1957)

IF THERE IS ONE IMAGE that dominates all others in the Western film, it is that of the lone rider, a small, isolated figure against the awesome natural background of mountains and plains. The Westerner may inhabit the ranches, the modest cabins, the saloons, and even the jails that are part of the scene, but essentially he is a man apart, moving to his own drummer in a world that expects to test him—or threatens to destroy him—at every turn in the trail. The American concept of rugged individualism has its apogee in the Western film.

Not that the Westerner is always literally alone. His isolation from others is often figurative; in the path he chooses in life, he may be bonded with others—the sheriff with his posse, the outlaw with his gang, the cowboy with the other drovers. Yet his loneliness remains pervasive, etching his grave and rugged countenance, affecting the way he sits astride his horse, the cautious, languid way in which he stalks down the main street of a dusty Western town. He understands, all too well, that despite the sheriff's badge or the marshal's gun, he inhabits a lawless society where sudden death lurks in the shadows. He knows, as we all do after years of watching him, that in the ultimate showdown, he will be required to stand on his own, confronting his final destiny. The strength, resilience, and underlying melancholy of the Western loner has been well embodied in such actors as John Wayne, Gary Cooper, and Randolph Scott.

Certainly one of the most ubiquitous loners in Western films has been the lawman. In the historical West, the lawman was indeed lone, and despite the fact that he could deputize as many men as he needed when the occasion warranted, he usually had to face trouble by himself. The town marshal, whose jurisdiction did not extend beyond the town or city limits, was especially vulnerable to gunfire. For most of each day, he was obliged to cope with the rowdy, dangerous element in the saloons, gambling houses, and brothels in the settlements. The sheriffs, whose jurisdiction extended over the entire county, had a far lower mortality rate since they did not have to tour the streets and saloons located within their bailiwicks, breaking up brawls and gunfights.

Most often the movie marshal or sheriff has taken the form of a righteous and unsullied leader, struggling by himself or with an ineffectual posse to preserve the peace and the status quo, a man whose badge and gun spoke much louder than his simple utterances of duty and responsibility. For the first few decades of sound, the lawman simply did his job, and in scores of minor Westerns, such popular actors as Gene Autry, Roy Rogers, and John Wayne often played one-dimensional characters whose rugged faces were seldom if ever clouded with doubt or genuine thought. They were merely symbols of law and order in a lawless land.

One particular characteristic appeared to mitigate against their zealous enforcement of the law: a sincere reluctance to carry out the more violent aspects of their work and even a genuine empathy with their quarry. The annals of Western films in the thirties and forties are filled with sheriffs and marshals who pin on their badges only when there is no other recourse or when violence directed at a friend or family member makes action essential. In Michael Curtiz's energetic

This photograph shows the actual O.K. Corral in Tombstone, Arizona, where the gunfight between the Earps and the Clantons took place on the afternoon of October 26, 1881.

PAGE 90   *Frontier Marshal (Fox, 1939). Randolph Scott starred as a taciturn Wyatt Earp in the second Western to be loosely adapted from Stuart Lake's book on Earp. When Earp's widow objected to the hero's romance with Sarah Allen (Nancy Kelly), the studio was obliged to make a settlement to appease her anger.*

Dodge City (1939), gunfighter Wade Hatton (Errol Flynn) rides into "a town with no ethics but cash and killings" and takes over the sheriff's job after a little boy is fatally caught in the cross fire of a shoot-out. James Stewart's Tom Destry, in George Marshall's *Destry Rides Again* (1939), assumes his late father's mantle as sheriff of Bottleneck and generates merely contempt for his nonviolent, gunfree ways until he succeeds in routing the villains. Drifting cowboy Wyatt Earp (Henry Fonda), in John Ford's *My Darling Clementine* (1946), surrenders his neutrality and becomes marshal of Tombstone only after his young brother is murdered by the evil Clantons.

Wyatt Earp, perhaps the most ubiquitous of reluctant lawmen to turn up in Westerns of the thirties and forties, had his origins in history. His true story has been obscured by time, but apparently he was, at various times, a law officer and a gunfighter who was more devious and crooked than heroic. Similar shadows hover over the figure of his often ambiguous colleague, Doc (John H.) Holliday, who was probably more of a petty gambler with an itchy trigger finger than the morose, tubercular figure of most of the films. Controversy still rages over the circumstances surrounding the famous gunfight at the O.K. Corral in which Earp and Holliday participated. On that fateful day of October 26, 1881, did Earp, Holliday, and their men kill a group of criminals, or were they themselves a gang of thieves and murderers?

Whatever the truth about Earp and Holliday, they were clearly the stuff of legend and ripe for Western heroics, whether under their own or assumed names. *Law and Order*, Edward L. Cahn's 1932 Western, fictionalized the Earp-Holliday characters while retaining the town name of Tombstone.

A novel by W. R. Burnett was adapted by John Huston and Tom Reed into a somber screenplay concerning the Earp-like Frame Johnson (Huston's father, Walter), who tames Tombstone with the help of a Holliday-surrogate (Harry Carey). During the course of events, which included the shoot-out at the O.K. Corral, Johnson is forced to hang a simple farmer (Andy Devine) who has killed someone accidentally. In keeping with Burnett's novel—he was best known for his hard-boiled contemporary crime fiction—the movie's cowboys behaved more like latter-day gangsters than range riders, dispensing violence with cold-blooded nonchalance.

A year earlier, the Earp legend had been given impetus with the publication of Stuart Lake's book *Wyatt Earp, Frontier Marshal*. Characterized by the publisher as "a stirring, action-packed account of one man's struggle against Old West lawlessness," the book was loosely used as the basis for Lewis Seiler's 1934 movie *Frontier Marshal*, which had Earp (George O'Brien), here named Michael Wyatt, fighting to clean up Tombstone while romancing demure Mary Reid (Irene Bentley). Actually, the film resembled *Destry Rides Again* more than its ostensible source, with a hero confronting corrupt town officials and being saved from death by the saloon singer (Ruth Gillette), who takes the bullet meant for him. A 1939 remake, also called *Frontier Marshal*, came closer to Lake's book, casting Randolph Scott as a stoic Wyatt Earp and Cesar Romero as a melancholy Doc Holliday.

It took master director John Ford to give durable form to the Earp-Holliday legend in his classic Western *My Darling Clementine*. Although formally derived from Stuart Lake's book, the evocative screenplay by Samuel G. Engel and Winston Miller is less interested in re-creating historical events than in celebrating the coming of civilization to the West. Ford's purpose is made instantly clear the moment we see his Wyatt Earp in the calm, stoic, and sturdy person of Henry Fonda. A nomadic cowboy whose only ties are with his brothers, Earp is wary of a lawless Tombstone ("What kind of town *is* this?"), but when his youngest brother, James, is brutally murdered by the amoral Clantons, led by the evil Ike (Walter Brennan), he agrees to become the new marshal. He forms an uneasy yet ultimately strong alliance with Doc Holliday (Victor Mature), the darkly brooding, hard-drinking, and tubercular man whose power he has usurped. Together, they come to represent the laws of honor and decency that had to prevail if Western America was to survive, and in the climactic shoot-out at the O.K. Corral, they succeed in destroying the vicious Clantons, who represent lawlessness. Doc loses his life in the fight, and Earp moves on, unable to accept the ultimate domestication embodied in his "darling" Clementine (Cathy Downs).

While bearing little resemblance to the truth about Wyatt Earp, *My Darling Clementine* is steeped in Ford's deepest feelings of veneration for America and the land, and for the civilizing influences of family and community. These feelings, which run truer to the film's intention than any of the shoot-outs or violent encounters, can be seen in the beautifully wrought sequences that draw Earp deeper into the life of Tombstone. He rescues Thorndyke (Alan Mowbray), a boozy, pathetic Shakespearean actor, from the humiliations of the Clanton clan, and in one of the film's most unforgettable scenes, he joins Clementine in the town's celebration of its new church. As they walk together down the street to the joyous sound of singing voices and clanging church bells, we can sense his pleasure at sharing in the event. Later, when

My Darling Clementine *(Fox, 1946). Held captive by the Clanton sons and their followers, Shakespearean actor Granville Thorndyke (Alan Mowbray) is humiliated and forced to perform Hamlet's soliloquy atop a saloon table. Earlier, he had caused a riot by failing to turn up at the Birdcage Theatre (which still exists in Tombstone).*

My Darling Clementine (Fox, 1946). Mexican vixen Chihua-hua (Linda Darnell) attends her adored Doc Holliday (Victor Mature; LEFT). Later, despite Doc's efforts to save her, Chihua-hua dies of wounds inflicted by one of the vicious Clanton gang. BELOW   Wyatt Earp (Henry Fonda) holds the body of his slain brother Virgil (Tim Holt), another casualty, as Morgan Earp (Ward Bond) looks on. One of John Ford's finest Western films, My Darling Clementine is steeped in Ford's ideas about the civilizing of the West.

OPPOSITE   A poster for Gunfight at the O.K. Corral (Paramount, 1957).

BURT LANCASTER · KIRK DOUGLAS

HAL WALLIS' PRODUCTION OF

GUNFIGHT AT THE O.K. CORRAL

VISTAVISION

TECHNICOLOR

A PARAMOUNT PICTURE

CO-STARRING RHONDA FLEMING · JO VAN FLEET · JOHN IRELAND DIRECTED BY JOHN STURGES · SCREENPLAY BY LEON URIS

Earp dances in comically stiff-footed fashion with Clementine, we know that the wanderer has found a temporary home. As in all his best films, Ford gives the simplest rituals (including the earlier funeral of Earp's brother) the stamp of truth. He remains surefooted throughout the film, erring only in the clichéd portrayals of the women, including the vapid Clementine and the hot-blooded, ill-fated Mexican girl Chihuahua (Linda Darnell).

Although *My Darling Clementine* abounds in Fordian themes and touches of serene, homespun Americana, Ford is not a director to ignore the possibilities for vigorous action, and the film contains a number of well-handled sequences in the Western tradition, superbly photographed in black-and-white by Joseph MacDonald and tightly edited by Dorothy Spencer. The showdown scene between Earp and Holliday (Earp has evidence linking Doc to his brother's murder) bristles with tension, and the climactic shoot-out at the corral, a

model of controlled filmmaking, remains the definitive version of that much-replayed incident. The cumulative impact of *My Darling Clementine* remains inseparable from Henry Fonda's central performance as Earp. Seated alone on a porch, his legs propped against a post, he exudes the quiet strength and authority of the Western loner who wears his proud isolation like a badge of honor.

Few Westerns on Wyatt Earp and Doc Holliday have approached the mythic quality of *My Darling Clementine* or matched its deeply felt portrait of the lone Westerner who must reluctantly assume the role of lawman. This did not keep other directors from continuing to mine this territory. One director, John Sturges, was so fascinated with the loner's story, transformed from reality into legend, that he offered two disparate versions a decade apart. His popular and large-scale *Gunfight at the O.K. Corral* (1957) retained the basic Earp-Holliday partnership—the consumptive, hard-drinking

This striking poster for High Noon *(United Artists, 1952) emphasizes the lone figure of Sheriff Will Kane (Gary Cooper) as he faces the showdown with Frank Miller and his gang.*

OPPOSITE   Gunfight at the O.K. Corral *(Paramount, 1957). While pensive Marshal Wyatt Earp (Burt Lancaster) faces dealing with the evil Clanton clan, his sardonic, fatalistic friend Doc Holliday (Kirk Douglas) is deciding whether to join him. Usually depicted as a brooding, alcoholic loner, John H. ("Doc") Holliday was actually a gambler who killed people he didn't like. He died of tuberculosis eighteen months after the legendary gunfight.*

Doc (Kirk Douglas) sides with Marshal Earp (Burt Lancaster) against the nasty Clantons and joins him in the expected shoot-out at the corral ("If I'm goin' to die, let me die with the best friend I ever had.") Well-staged and exciting, this climactic, six-minute episode compensates in part for a fairly perfunctory film, which, at least, enshrined its clichés in bright Technicolor. Ten years later, in a more cynical time, Sturges directed James Garner in *Hour of the Gun* (1967) as a bitter Wyatt Earp more obsessed with avenging the murder of his brother than in restoring law and order to Tombstone. Jason Robards played a Doc Holliday whose stature increased as Earp's decreased. Doc himself finally received his due in Frank Perry's *Doc* (1971), assuming a dominant role over Harris Yulin's Earp. The movie, however, worked too strenuously to demythologize the Earp-Holliday legend, with Pete Hamill's original screenplay turning Holliday (Stacy Keach) into a weak-willed drunkard and Earp into a corrupt opportunist.

Curiously, when the Western lawman was relegated to a supporting role, when he faded into the background instead of standing alone, his rugged enforcement of the law, however reluctant, frequently seemed to vanish, and he became either ineffectual or corrupt. Many a sheriff played by a minor actor could be counted on to bite the dust before the film's end, triggering the hero's vengeance. Or the sheriff might join the villains against the hero; figurehead sheriffs in thrall to the powerful town boss were staple characters in many Western movies. Some lawmen were aging or helpless—in George Marshall's *Destry Rides Again* (1939), the old sheriff (Charles Winninger), actually the town drunkard, appointed as a joke, cannot contain the corruption in Bottleneck, and he is ultimately shot dead. Other subordinate lawmen revealed a streak of sentimentality a yard wide—in John Ford's *Stagecoach* (1939), for example, the sheriff (George Bancroft)

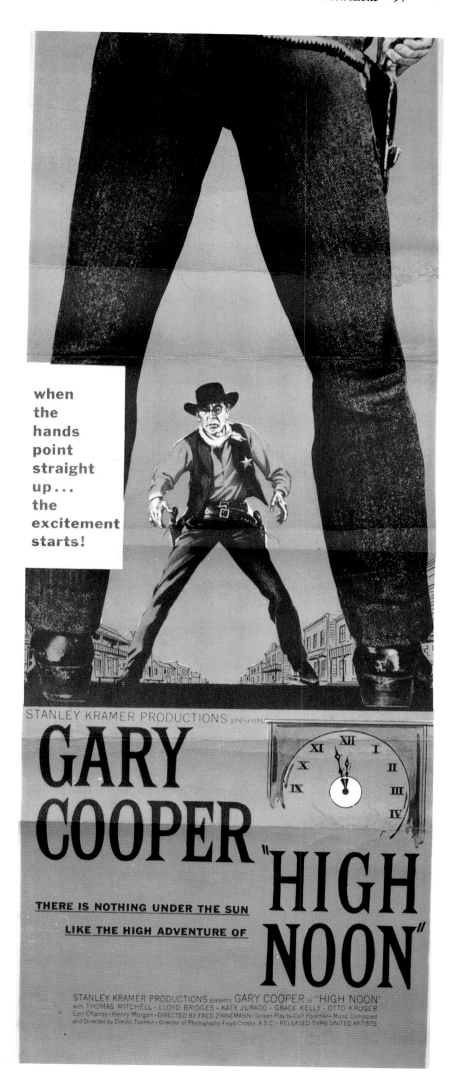

when the hands point straight up... the excitement starts!

STANLEY KRAMER PRODUCTIONS presents

GARY COOPER "HIGH NOON"

THERE IS NOTHING UNDER THE SUN LIKE THE HIGH ADVENTURE OF

STANLEY KRAMER PRODUCTIONS presents GARY COOPER in "HIGH NOON" with THOMAS MITCHELL · LLOYD BRIDGES · KATY JURADO · GRACE KELLY · OTTO KRUGER · Lon Chaney · Henry Morgan · DIRECTED BY FRED ZINNEMANN · Screen Play by Carl Foreman · Music Composed and Directed by Dimitri Tiomkin · Director of Photography Floyd Crosby, A.S.C · RELEASED THRU UNITED ARTISTS

High Noon (United Artists, 1952). In the film's famous cli-max, Sheriff Will Kane (Gary Cooper) approaches the ultimate confrontation with his sworn enemy. After a quarter-century as a popular actor, Cooper finally won an Academy Award for his performance in this film, as the troubled, tenacious lawman.

allows John Wayne's wanted cowboy, the Ringo Kid, to ride off into the sunset with Claire Trevor. Even legendary out-laws could earn the sympathy of their pursuers—the marshal (Randolph Scott) commiserates with the plight of Jesse James in Henry King's *Jesse James* (1939), and the sheriff (Brian Donlevy) pursues Robert Taylor's *Billy the Kid* (1941) with a heavy heart. Most often, the Western movie sheriff was shown as too soft-centered—or too single-minded—to har-bor any doubts about his calling.

A major turning point in characterizing the loner with a badge came in 1952 with the release of Fred Zinnemann's *High Noon*. The monochromatic sheriff, stalwartly retaining or restoring law and order in his town, gave way in this important instance to Sheriff Will Kane (Gary Cooper), a troubled, somber man facing imminent death when he is forced to stand by himself against a gang of killers. Although he remains true to the Western code of honor ("I've never run from anybody before!"), Kane finds himself assailed on all sides by cowardice, self-serving equivocation, and mendacity. He becomes the ultimate Western loner, the sole representa-tive of courage and justice in a weak, corrupt society. He perseveres, but he can take no pleasure in a bitter and hollow triumph. Clearly, this was no conventional Western lawman, and *High Noon* was no ordinary Western drama.

The stark, simple tale of *High Noon* unfolds in a single day. On his last day as the sheriff of Hadleyville, Kane learns that Frank Miller (Ian MacDonald), newly released from prison, is returning to town on the noon train; his sworn goal is to kill Kane for "sending him up." Scheduled to marry Amy (Grace Kelly), a lovely young Quaker girl, Kane has the choice of leaving quickly, but he decides to stay and face Miller; he refuses to "lie like a coward in his grave." When he asks for help, he finds betrayal—nobody will stand with him against the enemy. ("This ain't our job." "It's the fault of the politicians up north!") As the minutes tick away, Kane's disil-lusion and despair bite more deeply into his face, and after surviving the shoot-out, he flings his badge to the ground and rides away with his new bride.

As a Western drama, *High Noon* impresses with firm direction by Fred Zinnemann, Floyd Crosby's austere black-

and-white photography, and the superb editing by Elmo Williams and Harry Gerstad, which succeeds in building tension through repeated shots of the town clock and the deserted railway station. As Kane, Gary Cooper makes apt use of his stoic demeanor and understated acting style; as the day progresses, his craggy face registers darker shades of anger and disbelief. And if the repeated lyrics of the ballad "High Noon" (by Dimitri Tiomkin and Ned Washington) become oppressive after a while, there is no denying the song's impact on the film's commercial success. (The song and Tiomkin's musical score received Oscars, as did Cooper and the editors.)

Over the years, these considerable virtues of *High Noon* as a film have often been obscured by its status as a parable, a cautionary tale, of American political life in the early fifties. At the time that Carl Foreman was writing his screenplay, Hollywood was deeply in the throes of investigation by the House Un-American Activities Committee, and Foreman himself expected to be called before the committee as an uncooperative witness. Shunned or deserted by many friends, Foreman, without telling any of the other participants, bitterly expressed his feelings through the script's events at Hadleyville. In effect, his screenplay was a submerged protest at the cowardice and vacillation of many in Hollywood in response to the onslaught of the HUAC investigation. Implicitly, it called for standing up to government oppression

High Noon (United Artists, 1952). In the climactic shoot-out (ABOVE), Sheriff Will Kane (Gary Cooper, right) finally confronts Frank Miller (Ian MacDonald), the man who has sworn to kill him. His wife (Grace Kelly, center) has abandoned her Quaker principles of nonviolence to come to his aid. In the heat of the fight, the felled Kane (OPPOSITE) tries to fire off a few rounds. Many directors of more traditional Westerns, such as Howard Hawks, were angry with the film for what they claimed was its false view of frontier life and justice.

despite one's peace-loving nature—at the movie's end, Kane's gentle Quaker wife must shoot one of the villains to save her husband's life. Not surprisingly, the movie was condemned by Western purists, who believed that "messages" do not belong in the Western, especially a message that cast even the mildest aspersions on America's honor and bravery.

Despite the open contempt with which *High Noon* was regarded by many (John Wayne remarked, "What a piece of you-know-what *that* was!"), its influence was widespread and unmistakable throughout the fifties, unquestionably due more to its box-office success than to its social conscience. Alfred Werker's *At Gunpoint* (1955) was, in fact, a virtual clone of the original, dealing with Jack Wright (Fred MacMurray), a mild-mannered storekeeper who shoots a bank robber by accident and is proclaimed a local hero—until the robber's friends vow revenge. Then the good citizens shun him entirely and even boycott his store when he insists on remaining steadfast. "I've got to defend my right—our right—to live decently and honestly in a place of my own choosing," he tells his troubled wife (Dorothy Malone). Once again, a weak society, easily intimidated by brute power, forces a man of integrity into choosing between taking a lone stand against tyranny and evil or going against his grain by knuckling under. Eventually, of course, in a not entirely believable ending, the townsfolk line up on the side of Wright.

One of the more blatant imitations of *High Noon*—and a trim, intelligent Western in its own right—was Delmer Daves's *3:10 to Yuma* (1957). Van Heflin starred as Dan Evans, a sturdy rancher who agrees to take captured outlaw Ben Wade (Glenn Ford) to Yuma to stand trial, knowing that Wade's gang has sworn to release him. (Evans needs the reward money to pay the debt on his failing ranch.) With admirable attention to the precisely observed detail—one memorable shot encompasses Evans's ranch and family as he

rides off to town—Daves frames a surprisingly compelling story of a man who is forced into heroics when everyone around him has failed to help. Halsted Welles's screenplay generates tension as the minutes tick away and Evans moves toward the inevitable deadly confrontation with Wade and his men. Unfortunately, the resolution—Wade, chastened by Evans's heroism, comes to his aid during the shoot-out—fails to convince.

By the end of the fifties, Westerns were beginning to add other ingredients to the *High Noon* mix. John Sturges's *Last Train from Gun Hill* (1959) combined elements of *High Noon* with those of the traditional revenge Western. Playing in his most intense style, Kirk Douglas appeared as Matt Morgan, a marshal whose wife was raped and killed by Rick Belden (Earl Holliman), the scurrilous young son of an old friend, Craig Belden (Anthony Quinn). A prosperous rancher, Belden refuses to allow Matt to hold his son for the murder. He organizes his forces to keep Matt from getting his son on the last train to prison. (The importance of the time element—a central occurrence at a precise time—echoes both *High Noon* and *3:10 to Yuma*.) In the violent show-

down, Craig Belden and his son are killed. Sturges staged the key scenes with dispatch, especially in one fierce encounter in which a bitter, vengeful Matt describes to young Rick in brutal detail how he will be brought to trial, sentenced, and hanged. The film, however, offers few surprises—we know that Matt, "that poor fool with his high-flown ideals," as one character describes him, will persevere and triumph. In the Western vision, the Western scheme of things, only the righteous can prevail, no matter how lonely the trail they are forced to ride.

Edward Dmytryk's *Warlock*, also released in 1959, offered yet another variation of the *High Noon* theme. A

3:10 to Yuma (Columbia, 1957). Peace-loving farmer Dan Evans (Van Heflin) is compelled to deal with outlaw Ben Wade (Glenn Ford), who is being held at bay. Saloon girl Emmy (Felicia Farr), who loves Ben, looks on. This High Noon *clone boasted a trim screenplay by Halsted Welles and firm direction by Delmer Daves.*

shade subtler than the standard marshal-versus-villains confrontation, the film's principal conflict involved contrasting attitudes toward law and order in the West. Blaisdell (Henry Fonda), a melancholy gunslinger with a killer's reputation, is hired by the people of Warlock to defend them against a band of brutal ranch cowboys. He represents the primitive code of Western justice: swift, deadly, and beyond the law. When one of the cowboys (Richard Widmark) changes sides and becomes the town's sheriff, the stage is set for an inevitable clash between legal justice (Widmark) and sanctioned lawlessness (Fonda). Others become heavily involved in the furious action: Anthony Quinn as Fonda's clubfooted friend, whose admiration for Fonda holds a hint of homosexual feeling, and Dorothy Malone as a revenge-minded girl. Widmark's sheriff, impotent at first but later assured and righteous, marked a direct line from Gary Cooper's Will Kane.

The influence of *High Noon* extended well into the sixties, and even toward the end of the decade the concept of the

Usually, the lone Western lawman stood for honesty, rectitude, and righteous indignation, blurred only by the ambiguity of the fifties and sixties. Occasionally, however, the job of determining or carrying out the law fell into the hands of someone who was not too scrupulous about its dictates. The Western film is sprinkled with corrupt or opportunistic sheriffs who were allied with the chief villain in holding sway over the community, or marshals who were too weak—or too drunk—to carry out their responsibilities. Sometimes, the corruption or the weakness extended to the judges who exercised their authority over the law.

Warlock (Fox, 1959). In Edward Dmytryk's feverish Western, Anthony Quinn played one of the most unusual roles of his career as Morgan (LEFT), Blaisdell's blond, clubfooted, and perhaps excessively devoted friend. Henry Fonda portrayed Blaisdell (BELOW), the quick-fingered gunman hired by the people of Warlock to defend them against a band of nasty cowboys. Blaisdell's rough version of law and order is pitted against the legal justice of cowboy-turned-sheriff Gannon, played by Richard Widmark.

sole representative of law and order, besieged or despised but finding unexpected reserves of strength, persisted in Western films. Burt Kennedy's exceptionally grim *Welcome to Hard Times* (1967) cast Henry Fonda against type as a cowardly mayor who finally guns down the evil Man from Bodie (Aldo Ray) when he tries to destroy the town a second time. In Vincent McEveety's *Firecreek* (1968), a timid part-time sheriff (James Stewart) who would prefer to tend his farm returns to the law with guns blazing when Henry Fonda (in his first fully villainous role) and his gang murder a deputy and terrorize the town. ("The day a man decides not to face the world," he proclaims, "is the day he better step out of it!") Allen Smithee's moody *Death of a Gunfighter* (1969) starred Yul Brynner as a gunslinger-turned-sheriff who is despised by the town's corrupt hypocrites after he kills in self-defense. (Smithee was a pseudonym for Robert Totten and Don Siegel, who both directed the film at different times.) The message of these Westerns sounded as clearly as it had in other decades: evil must be routed, even by the isolated loner, and vacillation and cowardice have no place in a man's world. Somehow, in a decade dominated by "love power" and protest, the message seemed anachronistic, and audiences in the sixties preferred their Westerns to be comic or, in the style of the popular "spaghetti" Westerns from Italy, excessively lurid.

One judge who carried out his own form of "frontier justice" came from the pages of history. Crude and portly Roy Bean had moved west with the coming of the railroads and, armed only with his gun and credentials as a scoundrel and swindler, had established himself as the ruling force of a town he called Langtry, in honor of Lillie Langtry, the beautiful British actress he worshiped. Setting himself up in a saloon, he held court in his barroom, hanging every defendant who refused to pay the price of his justice. Occasionally, he would fine a corpse for whatever money was found on the body, and he often found reason to hang a man on the tree near the court. Jurors had little to say about the court's decisions, but each man was guaranteed a drink at the bar before the case was heard.

Film producers could hardly be expected to resist someone as colorful as Judge Roy Bean. He became the principal character of two contrasting movies. Samuel Goldwyn's leisurely and flavorsome production of *The Westerner* (1940) transformed Bean from his true pudgy person into a lean, cantankerous rogue, played with authority by Walter Brennan. Under William Wyler's expert direction of a screenplay by Jo Swerling and Niven Busch, Bean was portrayed as the self-appointed law "west of the Pecos," determined to keep homesteaders from settling on his range. Brennan's skilled performance, which earned him an Academy Award for Best Supporting Actor, transformed the scoundrelly judge into a sympathetic figure, despite his questionable notion of justice.

OPPOSITE   *Firecreek (Warner Bros., 1968). In a departure from his usual benign persona, Henry Fonda (right) starred as Larkin, leader of a band of killers who terrorize the tiny Western town of Firecreek. James Stewart costarred as the part-time sheriff whose righteous wrath finally brings them to heel.*

The Westerner (United Artists, 1940). Fatally wounded by Cole Harden (Gary Cooper), Judge Roy Bean (Walter Brennan) expires after seeing a blurred vision of his lifelong idol, actress Lillie Langtry. Brennan won his third Oscar as Best Supporting Actor for his performance.

Nominal star Gary Cooper played Cole Harden, the drifter who saves himself from a hanging by claiming that he knows Bean's beloved Lillie Langtry. In keeping with the tenor of the thirties and forties, Harden becomes the champion of "the little people" who are powerless to defy Bean. Cooper's laconic, understated performance contrasted beautifully with Brennan's colorful, fascinating rascal, and their scenes together crackled with a knowing humor and rapport.

In addition to these well-matched performances, *The Westerner* benefits from Gregg Toland's superb photography, which bathes many of the key scenes in a warm glow. His expertise shows to best advantage in the film's well-remembered climax in which Bean, alone in the theater and dressed in his Civil War uniform, waits for a performance by his adored Lillie, only to find Harden at center stage, guns at the ready. Mortally wounded in the shoot-out, Bean beholds the Jersey Lily in a soft haze that fades as he dies.

When Roy Bean returned to the spotlight over three decades later, the world had turned in a different direction. In *The Life and Times of Judge Roy Bean* (1972), director John Huston and writer (later director) John Milius collaborated to create a distinctly modern view of the hanging judge—ironic,

The Westerner *(United Artists, 1940). The crowd, including cowboy Cole Harden (Gary Cooper), contemplates another victim of Judge Roy Bean's one-man "justice." Gregg Toland's superb black-and-white photography gave the film a visual sheen.*

iconoclastic, and essentially tongue-in-cheek. In the person of Paul Newman, still handsome and blue-eyed behind the stubble, Bean remained the sole dispenser of justice west of the Pecos, but his story was told as a series of picaresque and absurd adventures that bordered occasionally on surrealism. Milius's screenplay retained the basic elements of the Bean legend—his summary "justice" and his worship of Lillie Langtry—then mischievously twisted them so that in the end the hanging judge becomes the champion of the old order, an avenging angel who destroys the trappings of advancing civilization, greedy and mean-spirited.

Like *Butch Cassidy and the Sundance Kid*, which it occasionally resembles in its contemporary approach (even to the extent of the interpolated song), *The Life and Times of Judge Roy Bean* blends boisterous comedy and Western action with touches of sentiment and satire. In a series of episodes, Newman's Roy Bean, after setting himself up as the sole judge in the area ("God must have directed my bullets"), encounters colorful characters who either accept or fatally defy his brand of "justice"; these include a self-styled traveling preacher (Anthony Perkins), an eccentric trapper named Grizzly Adams (John Huston), and a blustering albino gunman called Bad Bob (Stacy Keach), who gets blown away by the judge. Bean also finds a kind of serenity and stability in his relationship with the gentle Mexican girl Marie Elena (Victoria Principal), who dies in childbirth, and with a beer-swigging bear that becomes a kind of family pet. As in *The Westerner*, Bean's overriding obsession is Lillie Langtry; he destroys anyone who defiles her name or image.

Like the Roy Bean of history, Newman's judge has no compunction about dispensing his summary justice—he hangs anyone he chooses, fines corpses for "laying around," and rages when the bear places his "profane paws" on the poster of the Jersey Lily. Perversely, however, this Bean is also a romantic dreamer with a vision of a civilized West that does not include oil wells or greedy land barons. Yet the moment lawyer Frank Gass, played in properly snide fashion by Roddy McDowell, enters the scene, Bean's vision begins to fade. The attempt on the judge's life, the deaths of Marie Elena and the bear, the censure of the town's women— ironically, they were among the first prostitutes to arrive— all conspire to send Bean away. Twenty years later, like a ghostly wraith, he returns to join his feisty daughter, Rose (Jacqueline Bisset), in wiping out Gass's "civilized" town. "For Texas and Miss Lillie!" he cries as the town goes up in flames. Much later, in an ironic coda to Bean's story, Lillie Langtry (Ava Gardner) actually comes to visit the fragmentary remains of the town named for her.

One of the best Western films of the seventies, *The Life and Times of Judge Roy Bean* pleased many critics and film-

The Life and Times of Judge Roy Bean *(First Artists Productions, 1972). Judge Bean (Paul Newman) poses with one of the victims of his brutal, self-styled "justice." John Huston's quirky and colorful film gave a satirical edge to the story.*

goers who responded to its playful, idiosyncratic approach to Western lore, while irritating those who favored a more traditional approach. Whereas *The Westerner* was rooted in the populist tradition of the thirties, in which a defender of the "little folk" routs the ruthless capitalists who make their own laws (Harden versus Bean), Huston's film, in the wickedly irreverent style of the seventies, turns the tables by making its amoral protagonist the ultimate defender of old but fading values, the independent man against the corrupt establishment (Bean versus the twentieth century). In a sense, the two Beans, Brennan's and Newman's, became talismen of their times.

The Judge Beans notwithstanding, the Western lawman usually stood firmly on the side of right. Conversely, it might be said that the desperado or outlaw pursued by the lawman would represent the "bad" side, or unregenerate evil. In the annals of the true West, this was usually the case. Cold-blooded, vicious, and short-lived, the outlaw had little com-

The Life and Times of Judge Roy Bean (*First Artists Productions, 1972). Paul Newman (left) starred in John Huston's oddball Western as the infamous hanging judge Roy Bean. The bear, being bottle-fed by a follower, is the judge's good friend. It meets a sorry end later in the film.*

punction about killing anyone in his line of fire as he robbed banks and stagecoaches or rustled cattle. The money he stole was quickly spent on whiskey, women, and gambling; none of it went to impoverished families, even his own. Ultimately, if the outlaws failed to kill each other in vendettas, they were hanged at "necktie parties" by outraged citizens.

In Western movie lore, however, the truth vanished in a rose-colored haze. Very often, the outlaw was depicted as the equivalent of an urban delinquent, a kind of Dead End Kid in spurs and chaps who was misunderstood or condemned by society; fundamentally, he was an honorable sort in the wrong business. This sentimentalized view of the outlaw eventually took on a darker coloration as the years passed, but it has prevailed, even to recent times.

In the silent years, the concept of the outlaw as a basically decent man who could be redeemed by the love of a good woman had been epitomized by William S. Hart. When sound arrived, the concept persisted from the start.

The very first important sound Western, Raoul Walsh's *In Old Arizona* (1929), introduced Warner Baxter as the colorful bandit the Cisco Kid, who seems less concerned with plying his trade than with battling a Texas ranger (Edmund Lowe) for the love of a girl. Baxter, in the role that Walsh had intended to play himself until he lost an eye in an accident, received the second Oscar for Best Actor for his performance as the dashing Cisco. However, Walsh's use of sound, including hoofbeats and gunshots, to enhance the Western action was much more interesting than Baxter's none-too-convincing portrayal.

Unrepentent and happy-go-lucky, the Cisco Kid has a corporate view of banditry. "I never rob . . . the individual," he says as he divests the stagecoach company of its gold. He even harbors a sentimental streak, at one point speaking warmly about his loving parents and his dreams of settling someday in Portugal. When his beloved Tonia (Dorothy Bur-

In Old Arizona (Fox, 1929). The dashing Cisco Kid (Warner Baxter) holds up a stagecoach, with his girl, Tonia (Dorothy Burgess), at his side. Baxter played the Kid twice more, but in later years, Cesar Romero assumed the role.

gess) betrays him, he expresses sadness and disillusion rather than rage. Cisco's sense of fate ("I know in the end I will pay") appears to foreshadow his doom, and yet the ranger who pursues him throughout the film, and who is his rival in romance, permits him to escape at the end, recognizing the bond of honor that unites lawman and outlaw. This bond has its roots in American soil. In Europe, a bond of honor existed only among the upper strata of society; duels were fought and lives were lost in an effort to uphold the bond or to remove any stain on it. In a democratic America, those on opposing sides sometimes forged a link of understanding, recognizing their common humanity. In a sense, they were mirror images of each other, intimately involved in the same vision of the land. The movies may have romanticized the bond, but it unquestionably existed.

A rose-colored view of the outlaw as a lonely figure at odds with society continued throughout the first decade of sound, well into the thirties. (The view extended to other genres, especially the crime and gangster movies of the period.) A typical—and underappreciated—Western film, Christy Cabanne's *The Last Outlaw* (1936), focused on a crusty old outlaw called "Pop" (Harry Carey), who helps to

Three Godfathers *(MGM, 1948). In this allegory of the Nativity in Western dress, the three bank robbers bury the woman they found dying in the desert, having promised to take care of her baby. The story had been originally filmed as* Marked Men *by John Ford in 1919, then remade (not by Ford) in 1930 as* Hell's Heroes *and again in 1936 as* Three Godfathers.

rid the range of racketeers while confronting the perils of a new civilization.

For most of the forties, the "good" outlaws continued to be relatively pure of heart, although their reformation was less inevitable. In *The Desperadoes* (1943), Columbia's first color film, Glenn Ford had a rough time as Cheyenne, a young outlaw trying to reform. He falls in love with a girl (Evelyn Keyes) whose father (Edgar Buchanan, in an uncharacteristic role) secretly leads a gang of desperadoes. Framed for a bank robbery, Cheyenne must battle for his vindication. In a well-staged climax, he stampedes a herd of wild horses to free his sheriff friend (Randolph Scott), falsely accused of assisting in the robbery. Ultimately, of course, he wins admiration, respect—and the girl. Charles Vidor directed briskly, and Robert Carson's screenplay even contained a few snippets of

subtlety, allowing some of the principal characters to reveal hidden aspects of their identity behind the masks of the conventional characterizations.

Outlaws in forties Westerns continued to reveal a softer side: in George Sherman's *Renegades* (1946), Larry Parks (just before he appeared as Al Jolson in *The Jolson Story*) played the reluctant member of an outlaw family who meets a tragic end when he is unable to sever family ties. Perhaps the summit for sympathetic outlaws was reached in John Ford's version of *Three Godfathers* (1948), in which the clear references to the Nativity become oppressive. The Western town to which the outlaws are headed is called New Jerusalem, the three outlaws (read wise men) attempt to deliver the (Christ) child they rescue to the town at the cost of their freedom, and there is much pointed quoting from the Bible. Ford's pictorial sense, Winton C. Hoch's superb color photography, and lean performances by John Wayne, Ward Bond, and other familiar Ford players cannot compensate for the prevailing mawkishness.

As the forties waned, the long-established pattern of misunderstood outlaws, noble despite their sins, no longer seemed valid. The darker hues of *film noir* began to seep into the Western, producing a brooding sense of unrepentent evil or unavoidable doom that would have dismayed or baffled most of the earlier and saintlier outlaws. Actors suitable for *noir*'s shadowed city streets took on prominent Western roles. In George Sherman's *Black Bart* (1948), Dan Duryea, playing a historical outlaw who occasionally left doggerel verse in his wake, begins the film on the verge of being hanged and finally dies in a hail of bullets as he flees a burning shack; at

no point does he indicate the slightest intention of mending his criminal ways. Richard Widmark, who, like Duryea, seemed more at home in urban *film noir*, also surfaced as a nasty outlaw, in William Wellman's harsh Western *Yellow Sky* (1948). Brutish and snarling, Widmark's Dude clashes ultimately with his fellow bank robber Stretch (Gregory Peck) as they stumble into a ghost town inhabited by a crazy old prospector (James Barton) and his daughter (Anne Baxter). The movie's *noir* origins could be traced to the original story by W. R. Burnett.

An early-forties film with *noir* aspects was even remade into a Western during this period. Raoul Walsh's *High Sierra* (1941) had given Humphrey Bogart one of his strongest roles as a gangster who finds himself out of place in society after his release from prison. Walsh himself restructured the film as *Colorado Territory* (1949), changing Bogart's surly

Yellow Sky (Fox, 1948). Fleeing bank robber Stretch (Gregory Peck, right) comes upon a ghost town inhabited by tomboy Mike (Anne Baxter) and her grandfather (James Barton). William Wellman's tough, blistering little Western was enhanced by Joseph MacDonald's photography.

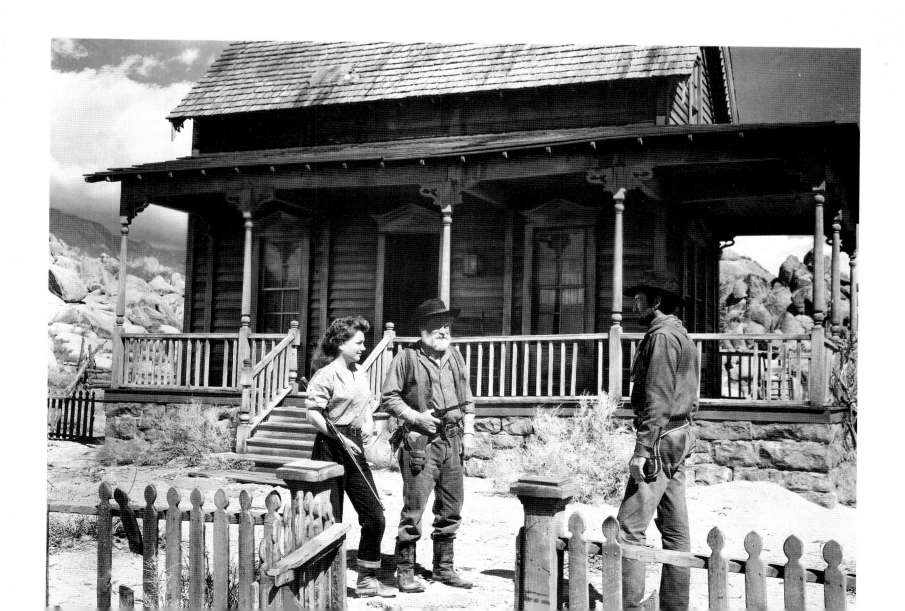

Bandolero! *(Fox, 1968). Dee Bishop (Dean Martin) engages in a gunfight in Andrew McLaglen's Western. A popular singer and partner to comedian Jerry Lewis in the fifties, Martin turned to a variety of roles as a solo actor in the sixties and beyond.*

Roy ("Mad Dog") Earle into an equally grim-visaged Wes McQueen (Joel McCrea). Like Earle, McQueen makes the fatal mistake of taking on one last robbery and ends his days atop a bleak mountain range that reduces him and even his pursuers to the size of ants. The *noir* concept of man as an insect trapped in a spider's web of his own making reverberates throughout this hard-edged Western.

By the early fifties, the *noir* atmosphere began to dissipate, and as the decade waned, the bleak view of the outlaw as doomed outcast was replaced for a while with more traditional conceptions. For most of the sixties, the lone Western outlaw returned to riding largely familiar trails, either touched with the glamour of the renegade or suffused with a primitive,

unregenerate evil. Often he appeared in the guise of a no-longer-young but still agile film star who enjoyed playing roles on the wrong side of the law. James Stewart and Dean Martin, for example, starred in Andrew McLaglen's 1968 Western *Bandolero!* as unlikely train-robbing brothers who are pursued by both a posse and Mexican bandits. Another seasoned veteran, John Wayne, found audience and critical approbation when he took on the role of outlaw-turned-marshal Rooster Cogburn in Henry Hathaway's film version of Charles Portis's best-selling novel *True Grit* (1969). As the fat, aging, one-eyed Cogburn who defeats the villains and helps a young orphaned girl (Kim Darby) avenge her

father's murder, Wayne so enchanted critics and moviegoers with this variation on his usual stoic, hard-bitten hero that he won new acclaim and an Academy Award. The view of Wayne, a pistol in one hand and a rifle in the other, as he charges the villains with a cry of "Fill your hands, you sons-of-bitches!" made an indelible impression. Six years later, Wayne reprised his role in *Rooster Cogburn* (1975), which costarred Katharine Hepburn as a feisty spinster who assists him in routing a gang of thieves and murderers.

One 1976 film that managed to preserve at least a measure of the isolated outlaw's folkloric quality was Clint Eastwood's *The Outlaw Josey Wales*. Acting the title role as well as directing—he replaced coscenarist Philip Kaufman as director—Eastwood played a farmer who becomes a Confederate guerrilla raider in order to track down the soldiers who murdered his wife and children. When he refuses to surrender at the end of the war, he becomes a hunted man and gathers a band of outcasts and losers around him. Eventually, the outcasts form a thriving community and gradually wean Josey Wales from his obsessive dream of revenge. At the end he has come full circle, tending a farm again.

*True Grit (Paramount, 1969). Rooster Cogburn (John Wayne) looks on as young Addie Ross (Kim Darby) stands at her father's grave (*BELOW*). Wayne's performance as the tough old Rooster, heavy in the saddle (*OPPOSITE, BELOW*), won him an Academy Award after more than four decades of making movies.*

Although *The Outlaw Josey Wales* contains the requisite number of action scenes, there is a surprising gentleness and hopefulness at the heart of the film that offset and dilute the violence. When his young son dies, Josey delivers a moving eulogy: "This boy was brought up in a time of blood and dyin'. . . . He never turned his back on his folks and his kind." Josey's wanderings lead him to the film's most original character, a "civilized" old Indian (Chief Dan George) who mixes whimsical humor with stinging truth. ("They call us civilized because we're easy to sneak up on.") Ultimately, Josey recognizes that the patchwork community he has built around him is his only true path to redemption from hate and vengeance. He tells the people of the community, "I came here to die with you . . . or live with you." He concludes, "Men can live together without butchering each other." At the film's end, he must leave the farm, but his archenemy, who has pursued him throughout the film, realizes his worth and allows him to get a head start. By transforming a bitter, hunted outlaw into both the redeemer and the redeemed, *The Outlaw Josey Wales* returned the figure to some of his old mythic glory before new attitudes moved him in the direction of evil.

The outlaw as mythic figure also appeared in Australian director Fred Schepisi's first American film, *Barbarosa* (1982). Folksinger Willie Nelson, his grizzled face as rugged and timeworn as the landscape, played the outlaw Barbarosa, who enjoys both a legendary status and a charmed life. On the way to his final destiny, Barbarosa meets and strikes up a shaky alliance with Karl (Gary Busey), a callow farm boy who is being pursued by the family of his brother-in-law, whom he killed accidentally. Since Barbarosa has been hunted for thirty years by the vengeful Mexican leader Don Braulio (Gilbert Roland), the two men are in constant flight, wandering through the bleak desert. Ultimately, Barbarosa meets an elegiac death and young Karl replaces him as a living legend.

Rooster Cogburn *(Universal, 1975). Katharine Hepburn and John Wayne costarred for the first time in Stuart Millar's sequel to* True Grit *(1969). Although Hepburn's tough-fibered spinster played well against Wayne's one-eyed codger, the movie was only moderately entertaining.*

The Outlaw Josey Wales *(Warner Bros., 1976). Clint East-wood (foreground) starred as the farmer who becomes an out-law and an avenging angel in the years after the Civil War. Under Eastwood's own direction, Josey's painful journey back to civilization made for a strikingly effective film.*

Barbarosa *(Universal/AFD, 1982). Karl (Gary Busey), a naive farm boy on the run, and Barbarosa (Willie Nelson), a wily, legendary outlaw, join forces in Fred Schepisi's well-made, undervalued little Western. Folksinger Nelson gave an ingratiating performance as a man who knows his precise place in a dangerous world.*

The Culpepper Cattle Company *(Fox, 1972). During a brief rest from the rigors of the cattle drive* (ABOVE), *young Ben Mockridge (Gary Grimes, center) listens in rapt fascination to the cowboys' tales. At one point, he poses (standing at right) with the cowboys* (OPPOSITE, BELOW). *Yet another rite-of-passage film, it followed Ben's progress from cook's assistant to a gunman who understood the violent ways of the West.*

While clearly limited in its budget, *Barbarosa* makes excellent use of the Texas landscape, and William D. Wittliff's screenplay contains some agreeably quirky touches and even a few surprising complexities. Barbarosa holds firm to his sense of values ("I don't kill for amusement—man or rabbit"), and he is also fully aware of his inevitable fate. He dies unflinchingly, with a precise awareness of his status as a Western legend. Nelson gives the role a quiet grace and dignity, and Busey makes Karl an appealing figure who develops from an ingenuous, principled youngster into a man feared and revered by the Mexicans.

Whether mythic or murderously real, the Western outlaw often struck a solitary figure on the plains, clashing with the lawman who also stood alone. Curiously, however, the loneliest man on the Western scene may well have been

the cowboy. While the sheriff or marshal might ride with his posse and the outlaw with his gang, the cowboy was frequently an isolated figure, drifting from ranch to ranch, enduring extraordinarily harsh winters as he moved cattle from one grazing land to another. Young and tough, he was obliged to be in the saddle fifteen hours a day, seven days a week, continually testing his skills at roping, shooting, and bronco busting. If he gathered in the bunkhouse or around a campfire with other cowboys, it was not to exchange anecdotes or to croon cowboy ballads but to eat his meager rations and catch a few hours of badly needed sleep. Contrary to Western movie lore, he did not often get to town, to play cards or to flirt with the bar girls, and in particularly bad times he drifted into gunfighting or bounty hunting in order to survive. By the last quarter of the century, his poor lot had worsened: severe storms had destroyed many cattle ranches, and homesteaders (called sodbusters or nesters by the cowboys) had taken over much of the land where the cattle had once roamed. Once again, the encroachment of civilization— the need for a kind of communal domesticity in a new land— was turning the isolated loner into an anachronism.

Although cowboys, ranging from the clean-living Roy Rogers variety in designer clothes to the hard-bitten, grizzled cowpokes personified by Ward Bond or Ben Johnson, clut-

Cowboys gather in front of the chuck wagon around 1890. At dusk, the cattle drive was stopped, and the horses were placed in an improvised rope corral while the cook prepared the evening meal. After the meal, the cowboys were sent on night watch, usually in two-hour shifts, with the job of riding around the herd.

tered the Western movies of every decade, not many films have dealt expressly with the life of the American cowboy in the Old West. When a film chose to convey some of the unromantic and everyday aspects of the cowboy's experience, it did so through the eyes of the very young and the very naive, who had to discover its many hardships and few rewards. Hugo Fregonese's likable little Western *Saddle Tramp* (1950) had an older cowboy (Joel McCrea) finding himself suddenly saddled with the care of four homeless boys whom he teaches, reluctantly, to survive. In Dick Richards's *The Culpepper Cattle Company* (1972), young Ben Mockridge (Gary Grimes) loses his romantic notions about the West in a series of incidents that take him from cook's helper to gunslinger. He finally defends a sect of religious pacifists against a cruel landowner, and it is his ultimate disillusionment with

the pacifists' leader that brings him closer to maturity. At the film's end, to the sound of a choir, he rides off alone into the horizon, his own man at last.

By far the most disturbing of these coming-of-age Westerns was Mark Rydell's *The Cowboys* (1972), which advanced the notion that the path to manhood requires initiation into violence. It concerned a group of young teenagers who are hired by Wil Anderson (John Wayne) as a last-ditch measure to bring his cattle to the market. En route, the boys learn the Western ways from their surrogate father. After the evil Long Hair (Bruce Dern) shoots Wil in the back (the sudden killing of a seemingly indestructible icon like Wayne is a shocking moment), the boys embark on a bloody campaign of revenge, shedding their innocent childhood along

the way. Although the film contains much authentic detail and some brutal but effective sequences, its schematic construction—the boys include every possible ethnic type, and the cook on the cattle drive is black—weakens the story's credibility. And the sight of barely pubescent boys implacably engaged in a violent orgy of revenge is difficult to watch.

One film that dealt directly and, to a degree, realistically with the life of the cowboy was Delmer Daves's 1958 Western *Cowboy*. Derived from Frank Harris's book *My Reminiscences as a Cowboy*, the movie starred Jack Lemmon as Harris, a naive hotel clerk in Chicago who signs on with a two-thousand-mile cattle drive led by Tom Reece (Glenn Ford). By the time Harris has returned to civilization, he has learned that the cowboy faces an almost daily threat of extinc-

OPPOSITE   The Culpepper Cattle Company *(Fox, 1972).*
Dick Richards's Western concerning the coming of age of a
young boy (Gary Grimes) offered atmospheric photography.
On a cattle drive to Colorado, young Ben learns about the need
to take a stand.

The Cowboys *(Warner Bros., 1972). Aging rancher Wil*
Anderson (John Wayne) rides with one of the boys he has taken
under his wing, who will soon learn about the code of the West.

Cowboy *(Columbia, 1958). Range boss Tom Reece (Glenn*
Ford) takes a tumble from his horse. The film focused on the
rugged Western education of a true-life Chicagoan named
Frank Harris, who wrote about his experiences in My Reminiscences as a Cowboy. *Ford played his stern and tough-*
minded mentor.

tion as he confronts the hostile elements of man and nature. (Even cows, he is told, are "miserable, slap-sided fleabags!") Harris discovers that death is an all too familiar companion on the open plains; over the grave of one of his men, Reece offers a quick, blunt eulogy: "A man's dead and that's that," adding, "He was a good man with cattle." (The stoic acceptance of death remains one of the cardinal rules of male-oriented action films.) Ultimately, Harris's resilience cracks, and he accuses Reece and his men of being "a pack of animals" without "a shred of decency." By the time the movie ends, however, he has come to understand and accept Reece's fatalistic, clear-eyed approach to living in an untamed West. In one powerful moment, Reece lets his feelings show: "I'm tired of burying people," he tells Harris, his face grim and ashen.

While many of the men who stood alone against the imposing Western vistas were lawmen, outlaws, and cowboys, many others remained totally unattached, unwilling to make even the smallest commitment, to link themselves with any other person or group. These were the completely iso-

The Oklahoma Kid (*Warner Bros., 1939*). *The tough, urban, modern personas of James Cagney and Humphrey Bogart did not play well out on the prairie. Here they are enemies in Lloyd Bacon's fast-moving but scarcely credible Western.*

lated loners, answering to nobody but themselves, and often they lived on the shady side of the law as gunslingers, saddle tramps, and bounty hunters. Hardened, taciturn, and wary, these men populated the Western films of every decade, either rejecting all codes of behavior or fashioning their own out of bitter experience.

Not that these loners were all alike. Many of them, especially from the thirties to the fifties, were fiercely obsessed with one motive: revenge for the killing of a member of their family. (As always, no film genre stressed the binding force of the family as much as the conservative traditional Western.) Others of these isolated figures resembled knights in shining armor, hiding their willingness to help others behind a mask (sometimes a literal mask) of placidity and conformity; these were the Robin Hoods in chaps and spurs. Still others were men whose mysterious pasts had set them apart from the norm and who, during the course of events, felt obliged to confront the past and take a stand against evil. These were the eagles who became hawks: the men who usually gave up their isolationism or their bad ways for a cause, even if only temporarily.

When the motive of revenge governed the life of a Western loner, like a figure in a Greek tragedy—an Orestes of the plains—he was driven by its compelling force until the end of the movie, when he usually realized its destructive power. The theme of revenge became a staple in Western films, starting with William S. Hart's fierce vendetta against an entire corrupt town in *Hell's Hinges* (1916) and continuing into the sound years. John Wayne's Westerns in the early thirties continually resorted to young Duke's search for the killer of a relative, and Gene Autry's first starring movie, *Tumbling Tumbleweeds* (1935), used this plot gambit. Even James Cagney, as an independent-minded but basically decent gunman in Lloyd Bacon's *The Oklahoma Kid* (1939), applied his urban toughness to exacting revenge for the lynching of his father, dispatching the perpetrator (Humphrey Bogart) and his gang in a whirlwind of gunplay.

Although the theme of revenge continued to appear in Western movies, cropping up continually in low-budget as well as epic-size films, it reached a peak in the fifties, when movie after movie saw the hero relentlessly determined to seek out and destroy those who had killed or kidnapped someone in his family. The fact that a decade largely noted for its bland conformity contains so many films concerned with vengeance for blood spilled suggests a split between societal attitudes and the private fantasies implied in the dream world of the movies: an updated version of sanctioned Victorian morality versus forbidden Victorian proclivities. In other words, the tight button-down collar in the advertisements turned into a noose on the screen.

Winchester '73 (Universal-International, 1950). Lin McAdam (James Stewart) and Dutch Henry Brown (Stephen McNally) compete for the coveted Winchester '73 rifle during a Fourth of July contest in Dodge City (RIGHT). It turns out that Dutch Henry is Lin's evil brother, whom Lin has been pursuing vengefully for killing their father. BELOW Lin McAdam gets the better of vicious gunman Waco Johnny Dean (Dan Duryea). Stewart's first film with director Anthony Mann set the pattern for the well-made Stewart-Mann Westerns to follow.

Winchester '73 (1950), Anthony Mann's first Western with James Stewart, kept revenge within one family; Stewart spent the movie tracking down and finally shooting his brother (Stephen McNally), who had murdered their father. The rifle of the title passes from hand to hand as the story progresses. The climactic shoot-out, with a frenzied Stewart stalking his unregenerate sibling in a forbidding mountain setting, fairly blisters the screen. Alfred Werker's *Three Hours to Kill* (1954) starred Dana Andrews as a stagecoach driver who is accused of killing his ex-fiancée's brother. After he is nearly hanged by a drunken posse before his innocence is proved, he turns angry gunfighter, tracking down the true killer with single-minded ferocity.

Revenge for a brother's murder (a theme, incidentally, as old as William S. Hart's *Riddle Gawne* of 1918) also emerged as the center of *The Man from Laramie* (1955), a superior Anthony Mann Western. The last of Mann's fruitful collaborations with James Stewart, the film starred Stewart in one of his best Western roles as Will Lockhart, an army officer out of uniform as he relentlessly stalks the man who sold rifles to the Indians and precipitated a bloody raid in which his brother was killed. His search leads to the powerful Waggoman family, ruled by the nearly blind Alec Waggoman (Donald Crisp). Alec's nasty, psychotic son Dave (Alex Nicol) has an ambitious rival in his adopted brother Vic (Arthur Kennedy), leading to a bitter and ultimately fatal family rivalry. (The story line's resemblance to *King Lear* is not accidental.) After a number of violent confrontations between Will and the Waggomans, Will squares off with Vic, who turns out to be the man guilty of selling rifles to the Indians. Although Will has "come a thousand miles to kill" Vic, he is unable to pull the trigger, instead leaving Vic to die at the hands of the Apaches.

Skillfully scripted by Philip Yordan and Frank Burt, *The Man from Laramie* has the pace, the vigor, and the intelligence of Mann's best Western films. Although Stewart domi-

The Man from Laramie *(Columbia, 1955). James Stewart (foreground) starred as Will Lockhart, an army officer out of uniform who is bent on a mission to avenge his brother's death. Stewart's final Western with Anthony Mann, the movie unfolded its violent story with Mann's customary vigor and attention to detail.*

nates with his portrait of a fiercely single-minded cowboy, the complex family relationships of the Waggomans provide much of the film's fascination. Vic's scenes with his adoptive father, played by two unusually able actors, have an intensity rare in Westerns ("I was your only true son!" Vic cries before they grapple fiercely, leaving Alec critically hurt and blind). The film also contains several scenes of shocking brutality: one in which Stewart is dragged at the end of a rope by Dave and his men, while his wagons are burned and his mules

shot, and another, later in the movie, in which Dave, in a rage at Will, shoots him in the hand at point-blank range: in a sense, the Western equivalent of castration.

Henry King's *The Bravados* (1958) also hinged on revenge: in this case, one man's revenge for his wife's murder and his painful discovery that all is not what it seems to be. Gregory Peck played the stern-visaged stranger looking for the four men he believes raped and killed his wife. He destroys them one by one, until the last (Henry Silva) convinces him that they were not truly responsible for his wife's death. Once again, as in many Westerns, revenge turns out to be neither sweet nor justified. The film ends ironically: Peck is proclaimed a hero at the same time that he faces the horror of his act ("I killed three men! I killed them for revenge . . . revenge for something they didn't even do!"). Bitterly, he denounces himself as "judge, jury, executioner," although this being a commercial-minded movie, such a strongly downbeat

The Bravados (Fox, 1958). Gregory Peck (right) visits the four outlaws (from left: Stephen Boyd, Albert Salmi, Lee Van Cleef, and Henry Silva) who, he believes, have raped and murdered his wife. Henry King's film centered on Peck's moral dilemma: after the men escape from prison, Peck pursues and kills three of them—then learns that they are innocent of the crime.

ending cannot exist without a ray of hope—there is a suggestion that Peck will find redemption and peace of mind with an old girlfriend (Joan Collins).

Certainly the finest expression of one Westerner's obsessive mission can be found in John Ford's towering film *The Searchers* (1956). Here, a combination of revenge, shattered family ties, and a hatred born of bigotry drives Ethan Edwards (John Wayne) to find the nieces who have been kidnapped by Comanches. In Frank S. Nugent's adaptation of Alan LeMay's novel, Ethan returns to his brother's family in Texas in 1868 after a long and mysterious absence. When his brother and sister-in-law and their son are savagely murdered by marauding Indians and their daughters abducted, Ethan begins a five-year search for the girls, fired by his loathing for Indians. Accompanying him is his brother's adopted son Marty (Jeffrey Hunter), who is part Cherokee and therefore not to be fully trusted or confided in. When Ethan con-

firms to his bitter despair that his surviving niece, Debbie (Natalie Wood), has become an Indian squaw, a festering determination to kill her, rather than rescue her, takes hold in him.

The most widely admired of Ford's Westerns (and perhaps of all Westerns), *The Searchers* warrants—and has received—close scrutiny. In addition to Winton C. Hoch's dazzling photography, which conveys a true sense of the numbing isolation and imminent danger that pervade the

characters' lives, the film contains sequences that remain models of the screen's collaborative art: a brilliant fusing of editing, camerawork, and performance as filtered through a master director's eyes. The early scene in which Ethan's family faces an Indian attack terrifies with a succession of vivid images: birds in sudden flight, a barking dog, and a nervous Martha Edwards watching her gun-toting husband as he tries to remain calm ("Think I'll kill some sage hens before supper"), ending with the shocking view of a Comanche looming ominously over young Debbie. The reiterated views of Ethan and Marty riding together against the majestic background of Monument Valley have an unmatched purity and grandeur. And the climactic battle, in which Marty insists on rescuing the reluctant Debbie and Ethan scalps the dead Indian chieftain Scar, generates an excitement that few other Ford Westerns can match. Above all, the film impresses with its economy: gestures and facial expressions used more eloquently than words, as in the sad, reflective look on Ethan's face as he sits alone on the porch, or the elation with which Debbie rushes to hug Marty for the first time in five years.

The Searchers abounds in so many virtues that one tends to overlook its undeniable faults: stretches of tedium, mostly involving the triangular relationship of Marty, Laurie Jor-

genson (Vera Miles), his longtime sweetheart, and Charlie McCorry (Ken Curtis); the characterization of Indians as savages or clowns; and the patently fake scenery for some of the outdoor scenes. One prefers to remember the Fordian rituals that punctuate the narrative, such as the funeral for Ethan's kin, with the singing of "We'll Gather at the River" as the group huddles about the graves, or the communal gathering for Laurie's intended wedding to Charlie.

Richly textured and varied, *The Searchers* draws much of its power from John Wayne's central performance as Ethan Edwards, which may well be his finest. Wayne's Ethan is a complex man: stubborn, fiercely independent, and relentless in pursuit of his goal. There is something hidden and unspoken in his face: the suggestion of a dark past we can never really fathom. As he spends the years searching for his kidnapped niece, Ethan undergoes his own voyage of self-discovery—his own search for inner peace—that turns him from a driven bigot who shoots out the eyes of a dead Indian so that his soul will wander forever into a man who lifts his Indianized niece high in the air and exclaims, "Let's go home, Debbie."

Wayne succeeds in capturing every nuance of Ethan's character, whether he is gazing with love at his brother's fam-

The Searchers *(Warner Bros., 1956). At the beginning of the film* (OPPOSITE), *the eternal loner Ethan Edwards (John Wayne) is greeted by his sister-in-law Martha (Dorothy Jordan) as he returns home from a long and mysterious absence.* BELOW *Young Martin Pauley (Jeffrey Hunter), who is "one-eighth Cherokee," is reunited with Debbie (Natalie Wood), the young girl who has been held captive for years by the Indians. John Ford's towering Western explored the anguish and the shifting attitudes of her Uncle Ethan* (RIGHT) *during the long years that he searches for her.*

ily, reacting with sick horror to the discovery of one niece's body ("Don't ever ask me! As long as you live, don't ever ask me more!"), or destroying a herd of buffalo (potential food for the Indians) with a frenzy that almost rages out of control. Those who would question Wayne's acting ability might watch the expression of loathing, sorrow, and pain that passes across his face when he finds young girls who have been turned into Indian maidens ("They ain't white any more. They're Comanche"). At the end, Ethan has become a lost soul, out of place in the advancing forces of civilization. Ironically, despite his increasing humanity, he has been rejected by home and hearth. As the door closes on him, possibly forever, Ethan has assumed an almost tragic stature.

With *The Searchers,* the recurring theme of revenge found its strongest expression, and by the sixties, the theme required at least a suggestion of originality and freshness to pass muster in a Western film. The film cryptically entitled *One-Eyed Jacks* (1961) provided this suggestion in its tale of a revenge-bent hero and his target. Directed by its star,

Marlon Brando, with surprising flair as well as almost total self-absorption, the movie traces the long search of Rio (Brando) for Dad Longworth (Karl Malden), the surrogate father who betrayed his love and trust. Fleeing from the authorities after a robbery, Longworth had abandoned Rio in the desert without a horse, leaving him to be caught and imprisoned. Rio's dream of revenge becomes complicated when, five years later, he learns that Longworth has become a sheriff; he also meets Longworth's Mexican wife, Maria (Katy Jurado), and pretty stepdaughter Louisa (Pina Pellicer), with whom he falls in love. In the inevitable show-down, Longworth is killed.

Reportedly, Brando, who replaced Stanley Kubrick as director, shot a million feet of film for an original version that ran nearly five hours, even after extensive cutting. The final release print, running over two hours, shows evidence in the continuity of the severe cuts by editors after Brando relin-quished the reins, but it contains a number of well-con-structed sequences as well as a feverish intensity rare in Westerns. Rio's first reunion with Longworth—the older man watching warily from his hammock as the younger

The Searchers *(Warner Bros., 1956). Ethan Edwards (John Wayne) and Martin Pauley (Jeffrey Hunter) ride through a snowstorm on their search for Ethan's kidnapped niece, Debbie. Among the many virtues of John Ford's classic Western is the beautiful color photography by Winton C. Hoch, who won an Academy Award seven years earlier for Ford's* She Wore a Yellow Ribbon.

OPPOSITE One-Eyed Jacks *(Paramount, 1961). Rio (Marlon Brando) embraces Louisa (Pina Pellicer), the daughter of the man who is the target of his obsessive revenge. Originally scheduled to be filmed in sixty days, the movie took six months to complete, largely due to complications created by star-director Brando.*

approaches—has a quietly sinister feeling, and a remarkable amount of heat is generated in the scene, spoken entirely in Spanish, in which Maria confronts Louisa and forces her to admit she is pregnant by Rio. Also, the climactic scene in which Longworth and his deputies arrest Rio for murder— Rio has killed a nasty, drunken gunman (Timothy Carey) in a barroom brawl—vibrates with tension and a sense of passions out of control. Publicly thrashed by Longworth, a bitter Rio retaliates by spitting in Longworth's face, whereupon Longworth breaks Rio's gun hand and forces him to ride out of town alone.

Despite the occasional subtleties in Guy Trosper and Calder Willingham's screenplay—reportedly, Brando also worked on it for long periods—*One-Eyed Jacks* lacks the sustained and unified force of a great Western film. Its princi-

pal deficiency appears to be the director's indulgence of his star; Brando's Rio is shot in frequent close-up or at symbolic angles that continually remind us of his threat to Longworth's peace of mind. After a while, his brooding, sensitive face becomes more than a mite oppressive, so that we welcome the few scenes in which he does not appear. Apparently, Brando also indulged himself as director; filming a scene in which Rio sits on a rock and gazes out at the surf, Brando spent hours waiting for "the right wave" (Charles Higham, *Brando: The Unauthorized Biography*, New York, 1987, p. 139).

If a thirst for revenge consumed many a Western loner, not all of them rode the plains with burdens heavier than their saddlebags. Occasionally, as in Sydney Pollack's *Jeremiah Johnson* (1972), the loner (Robert Redford) sought to retreat

Angie, he brings them safely through the ordeal; ultimately, his courage earns her forgiveness and understanding. Embittered doctor Gary Cooper, the ambiguous hero of Delmer Daves's *The Hanging Tree* (1959), carries the burden of his wife's suicide, committed after he killed her lover in a rage. He heals old wounds by helping a blinded woman (Maria Schell) and educating an impressionable youngster (Ben Piazza) in the straight and narrow. And in Robert Parrish's leathery Western *The Wonderful Country* (1959), a cynical hired gun (Robert Mitchum) finds redemption by becoming a Robin Hood to the poor Mexicans whose land is being overrun.

No sense of fatalism or cynicism, or even a hint of irony, pervaded the Western film that, more than any other,

Jeremiah Johnson (Warner Bros., 1972). Jeremiah (Robert Redford) cuts his way through a murky swamp (LEFT) in Sydney Pollack's film about one man's confrontation with the terrors and rewards of the Western wilderness (OPPOSITE, ABOVE).

from civilization and to conquer the wilderness, with results that both gratified and terrified him. More often, however, in keeping with the mythic quality of many Western films, a number of these solitary figures burned with a flame of righteousness, seeking to perform good deeds in a corrupt world. Like the legendary Lone Ranger, whose masked presence on the side of law and order spanned radio, television, and the movies, these were knights not in shining armor but in Western garb. If some of them did not lead lives of ascetic purity, their intentions were indisputably noble. Most of these paragons found their way into the series Westerns, where, in the space of little more than an hour, they could best the villains, smile chastely at the heroine, and ride off into the sunset, if not alone, then with their loyal sidekicks. Western aficionados found comfort and a measure of entertainment in the exploits of such stalwart figures as Gene Autry, Roy Rogers, and "Hopalong" Cassidy (actually William Boyd).

When the budgets grew larger than those required by the assembly-line series, the knight on horseback usually took on more complex dimensions: suggestions of human failings or a tarnished, mysterious past sometimes colored his good works. In John Farrow's *Hondo* (1953), taciturn lone rider John Wayne, his face lined by unspoken sorrows and regrets, rescues Angie Lowe (Geraldine Page) and her young son (Lee Aaker) from marauding Apaches in the New Mexico desert. Later, he shoots her husband in self-defense, not knowing the man's identity. Sublimating his growing love for

Hondo (Warner Bros., 1953). John Wayne played the United States Cavalry dispatch rider Hondo Lane. A very Ford-like Western (John Ford actually directed several sequences), the film was originally made in the three-dimensional (3-D) process but was released in the standard flat-screen format.

embodied the concept of the Western knight riding out of a mysterious past to defend and protect the helpless. From the moment we view the single-named Shane astride his horse, quiet-spoken and blondely handsome, we know that we are in the presence of no less than a Western prince. As he settles for a while on the Starrett ranch, then helps Starrett and other homesteaders fight for their place in the sun, Shane becomes the golden center of young Joey Starrett's life, the focus of all things good, strong, and fearless. In the bland and taciturn person of Alan Ladd, Shane is every Western hero rolled into one.

One of the durable Western films, despite some long-standing critical disapproval, *Shane* (1953) represents director George Stevens's attempt to synthesize on a lavish scale all of the established aspects of the legendary West—not the true West—as developed in films over the years. It is, in fact, a conscious (perhaps a mite self-conscious) and loving tribute to the Western Legend as we have come to perceive it in films: the settling of the wilderness, the fight for control of the land between cattlemen and homesteaders, the deeply rooted

Shane (Paramount, 1953). Stars Alan Ladd, Jean Arthur, and Van Heflin pose for a publicity shot. George Stevens's film gave a fully rounded treatment to fundamental situations in the Western, from community dances and funerals to climactic shoot-outs.

Shane (Paramount, 1953). Shane (Alan Ladd), a Western knight in buckskin rather than armor, instructs his most ardent admirer, young Joey Starrett (Brandon de Wilde), in the proper way to handle a gun (OPPOSITE). One of the definitive Westerns, George Stevens's film merged Western myth, ritual, and action in its tale of good versus evil. One of the recurrent rituals in Western films, the funeral (ABOVE) epitomized the threat of imminent death faced by pioneers every day of their lives.

family ties, and the constant threat of destruction or sudden death, at the hands of man or the whims of the elements. But if it is all a created myth, then what better way to see it than through the eyes of a young boy? Shane is a boy's dream of the West, a fable constructed out of time-tested materials.

Furthered by the beautifully crafted screenplay by novelist A. B. Guthrie, Jr., and direction by Stevens that seldom falters, Shane moves steadily through its basically simple story: striving to build a home in the inhospitable wilderness, the Starretts (Van Heflin, Jean Arthur, and Brandon de Wilde), along with other homesteaders, find themselves threatened by a powerful rancher named Ryker. Help appears in the form of a mysterious gunman named Shane, who becomes the idol of young Joey Starrett. After some setbacks,

Shane succeeds in routing or killing Ryker and his men, especially a cold-blooded hired gun named Wilson (Jack Palance), then rides off forever, to the echoing pleas of Joey to "come back!"

Shane constructs a mosaic of themes around this archetypal story, giving many of the sequences an immediacy and excitement by having them viewed from Joey's perspective. He is present at Shane's first fight, when Shane faces up to Ryker's hoodlums ("I saw it all, Mother! Every bit of it!"), and he hides in the saloon for Shane's last fight when the weary gunman kills the heavies in a violent shoot-out. Along the way, Joey observes some of the familiar rituals of Western life: the funeral of hotheaded homesteader Tory (Elisha Cook), murdered by Wilson in a brilliantly staged scene (Tory's sudden fall backward as the bullets strike him is one of the best-remembered Western moments); a lively Fourth of July party by the homesteaders; quiet dinners in a simple, loving home. By the time Joey cries for Shane's return, we understand that he is crying for his lost innocence and, in a sense, our own.

Photographed by Loyal Griggs with a lustrous sheen that emphasizes the majesty of the Grand Teton Mountains, where much of the film was made, *Shane* often transcends every familiar Western element it includes. We can even forgive and admire Shane's stylish light buckskin versus Wilson's somber black costume. The film falters only in its attempt to suggest a romantic tension between Shane and Mrs. Starrett. Ladd's inexpressive acting style and Arthur's somewhat too sophisticated appearance do not combine to generate erotic sparks, no matter how clear the intention. Still, objections to *Shane*'s idealizing of the West, its enshrinement of Western clichés, and its unambiguous characters dim beside the luster of its many fine scenes.

Greatly contrasting with Shane's golden purity, two of the least likely Western knights-to-the-rescue appeared years later in the lean and surly person of Clint Eastwood. These men are not blond gods; the uncommunicative stranger of *High Plains Drifter* (1973) and the mysterious gunman of *Pale Rider* (1985) have been clearly scarred by life and are intimately acquainted with sudden death. Their eyes burn with an intensity that seems almost otherworldly, and indeed it is suggested that both of them may be wraiths returned from beyond the grave to right wrongs and wreak vengeance. Eastwood, who had become a major star in the sixties playing the "Man with No Name" in Sergio Leone's Italian Westerns, here paid homage to these Westerns, retaining their overblown, almost operatic style but also adding an odd, metaphysical touch of his own.

High Plains Drifter begins as near-parody, as the Stranger (Eastwood) appears in the town of Lago, where he is

taunted by the populace until he abruptly shoots three of his most conspicuous tormenters. Impressed by his prowess with a gun, the townsfolk (a sneaky lot, as usual, in Westerns of this stripe) offer to hire him to rid the town of killers who are on their way from prison. He agrees, but mockingly forms a "regiment" of his own, enlisting the town's pompous, ineffectual mayor and making the town's midget into a "sheriff." Eventually it becomes apparent that the Stranger is no ordinary mortal but a reincarnation of the sheriff who had been bullwhipped to death with the silent acquiescence of the good citizens of Lago. He fulfills his promise to destroy the killers and then, in a gesture of contempt, insists on the town being painted red and renamed Hell. As the town is engulfed in flames, he rides away. Curiously, this ending recalls the flames that destroy the corrupt town in William S. Hart's *Hell's Hinges* (1916), filmed over half a century earlier. Apparently, the basic concept of good versus evil, angel versus devil, has never faded in the Western genre.

Darkly forbidding and a force to be reckoned with, this avenging angel is the reverse side of Shane: Shane's purity of intention has been replaced by the drifter's submerged bitterness and rage. Eastwood himself directed *High Plains Drifter* (his second effort as a director), tempering Leone's overwrought style with some of his own restraint.

Eastwood's Preacher in *Pale Rider* moves closer to Shane in his righteous, single-minded pursuit of the villains, although the film's title (death comes on horseback) and the name given to Eastwood's character signal that something more supernatural was intended. Even the film's opening scene hints at the imminent arrival of an otherworldly being. Members of a poor mining community under the heel of a swaggering gang cry, "We need a miracle. Just one miracle." Enter Preacher, dressed as a man of the cloth but with a quick gun and fists of iron. (He also has some highly visible bullet holes in his back.) Soon he is the community's defender against the wealthy Le Hoods, who covet the land. The situation worsens when Preacher suddenly disappears, until he returns in a blaze of righteous rage to wipe out the Le Hoods and their henchmen. As he rides away, the ques-

High Plains Drifter *(Universal, 1972). Echoing his roles in the "spaghetti" Westerns, Clint Eastwood starred as the mysterious Stranger (*ABOVE *and* BELOW*) who has returned from the beyond to exact revenge in his own dark fashion. Eastwood himself directed this odd but arresting Western.*

Pale Rider *(Warner Bros., 1985). Star-director Clint Eastwood paid homage to Sergio Leone's* Once upon a Time in the West *by dressing the villain's murderous henchmen (*ABOVE*) in the same long brown coats worn by Henry Fonda's men in Leone's "spaghetti" Western. The mysterious Preacher (Eastwood) will soon be along to rid the town of these killers (*BELOW*).*

tion lingers: Was he real, or was he the reincarnation of a murdered man, sent back to earth to exact his revenge?

Around a plot that is fundamentally simplistic and awkwardly realized, Eastwood, as star and director, performs some fancy footwork, photographing Preacher at odd angles or in tight close-up and orchestrating scenes that either teeter precariously on the edge of parody or resemble scenes from early "spaghetti" Westerns. In one harsh but faintly absurd sequence, the villainous henchmen, all dressed in identical long brown coats that match the coats worn by Henry Fonda's men in Sergio Leone's *Once upon a Time in the West,* surround a hapless miner who has found gold and force him to dance before shooting him in cold blood. Too many lines of dialogue appear to be spoofing the genre—"You're a troublemaker, stranger!" Le Hood tells Preacher—and too many plot devices and moments suggest a metaphysical version of *Shane.* The ending even has a young girl running after Preacher as he rides away and shouting, "Preacher! Preacher! We all love you, Preacher! I love you!"

The Naked Spur *(MGM, 1953). James Stewart gave one of his best performances in a Western—fierce, intense, and entirely credible—as a bounty hunter in Anthony Mann's film. Janet Leigh played a woman with shifting loyalties who comes to understand his troubled mind.*

Apart from the Western loners of noble or ignoble intent, there were those who, at first, seemed to have no intent at all, men who prized their isolation from the familiar patterns of life. If not actively misanthropic, they still viewed compassion and caring as signs of weakness; human treachery awaited around every bend in the trail. Their guiding principle was: if every man is vile, then I must either stay apart from other men or surpass them in vileness. Of course, by the time his story ended, this species of loner could be counted on to reverse his attitude, to discover that far from being alone in a dangerous land, he had people who loved and supported him. He also learned a lesson entirely apt to the overall hawkishness of the genre: no man can isolate himself forever from the pervasive evil in the universe.

Westerners who turned from hermit to hawk appeared regularly in films of the late forties and fifties, most successfully in Anthony Mann's unusually complex *The Naked Spur* (1953). The film centered on James Stewart as Howard Kemp, a deeply troubled bounty hunter who is charged with bringing in outlaw Ben Vandergroat (Robert Ryan). When

others—a grizzled prospector (Millard Mitchell), a dishonorably discharged soldier (Ralph Meeker), and a woman (Janet Leigh)—join Kemp on the long journey, the situation becomes dangerously tense as Vandergroat works on dividing each person against the other. We eventually learn that Kemp is actually a rancher, bitter at losing his land because of a treacherous fiancée, and anxious to start again with the reward money. He finds, however, that he cannot control the situation until he controls his own tortured mind. The actual journey becomes Kemp's search for his lost innocence. At the end, after Vandergroat has died in a final confrontation, Kemp weeps in grateful release.

The Naked Spur contains the expected virtues of an Anthony Mann Western: an intelligent, Oscar-nominated screenplay, by Sam Rolfe and Harold Jack Bloom, photography, by William C. Mellor, that displays the awesome landscape against which the drama unfolds, and strong acting by a capable cast. Stewart's performance dominates the film: gone are the shy, awkward mannerisms he used for Jefferson Smith in *Mr. Smith Goes to Washington* (1939); his Howard Kemp is an obsessed man who is inwardly sick at being reduced to selling a man's life for money. In an extraordinary scene, following a nightmare in which he sweats and tosses fitfully, he relates the story of his unhappy past. When he engages in battle with the duplicitous members of his traveling party, he seems to be battling his own instincts more fiercely than the treachery of his opponents. At another point in the story, in an uncontrollable rage, he urges Ben to draw so that he can shoot him without compunction. Kemp's long-festering self-hatred spews forth in every word, every gesture.

Another troubled Mann hero appeared five years later in *Man of the West* (1958). Gary Cooper played Link Jones, an apparently timid Texan forced to deal with a sadistic gang of robbers made up of his uncle and cousins. Obliged to pretend that he wants to rejoin the gang, he manages to reduce their number, one by one, in a series of violent encounters, until he faces—and finally shoots—his now desolate uncle. As in other Mann Westerns, the interest stems not only from the surface action but also from the psychological involvement of the central character. As he abandons his safe, gentle life to go about the bloodstained business of shooting his relatives, Link begins to feel that he has become irrevocably corrupted, a man no better than his victims. Yet after the killing is done, he returns to his wife, softened by the love of the saloon singer (Julie London) the gang had repeatedly abused and humiliated. An unusually harsh and unsparing Western, with a blistering screenplay by Reginald Rose, *Man of the West* drew fire for some of its boldest scenes (especially one in which the woman is forced to strip for the gang), yet its primal force could hardly be denied.

One series of Westerns in the late fifties, starring William S. Hart's heir apparent, Randolph Scott, offered variations on the character of the redeemed isolationist or the transformed badman. In these films, trimly and confidently directed by Budd Boetticher, Scott created a freshly observed gallery of lonely, withdrawn men who, reasserting their honor and their pride, find themselves obliged to fight on the side of right. In *The Tall T* (1957), the best of the group, he played a proud but down-on-his-luck small rancher (characteristically, he is first seen riding alone in the desert) who must deal with

Man of the West *(United Artists, 1958). The vicious Coaley (Jack Lord), one of the sons of sadistic outlaw chief Dock Tobin (Lee J. Cobb), threatens to kill Link Jones (Gary Cooper), the retired gunman who has pretended to rejoin Tobin's gang. Anthony Mann's penultimate Western drew fire for its unrelenting violence.*

The Tall T *(Columbia, 1957). Clearly expecting trouble, rancher Pat Brennan (Randolph Scott) waits warily atop a stagecoach with the driver (Arthur Hunnicutt). In this and other Westerns directed by Budd Boetticher, Scott epitomized the strong, introspective Western loner with a code of honor.*

a band of outlaws when they hold him prisoner along with others. While subtle reversals in the usual Western characters (the rancher craves freedom from responsibility to others; the outlaw leader longs for a plot of land) keep the Burt Kennedy screenplay interesting, the final scenes show the rancher taking an expected stand: "Some things a man can't ride around!"

Boetticher repeated the pattern in other Scott Westerns, with satisfying results. In *Buchanan Rides Alone* (1958), Scott, somewhat less stolid than usual, played an easygoing, none-too-bright Texan, a former mercenary soldier in Mexico, who rides into Agry Town, known as Helltown-on-the-Border, where he proceeds to tangle with the vicious Agry brothers. Eventually, he learns that "a man's gotta be loyal to somethin'," in this case a young Mexican who has sworn to avenge his sister's dishonor. Some quirky touches in the screenplay (Buchanan addressing the dead body of his friend—"You died real good"—or the villainous brothers canceling each other out in the climactic shoot-out) give the film uncommon interest. *Ride Lonesome* (1959) starred Scott

as a former sheriff charged with bringing a young outlaw to justice before the outlaw's killer-brother can rescue him. Eventually he succeeds, but not before learning that he cannot take a stand alone. Not surprisingly, the Burt Kennedy screenplay repeated his line from *The Tall T*: "There are some things a man can't ride around!" This sentiment was echoed in *Comanche Station* (1960), the last of the Boetticher-Scott Westerns.

Apart from the Western loners—the lawmen, outlaws, and individualists who made their own way in the wilderness—the Western film also drew on the pages of history to fill its insatiable need for heroic figures who could fill no other shoes but their own. Hoisted from reality to legend by way of pulp fiction, word-of-mouth, and the strenuous efforts of flamboyant promoters, these men—and occasional women—provided endless grist for the Western mill. One of the most prominent of these Westerners was "Wild Bill" (actually James Butler) Hickok. Lauded as an adventurous pioneer and Indian fighter (at least until recent years, when darker hues were mixed into the rose-colored portrait), Hickok was actually neither heroic nor villainous. He had been a stagecoach driver, a Union scout, and a United States marshal of no particular repute when an article in the February 1867 issue of *Harper's New Monthly Magazine*, written by one Colonel George Ward Nichols, bestowed the mantle of a hero on Hickok's shoulders and changed James into the marksman known as "Wild Bill." Hickok spent a period of time in show business, gambled steadily, plotted a mining expedi-

Ride Lonesome *(Columbia, 1959). A small band of whites, led by bounty hunter Ben Brigade (Randolph Scott), tries to defend itself against a tribe of attacking Apaches. When not fighting off the Indians, Scott struggled to bring a young outlaw to justice in Budd Boetticher's compact little Western.*

OPPOSITE, ABOVE   *A portrait of the ever-popular "Wild Bill" Hickok. "Wild Bill" became a national celebrity after an interview with a Western journalist named George Ward Nichols, whose fanciful stories of Hickok's battles and skirmishes were taken as gospel by a gullible public. In silent and sound films, James Butler Hickok was treated as an authentic legend.*

OPPOSITE, BELOW   The Plainsman *(Paramount, 1936). Calamity Jane (Jean Arthur) bids farewell to her beloved friend "Wild Bill" Hickok (Gary Cooper), as Hickok's friend "Buffalo Bill" Cody (James Ellison, left) and army officers look on. The true "Calam" was a plain, hard-drinking virago named Martha Jane Cannary.*

tion, and was finally shot to death in August 1876 by an outlaw named Jack McCall, whose motives remain unknown.

These facts had little bearing on the figure created by Colonel Nichols, and "Wild Bill" soon became a familiar character in Western lore, especially in pulp Western fiction. In the silent years, William S. Hart portrayed Hickok in a 1923 movie that inspired unusually vituperative comments from the usually staid *New York Times*: its review called Hart's effort puerile and attacked Hart's performance for being of the "old, old school." By the time Cecil B. DeMille made Hickok the center of his 1937 Western epic *The Plainsman*, the legend was fully in place. Gary Cooper played him as a stoic, quietly forceful man whose brave deeds included rescuing the lovelorn Calamity Jane (Jean Arthur) from hostile Indians. His death scene, with "Calam" cradling his body as she kisses him goodbye, moved thirties audiences to tears. Although the film's historical distortions also turned "Buffalo Bill" Cody (James Ellison) into a bland and earnest nonentity and George Armstrong Custer (John Miljan) into a hero, DeMille's well-honed narrative sense—he often made up in storytelling ability for what he lacked in style—made the

movie reasonably entertaining and a virtual masterwork in comparison with the 1966 remake starring Don Murray as Hickok.

"Wild Bill" turned up repeatedly in Westerns of the forties and fifties, as a minor figure adding a semblance of historical verisimilitude (*Badlands of Dakota*, 1941; *Dallas*, 1950) or as a leading character in a standard Western adventure (*Wild Bill Hickok Rides*, 1941; *Pony Express*, 1953). In more recent years, the treatment has been much less kind, though hardly more accurate. In Arthur Penn's bitter, funny *Little Big Man* (1970), which viewed Western history through the eyes of a 121-year-old man, "Wild Bill" (Jeff Corey) turns up as a lethargic has-been who has one comic

saloon encounter with the protagonist, Jack Crabb, and then reappears later, to be shot dead by a boy. J. Lee Thompson's *The White Buffalo* (1977) transformed Hickok into an Ahab-like figure, played by Charles Bronson, who returns to the Western plains in search of the white buffalo that haunts his dreams. Chief Crazy Horse (Will Sampson) accompanies him on his mission.

Hickok's friend and erstwhile colleague William Frederick ("Buffalo Bill") Cody has also earned a decisive place in Western films. Unlike "Wild Bill," his true story contains colorful aspects—he was a pony express rider at fifteen, an army scout, and a buffalo hunter who supplied meat to railway workers (hence his nickname of "Buffalo Bill"). Like "Wild Bill," he was elevated to heroic status by a writer who turned his story into a myth. Ned Buntline (real name Edward Zane Carroll Judson) wrote a series of dime novels about "Buffalo Bill" Cody that stirred and delighted adventure-minded youngsters. On the strength of his newly found fame, "Buffalo Bill" toured with a play he wrote himself called *The Scouts of the Prairie*, and, starting in 1883, he traveled across America and Europe with a hugely popular show he called "Wild West." It offered live buffaloes, genuine Indians (including Sitting Bull) attacking a stagecoach, and

*Buffalo Bill (Fox, 1944). "Buffalo Bill" Cody (Joel McCrea) displays his expert marksmanship at his Wild West show (*BELOW*). The movie offered a mostly fanciful and whitewashed version of the life of the legendary army scout and buffalo hunter, depicting him as entirely upright in all his dealings with the government and the Indians. (*OPPOSITE, ABOVE*) Indians hold a ceremonial war dance. In Indian lore, the greatest honor came to the warrior who had put himself closest to danger during the battle.*

A cowboy tries his skill on a bronco in a Wild West show in North Dakota, 1919. Many years earlier, in 1883, "Buffalo Bill" Cody had introduced his popular Wild West show, which featured displays of marksmanship and horsemanship, and even a simulated scene of real Indians attacking a stagecoach.

authentic cowboys displaying their skills. Toward the end of his life, after years of bankruptcy, he made a film about the West he had known. (Only a part of the last reel has survived.) A heavy drinker and inept businessman, he died destitute in 1917.

As a film character, "Buffalo Bill" Cody surfaced many times in movies both major and minor. Two films, however, reveal widely contrasting attitudes toward his life and career. William Wellman's *Buffalo Bill* (1944) merely skimmed over the biographical data on Cody (Joel McCrea), depicting him as a staunch hero who becomes a Wild West showman after adventures as a scout and hunter. It showed him spending his last difficult years in vigorous protest against the ill treatment of Indians he had fought in earlier days, a rather unusual stance for a mid-forties Western. More than three decades later, Paul Newman offered quite a different characterization of Cody in Robert Altman's *Buffalo Bill and the Indians or Sitting Bull's History Lesson* (1976).

In Altman and Alan Rudolph's very loose adaptation of Arthur Kopit's play *Indians*, Buffalo Bill is no hero but an aging, flamboyant showman who is partly a fraud and partly a victim of his own legend, forced to indulge in Wild West

Buffalo Bill and the Indians or Sitting Bull's History Lesson (United Artists, 1976). William Frederick ("Buffalo Bill") Cody (Paul Newman) rides into the arena of his popular Wild West show. Robert Altman's film took a cynical view of Cody, portraying him as a florid and egotistical old man who begins to believe his own legend.

fakery to hold his audience. (Someone says, "Truth is whatever gets the most applause.") The brooding presence of Sitting Bull (Frank Kaquitts) was intended to provide a note of true as opposed to fraudulent Western history. Although Altman's affectionate and lavish re-creation of a Wild West show undercut some of the intended cynicism, the film's view of Cody was harsh and jaundiced, a far cry from Wellman's Buffalo Bill. Geraldine Chaplin's Annie Oakley, practicing her sharpshooting act with her increasingly nervous husband, Frank Butler, was equally far removed from the romanticized frontier maiden played by Barbara Stanwyck in *Annie Oakley* (1935) or Betty Hutton's leather-lunged bumpkin in *Annie Get Your Gun* (1950).

Among the historical Western figures who have weathered changes in film styles or survived approaches ranging from romantic to revisionist, none is more controversial than George Armstrong Custer. The general who led his troops into an Indian massacre at Little Bighorn on June 25, 1876, has been the subject of intense research over the years. Many books have been written in an attempt to explain his actions. Historians have asked: Why did he divide his meager command into three sections and then send them off in different directions? Why, after seeing the odds against him, would he shout, "Hurrah, boys, we've got them!"? Most recently, Evan S. Connell's book *Son of the Morning Star* (1984) sifted through all of the vast body of writings to reach what is regarded as the most reliable conclusion: only Custer himself will ever know the reasons for his legendary mistake. Apparently, before that fateful day at Little Bighorn, the attitude of this enigmatic general toward Indians ranged all the way from compassion to brutality.

Whatever the truth about "Old Yeller Hair," his image has appeared in many Western films, from the silent era to recent years. By far the most elaborate and most romanticized version of Custer's life and career can be found in *They Died with Their Boots On* (1941). Energetically directed by Raoul Walsh, the movie tossed history to the winds as it offered a Custer (Errol Flynn) who rises from a foppish, overbearing West Point cadet to a Civil War hero. According to the Wally Klein-Aeneas MacKenzie screenplay, Custer's daring deeds, in defiance of military rules, bring him nothing but trouble, and he also suffers from the treachery of an ex-cadet named Sharp (Arthur Kennedy). He finally leads his troops in a brave but futile battle at Little Bighorn. Staged in bravura fashion by Walsh, this climactic sequence must surely rank among the screen's greatest, as Bert Glennon's sweeping camera vivifies the clash of desperate cavalrymen and fierce Indian warriors. Flynn's flamboyant Custer was nicely balanced throughout the film by Olivia de Havilland as his sensible, devoted wife.

There were other Custers in the fifties (in *Warpath*, 1951; *Bugles in the Afternoon*, 1952; and *Tonka*, 1958); it was not until the sixties that films offered a revisionist view of Custer's contribution to military history. Robert Siodmak's *Custer of the West* (1968) was most conspicuous in this regard: a sprawling epic film, it characterized Custer not as a hero in buckskin but as a cold, ironic realist out of place in his time. Sickened by the army's murderously cruel treatment of Indians, he nonetheless reacts with cool detachment when the Indians' sacred hunting ground is stolen from them. He tells the Cheyennes: "Right or wrong, for better or worse, that's the way things seem to get done. That's history. I'm talking about history. You are paying the price for being backward." Throughout the film, despite Robert Shaw's intelligent performance, this George Armstrong Custer

Custer of the West *(Security/Cinerama, 1968). General George Armstrong Custer (Robert Shaw, center) leads his men into the fray. This film offered a more complex portrait of Custer than most, depicting him as neither a brave hero nor a self-serving, incompetent military officer.*

They Died with Their Boots On *(Warner Bros., 1941). General Custer (Errol Flynn) leads his soldiers in a charge against the enemy. Raoul Walsh's vigorous Western bore scant relation to history, but his staging of the battle at Little Bighorn was superb filmmaking.*

seems ambiguously motivated; it is never made entirely clear whether he is seeking personal military glory, honor in a dishonorable world, or justice for the Indians. By the time of the climactic Battle at Little Bighorn, in which Custer, as the sole survivor, forces the Indians to kill him, a confused audience cannot sort out its sympathies. Filmed in Spain, *Custer of the West* remains pictorially effective but dramatically inept, relying finally on a cluster of tricky Cinerama sequences, especially one involving a runaway train, for entertainment. It remained only for Arthur Penn's *Little Big Man* to complete the circle, portraying a demented, vainglorious Custer leading his troops to doom.

Lawman or outlaw, coward or hero, the Western man often stood as proudly alone as the mountain peaks he struggled to cross and conquer. The comforts of a good (or not-so-good) woman, the companionship of a drinking or gambling friend could make him forget his isolation for a while. Yet out of his loneliness came grit, determination, and the ability to withstand hardship and tragedy. Out of his isolation came the basis for many memorable Western movies.

The Return of Frank James *(Fox, 1940). Jesse's surviving brother Frank (Henry Fonda, right) rides into town with young Clem (Jackie Cooper). This sequel to the hugely successful* Jesse James *marked Austrian-born director Fritz Lang's first Western and first film in color.*

Men Together

"When you ride with a man, you stay with him. Otherwise, you're an animal."

—William Holden in *The Wild Bunch* (Warner Bros.-Seven Arts, 1969)

IF THE WESTERN LONER remained a ubiquitous figure in the genre, so did the figure of the Westerner who continually linked himself with others to form an immutable bond. In the real West, outside the families, which melded themselves into units as protection against the elements and enemies, hard-bitten men could find some respite from fear and loneliness by joining with other men in a common goal. Sometimes the goal was simple and direct. Young cowboys who rode the range for fifteen hours a day, seven days a week, continually testing their skills at roping, shooting, and bronco-busting, would gather in the bunkhouse or around a campfire to eat their meager rations or to catch a few hours of badly needed sleep. Occasionally, they would drift into town to play cards or to flirt with the bar girls. Often, loose bonds would form among the townspeople, citizens with different goals and interests, who organized in order to enforce the basic laws to overcome threats to their safety and well-being. Transposed to the Western film, such bonds were frequently seen in the image of the sheriff or marshal riding off with his hastily organized posse in pursuit of outlaws or desperadoes.

Yet the most prevalent bond by far among men of the Western genre existed not between the sheriff and his posse but among the outlaws they pursued. One Western movie after another focused on members of the outlaw gang who came together out of a variety of motives (revenge, greed, hostility toward society), then followed their destiny, usually to oblivion at the end of a rope. Not that these movie outlaws resembled the outlaws in the true annals of Western history, who robbed and murdered with impunity. Up on the screen,

these men were a tamer breed; although they occasionally bristled with nastiness or even unregenerate evil, more often they were depicted as wronged figures, forced into lives of crime by circumstances beyond their control. Like their gangster counterparts of the thirties, the Robinsons and Cagneys at odds with society, Western outlaws faced inevitable defeat. America, however, has always loved its outlaws, and, knowing this, many filmmakers over the years have latched onto the false legends surrounding such true-life desperadoes as Jesse James and turned them into screen legends that have persisted to the present day.

Jesse James, in fact, became one of the most familiar figures in Western films across the years, with each decade's film reflecting the attitudes of its particular time. Always linked with his more taciturn brother Frank, and more loosely allied with other well-known gangs of the period (especially the Daltons), Jesse rode the range in many a Western saga. The fact that he seldom if ever resembled the true Jesse apparently bothered nobody. In reality a vicious man with a darkly brooding temperament, James began his lawless career in 1866 with a bank robbery in Liberty, Missouri. Joined by his equally saturnine brother Frank and others, James continued to rob banks until 1873, when he branched into robbing trains as well. A staunch Confederate guerrilla during the Civil War, James blamed vengeful Northern enemies and relentless Pinkerton agents for driving him into outlawry; he often wrote to the newspapers denying his crimes ("I will never surrender to be mobbed by a set of blood-thirsty poltroons").

In 1875, when agents raided his mother's house, killing his younger brother and causing his mother to lose her arm, public sympathy for Jesse and his brother swept the country. For several years, he settled down in Nashville with his wife, Zee, then formed another gang. When a proclamation was made offering a reward for information leading to his arrest, Bob Ford, a treacherous former gang member, tracked James down to his hiding place and shot him dead on April 3, 1882. For weeks after killing James, Ford earned one hundred dollars a night appearing at theaters in Kansas City. The mythification of James can be attributed to one Major John Newman Edwards, a Missouri newspaperman and Confederate veteran who staunchly defended the Jameses in print and eulogized Jesse after his death. The law continued to pursue Frank James, who finally surrendered, saying, "I'm tired of running. Tired of waiting for a ball in the back. Tired of looking into the faces of friends and seeing a Judas." He was brought to trial for murder but acquitted after a series of trials.

From the beginning, Jesse and Frank James fascinated the moviemakers. As early as 1908, a movie called *The James Boys in Missouri* dealt with the brothers' exploits, and in 1921, two movies entitled *Jesse James as the Outlaw* and *Jesse James under the Black Flag* starred the outlaw's son Jesse Edward, who was billed as Jesse James, Jr. In 1927, popular cowboy star Fred Thomson, astride his horse Silver King, appeared in *Jesse James* as a purely heroic figure, forced into outlawry by circumstances. With the passing of time, the Jameses' arrogance and brutality were whitewashed out of existence. By the sound era, the authentic Jesse and Frank were virtually unrecognizable, and before long, the outlaw brothers were ennobled in movies that reflected the attitudes of the particular period in which they were made.

Jesse James (Fox, 1939). Fleeing from the law during one of his bank robberies, Jesse (Tyrone Power) gets caught up in a gunfight. Although Henry King's movie bore little resemblance to the truth, its energetic action and brilliant Technicolor photography made for a pleasurable Western.

The first major sound film to romanticize Jesse James came from 20th Century-Fox at the end of the thirties. A highly influential Western, Henry King's *Jesse James* (1939) culminated a decade of filmmaking in which a cold and/or hostile society was depicted as the villain, spurring mistreated, misunderstood citizens to lives of crime. Films such as *You Only Live Once* and *Let Us Live* showed hapless victims pursued by an indifferent, pitiless government. It was not difficult to transport this concept back to the days of the Old West, thus transforming a vicious hood into a wronged hero. In Nunnally Johnson's screenplay, Jesse James (Tyrone Power) becomes an honorable young man who turns outlaw with his brother Frank (Henry Fonda) only to wreak ven-

geance on the Saint Louis-Midland Railroad, whose nasty troubleshooter (Brian Donlevy) had killed their mother in trying to take over their land. Jesse and Frank are hailed as national heroes, celebrated in song and story, until Jesse is shot down by "that dirty little coward" Bob Ford (John Carradine).

Although it bears little relation to the truth, *Jesse James* qualifies as a superior Western, briskly directed by King, photographed in vivid Technicolor by George Barnes, and competently acted by Power, Fonda, Randolph Scott, Nancy Kelly, and a large cast of Fox regulars. Some scenes churn with vigorous action: for example, an ill-fated bank robbery by the James boys and their gang is played at a breathless pace that generates excitement. The attempt to portray Jesse's fatalistic state of mind, his inability to escape his past, works less well. At this relatively early stage in his career, Tyrone Power lacked the ability to suggest the depths of feeling in this brooding, self-loathing man; Henry Fonda's laconic, straight-talking Frank comes off much better.

The success of *Jesse James* prompted Fox to launch a sequel that would revolve around the surviving brother Frank. Henry Fonda was signed to repeat his role, the Technicolor cameras again moved into place, and the buckets of whitewash were retained to turn Frank James into a surly but basically decent man forced out of anonymity by circumstances beyond his control. In *The Return of Frank James* (1940), Frank tracks down his brother's murderer, Bob Ford, shooting him only after Ford has killed his young sidekick Clem (Jackie Cooper). He also sacrifices his own freedom to save a loyal black friend from the gallows. At his trial he is found not guilty; later, he is fully pardoned, in time to bid a quiet farewell to Eleanor Loomis (Gene Tierney), the young woman who befriended and supported him, and whom he secretly loves.

Rather solemn and low-key despite the Technicolor hues and the customary amount of gunplay, *The Return of Frank James* tries too hard to characterize and justify the motives of its hero. The ambiguities in Sam Hellman's screenplay are emphasized by the director, Fritz Lang, who hardly seemed an ideal choice to helm a Western adventure. (This was his first color film.) Infused with a gloomy fatalism, many of his films, both in Europe and America, portrayed the protagonist as either a hapless creature trapped like a fly in a spider's web made up of the social, political, and psychological strands of his time or an implacable figure obsessed with revenge. Applied to a strictly American genre, his dark point of view casts a certain glumness over *The Return of Frank James* that no relatively happy ending can mitigate. Nevertheless, the movie succeeded at the box office, and Lang was rewarded with another Western saga, *Western Union* (1941).

The Return of Frank James (Fox, 1940). In this Fritz Lang Western, Henry Fonda again took up the role he had in Jesse James *as Jesse's brother. Although the movie depicted Frank as more reflective and less violent than Jesse, in actuality, he was not much better than his notorious sibling.*

Virtually sanctified in celluloid, Jesse James turned up throughout the forties and fifties in such Westerns as *Jesse James at Bay* (1941), *Badman's Territory* (1946), and *The Great Missouri Raid* (1950), in every case unrecognizable as the murderous outlaw of history. Only one movie, Samuel Fuller's *I Shot Jesse James* (1949), veered from the conventional view, focusing on Jesse's assassin, Bob Ford (John Ireland)—he kills the outlaw to win a pardon so that he can marry his childhood sweetheart. Several films merely used the name Jesse James as a box-office lure, even failing to include Jesse as a character—*The Return of Jesse James* (1950) starred John Ireland as an outlaw who resembles Jesse, giving rise to the legend that Jesse has risen from the grave, and in *Jesse James vs. the Daltons* (1954), Brett King played a young gunman who, thinking he might be Jesse James's son, sets off on a search for his father.

This photographic portrait purportedly shows Jesse (left) and Frank James with their mother, Mrs. Zerelda Samuel. On a night in January 1875, operatives of the Pinkerton Detective Agency, hired to destroy the James gang, threw a lighted flare into their mother's home to illuminate those within. Alighting in the fireplace, it exploded and caused Mrs. Samuel to lose an arm.

The True Story of Jesse James (Fox, 1957). Jeffrey Hunter, shown with gun at the ready, played Frank James to Robert Wagner's Jesse in Nicholas Ray's CinemaScope Western. In keeping with the attitude of the period, the movie depicted the James boys as alienated teenagers trapped in a hostile world, not too far removed from the modern youngsters in Ray's movie Rebel without a Cause *(1955).*

One fifties film made a groping attempt at reality, but a reality filtered through contemporary concerns. Nicholas Ray's *The True Story of Jesse James* (1957), in keeping with the late-fifties interest in rebellious youth (*The Young Stranger*, *Dino*, and others) characterized Jesse and his brother Frank as misfits caught up in an unfriendly world that refuses to understand them. Ray, whose interest in youth at odds with society was evident in his earlier direction of *They Live by Night* and *Rebel without a Cause*, portrayed the James boys (Robert Wagner and Jeffrey Hunter) as Southern soldiers who are fired at as they surrender under a white flag. Refused work in a Union outpost because of their Southern sympathies, they turn to bank robbing, only to learn, like teenage rebels in every generation, there is no escape from a life of crime. Although the movie made a marked contrast to Henry King's romantic *Jesse James*, it hardly conveyed the "true" story of the outlaws.

A critical incident in the lives of the actual James brothers was their last, disastrous bank robbery in the small town of Northfield, Minnesota, on September 7, 1876, in which the townspeople lay in wait for the Jameses and their gang and opened fire on them, cutting them to pieces. The incident has figured importantly in many of the movies about the James boys; *The True Story of Jesse James*, for example, begins in the middle of the Northfield raid and relates the events leading up to it in a series of flashbacks. By the time of Philip Kaufman's *The Great Northfield, Minnesota Raid* in 1972, the long-standing romantic view of the Jameses had been replaced by the revisionist view of the brothers as murderous figures in a grubby and dangerous West, headed for oblivion in a time of rapid, devastating change.

Robert Duvall's Jesse is no staunch hero but an obsessed neurotic, goaded by his visions into destroying evil Northerners. As in other Westerns of the period, this film concentrated on harshly realistic details: Jesse's first vision of divine guidance, for example, occurs in an outhouse. This is not the simpler Old West of guns and horses, in which any respectable outlaw could count on ready cash at the local bank. This is the new West of steam-driven tractors, bank vaults with time locks, and a sport—baseball—that is rapidly replacing shooting as the national pastime.

The Northfield raid also turned up as the elaborately staged central sequence of Walter Hill's impressive Western *The Long Riders* (1980). Although Ric Waite's richly burnished photography and Ry Cooder's musical score give the movie a nostalgic feeling, Hill's intention, and the intention of writers Bill Bryden and Steven Philip Smith, is not nostalgia but rather a clear-eyed, unromantic depiction of outlaw life in frontier America, not only with all of its treachery and brutality, but also with the bonds that were often formed

The Great Northfield, Minnesota Raid (Universal, 1972). Philip Kaufman's unconventional Western came closer to history by giving Jesse James (Robert Duvall, right) a psychotic streak. Here he poses with brother Frank (John Pearce) and the old woman (Nellie Burt) who cares for them after they are wounded in the raid.

among men outside the law. Using a brothers-playing-brothers device, Hill cast James and Stacy Keach as Jesse and Frank James (they also assisted in the writing), Nicholas and Christopher Guest as Bob and Charlie Ford, David, Keith, and Robert Carradine as the Younger brothers, and Randy and Dennis Quaid as the Miller brothers. The screenplay portrays the outlaw gang as a wild bunch (Peckinpah's *The Wild Bunch* is a direct influence) made up of aimless, amoral men drifting into crime and notoriety, with each man using the others as shields against the outside world. Only the James boys are motivated by revenge, against the Pinkerton agents who burned down their house and killed their younger brother. The film's impact comes not from the telling of the familiar—if mythic—story but from the cumulative detail crowded into almost every scene, from rowdy encounters in a brothel to shoot-outs and bar fights that explode with violence. Like Philip Kaufman, Hill focuses on the gritty, realistic detail, an approach that is equally removed from the roseate Robin Hood attitude of the forties and the absurdist devices of the sixties, which tended to treat the Old West solely as a playground for knaves, buffoons, and opportunists. His directorial style reaches its peak in the Northfield raid, in which the gang shoots it out with the citizenry, mostly Swedish immigrants. Brilliantly staged and edited, the sequence uses slow motion, zoom shots, a cacophony of sound and, of course, a virtual river of blood to convey the terror and disorientation of the incident.

Other outlaws and outlaw gangs have been wrested from the pages of history to assume heroic proportions that would have astonished their contemporaries. Like the Jameses and the Youngers, who were occasionally given their

very own films (*Bad Men of Missouri*, 1941; *The Younger Brothers*, 1949), the Daltons arose out of the turbulence that followed the end of the Civil War. Impressed by stories of the adventures of the outlaw gangs, Bob, Grattan ("Grat"), Frank, Bill, and Emmett Dalton turned to banditry after serving the law in some capacity, and by the 1890s virtually every train robbery in the West was attributed to them. Their most notorious exploit was a reckless raid on Coffeyville, Kansas, in October 1892 that left many dead, including Bob and Grat Dalton. In 1940, Universal offered a highly fanciful version of the Dalton story entitled *When the Daltons Rode*, which starred Randolph Scott as a young lawyer who befriends the brothers after they are forced into a life of crime by dastardly railroad men. (The influence of *Jesse James* remained pervasive for several years.) Five years later, the studio reworked much of the same material in *The Daltons Ride Again* (1945), repeating the bloody shoot-out in Coffeyville that marked their end.

Outlaws of lesser reknown than the Jameses, the Youngers, and the Daltons have, on occasion, been transformed

The Great Northfield, Minnesota Raid (Universal, 1972). As in most Westerns, this view of a typical Hollywood Western street, complete with shops, riders, and coaches, offers a rather scrubbed, idealized version of the real thing.

The Long Riders (*United Artists, 1980*). Actor brothers played outlaw brothers in Walter Hill's unblinkered view of outlaw life in the West. From left: David, Keith, and Robert Carradine as the Youngers; Christopher and Nicholas Guest as the Fords; Dennis and Randy Quaid as the Millers; and Stacy and James Keach as the Jameses. The last two had a hand in the screenplay.

A horse team heads down a Western main street around 1905. By this time, the familiar Western street of countless Western movies was giving way to changing social conditions and increased political pressures. Often, the areas surrounding the towns were being taken over for dam sites by private power interests or were being depleted of their natural resources by lumbering, mining, and controlled grazing.

Belle Starr *(Fox, 1941). Belle Starr (Gene Tierney), aristo-cratic Southern girl turned gunfighter, joins with husband Sam (Randolph Scott), a Confederate guerrilla leader, in the fight against Yankee carpetbaggers. The true Belle was a disreput-able woman whose claims to fame included being the first woman ever tried for horse theft in a federal court.*

miraculously by movie legend. In such movies as *Al Jennings of Oklahoma* (1951), *Jack Slade* (1953), and *Blackjack Ketchum, Desperado* (1956), true-life figures with less than savory reputations have been transformed into victimized gunslingers trying to live down their criminal past. The West's most notorious female outlaw, Belle Starr, also turned up periodically in Western movies, cosmeticized from the disreputable woman she probably was into a heroine forced by circumstances into outlawry. Irving Cummings's *Belle Starr* (1941) distorted the truth most shamelessly, characteriz-

ing Belle (Gene Tierney) as a genteel Southern girl who turns gunfighter to continue the battle against carpetbagger Yankees. In 1952, Jane Russell played Belle in Allan Dwan's *Montana Belle* as a tough woman quite the equal of her male cohorts, who ends up being killed by the Daltons. Pamela Reed's sharp-tongued, forthright Belle in *The Long Riders* remains the closest the screen has gotten to veracity.

In many ways, these outlaws represented the opposite side of the Western coin. Unlike the sheriffs and marshals who were often called on to stand in isolated peril against the villains, or the gunslingers and saddle tramps who rode the lonely prairie, Western outlaws banded together to increase their gun power and their slim chances for survival. Frequently, they formed bonds that linked them strongly until the early death that seemed almost a certainty.

Two outlaws who epitomized this sort of male bonding in Western films were Butch Cassidy and the Sundance Kid. Earlier they could be spotted in minor roles, sometimes in disguised form, but it took George Roy Hill's *Butch Cassidy and the Sundance Kid* (1969) to thrust them into the spotlight. In reality, Butch Cassidy was a man named Robert LeRoy Parker, one of many jobless cowhands who had drifted into outlawry, joining at one time with the dangerous killer Kid Curry and later with a gunfighter called the Sundance Kid, whose true name was Harry Longabaugh. Together, Cassidy and Sundance had started robbing banks in 1896, separating and then reuniting as their fortunes changed. Their frequent traveling companion, Etta Place, who may have been a prostitute rather than a teacher as in the film, later became the Sundance Kid's common-law wife. Some of the incidents in Hill's film actually have a basis in fact: Cassidy and Sundance did pose as wealthy cattlemen in New York City during 1901, and they returned to robbing banks in 1906 after several years of seclusion in South America. As in the film, they were ultimately killed in a gun battle with the Bolivian army.

Whatever facts found their way into *Butch Cassidy and the Sundance Kid* were clearly beside the point; despite the introductory legend that "most of what follows is true," William Goldman's screenplay was intended as a lighthearted fable with contemporary allusions, focusing on two amiable, attractive outlaws who mock and defy authority and the establishment. As played by Paul Newman and Robert Redford, Butch and Sundance are movie stars in cowboy garb, buddies joined by a sense of mischief and a profound disregard for the law. When Butch tells Sundance, "Boy, I got vision, and the rest of the world wears bifocals," he is really paraphrasing every antiestablishment rebel of the late sixties, proud of his independence from convention and respectability.

As Butch and Sundance hurtle from one adventure to another, with Etta Place (Katharine Ross) in loving attendance for part of the way, the film sends up many Western movie clichés, turning each one merrily on its ear. Their first confrontation at a card game parodies the usual saloon shootout over card play, and Sundance's first scene with Etta mocks the familiar concept of the demure schoolmarm out West. (He lunges at her in the darkness, and after her initial surprise, she reveals herself not as the outraged virgin but as a woman who enjoys Sundance's amorous attention—and,

Butch Cassidy and the Sundance Kid (Fox, 1969). Pursued by the law, Sundance (Robert Redford) and Butch (Paul Newman) leap off a cliff into the water below. George Roy Hill's enormously popular movie mixed together breezy, impudent comedy, antiestablishment sentiment, and conventional Western action. Somehow, it all worked beautifully.

Butch Cassidy and the Sundance Kid *(Fox, 1969). To get at the safe and its money, Butch and Sundance (Paul Newman and Robert Redford) blow up the car that holds it—then watch the money fly away* (OPPOSITE). *Despite its opening legend— "Most of what follows is true"—the movie is a diverting mixture of fact and fancy, with generous dollops of whimsical Western parody as well. Sundance* (RIGHT), *actually named Harry Longabaugh, joined forces with Butch Cassidy (Robert LeRoy Parker) sometime in 1896. Their true careers resembled the film's counterparts only in the very broadest outlines.*

Butch and Sundance: The Early Days *(Fox, 1979). In this "prequel" to the popular* Butch Cassidy and the Sundance Kid, *released a decade earlier, Tom Berenger and William Katt played the jaunty outlaws as young men launching a career in crime. Director Richard Lester's buoyant touch made for an agreeable film.*

obviously, not for the first time.) Their robbery of a Bolivian bank, with Butch trying desperately to utter a few essential sentences in Spanish, becomes not a violent shoot-out but a slapstick caper in which the robbers are almost as bewildered as their victims.

Adding to the sense of spoof are Conrad Hall's Academy Award–winning but often overly busy photography and Burt Bacharach's jaunty musical score, with his and Hal David's Oscar-winning song, "Raindrops Keep Fallin' on My Head," featured in a scene in which Butch and Etta cavort on a bicycle. (Butch's fondness for bicycles is actually mythical.) At the film's close, Butch and Sundance, wounded and trapped by Bolivian soldiers, are obviously doomed to die,

but the film's essentially comic tone would never allow an ending in which we see them killed. They manage to keep a mocking, ironic edge to their conversation (Butch: "Is that what you call giving cover?" Sundance: "Is that what you call running?") before moving into the open, with guns blazing. The film ends with a freeze-frame.

Although some critics quibbled at the movie's facetious attitude, the ticket-buying public found *Butch Cassidy* extremely diverting, and it earned nearly $30 million in its American and Canadian release alone. Yet a decade later, when Fox created *Butch and Sundance: The Early Days* (1979), a "prequel" that dealt with events before the 1969 movie, audiences were much less responsive. Without charis-

matic stars in the leading roles—Tom Berenger and William Katt played Butch and Sundance—and with a rambling, episodic screenplay by Allan Burns that added unwarranted touches of sentiment to the comic mix, *Butch and Sundance: The Early Days* lacked spark and momentum. Still, helped by Laszlo Kovacs's stunning outdoor photography, director Richard Lester managed to bring his characteristic energy and style to some of the sequences, especially a train robbery in which Butch and Sundance discover that a troop of cavalrymen have been placed on board to trap them.

Curiously, in the same year that *Butch Cassidy and the Sundance Kid* was entertaining audiences with its send-up of the Western, another film appeared, unsparing and relentlessly violent, that moved the Western genre in general, and the concept of the Western outlaw in particular, in a new direction. It was not the first film to offer a bleak view of the outlaw as an embittered man doomed to extinction in a brutal land—John Sturges's *The Magnificent Seven* (1960), derived from Akira Kurosawa's Japanese classic *Seven Samurai*, tempered the heroism of its renegades with a sense of fatalism. Yet no film until Sam Peckinpah's *The Wild Bunch* (1969), set in the year 1913, offered such an unsparing portrait of a corrupt and dying West.

From its startling opening scene, in which a group of gleeful young children watch a swarm of red ants devouring a scorpion, to the blood-splattered shoot-out in a Mexican courtyard, *The Wild Bunch* gives no quarter. Although Lucien Ballard's photography includes images of breathtaking beauty, the outlaws, led by Pike Bishop (William Holden), are depicted with blistering clarity as a group of scroungy and amoral killers who somehow manage to retain a remnant of the old Westerner's creed ("When you ride with a man, you stay with him. Otherwise, you're an animal"). They still believe in loyalty among men, and although they would shoot a man in the back without blinking, they would give up their lives for one of their own.

Even the man who pursues the Bunch most relentlessly, a former colleague turned bounty hunter named Thornton (Robert Ryan), cannot fully sever his bond with these men. He may be as determined to destroy them as the vicious Mexican general and his men, who ultimately kill them in the bloody climax, yet after Pike Bishop lies dead, it is he who mourns his former friend, insisting on taking the body himself and refusing to let his scruffy and joking men even touch it.

The destruction of the Bunch is unquestionably one of the most violent scenes ever filmed. Still, these men meet their deaths if not heroically in the classic sense, then certainly with dignity and with full knowledge that their sacrifice, though futile, is for one of the Bunch, who is being held

The Wild Bunch (*Warner Bros.-Seven Arts, 1969*). *The Bunch strides into town* (OPPOSITE). *William Holden played the Bunch's leader, Pike Bishop* (ABOVE), *in Sam Peckinpah's powerful and extraordinarily violent Western. One of the most controversial films of its day,* The Wild Bunch *was either dismissed as repellent and unnecessarily brutal or hailed as a boldly innovative vision of the true West.*

captive. An ironic although unspoken aspect of their act is that Angel, the man they are attempting to save, is the youngest and most expendable of the Bunch, and they could have easily justified not going after him. Yet they accept their fate deliberately and knowingly, without flinching.

The excessive brutality—the blood spurts and gushes in many sequences—caused a storm of protest at the time of the film's release, countered by Peckinpah's assertion that it was intended as a cathartic that would precipitate a revulsion against violence. Yet, oddly enough, the revulsion it undoubtedly caused is almost perversely mixed with admiration for the beauty of the violent images. When a bridge collapses and men and horses fall into the water and drown, their

The Wild Bunch *(Warner Bros.-Seven Arts, 1969). Two of the Bunch—brothers Tector and Lyle Gorch (Ben Johnson and Warren Oates)—enjoy themselves in Mexico before their final shoot-out* (LEFT). *Death and destruction reign in the violent climax of Sam Peckinpah's harsh and stinging landmark Western* (BELOW). *Perhaps more than any film in recent years, Sam Peckinpah's film demythologized the movie West, offering a clear-eyed view of a brutal, corrupt, and totally amoral world.*

The Magnificent Seven *(United Artists, 1960). Akira Kurosawa's film* Seven Samurai *provided the source of John Sturges's Western, which strongly influenced the later "spaghetti" Westerns from Italy. Here the seven outcasts, led by Yul Brynner (kneeling at left), are clearly ready for action (although their artful poses suggest a publicity still).*

descent is shown in slow motion, creating an unsettling double reaction of horror and aesthetic pleasure. After a while, the shocking scenes of bloodletting become tempered by the nearly choreographic style in which they are filmed. Bloodbath or cathartic, *The Wild Bunch* remains a landmark film, brilliant and audacious, that made previous Western outlaws seem hollow by comparison.

The hard-edged realism that pervaded *The Wild Bunch* found its way into many of the Western films that followed in the seventies. Seldom did a Western outlaw assume the romantic stance of a Cisco Kid or the quiet humanity of John Ford's godfathers, escorting an orphaned newborn baby across the desert. At best, he was a scruffy rascal, like Frank Sinatra in the title role of *Dirty Dingus Magee* (1970), or at worst the murderous, dim-witted psychopath of Michael J. Pollard's Billy the Kid in *Dirty Little Billy* (1972). Romantic views of the Old West gave way to the harsh and unflattering "truth"—in Robert Benton's *Bad Company* (1972), two youngsters (Jeff Bridges and Barry Brown) who head West with the intention of becoming outlaws find disenchantment at every turn. The idea of the outlaw as a colorful, free-living spirit vanishes in the presence of sudden death and primitive

Bad Company *(Paramount, 1972). To avoid being drafted by the Union Army, Jake Rumsey (Jeff Bridges) and Drew Dixon (Barry Brown) head west with other draft dodgers and deserters, with the intention of becoming outlaws. Robert Benton's widely praised Western centered on their coming into manhood after a series of violent and comic adventures.*

Western justice. (Reflecting the antiestablishment, antiheroic attitude of the late sixties and early seventies, the movie's juxtaposition of brutal violence and raucous comedy suggests the screenplay that Benton and David Newman wrote for the 1967 film *Bonnie and Clyde*.) Richard Fleischer's *The Spikes Gang* (1974) also concerned youngsters (Gary Grimes, Ron Howard, and Charlie Martin Smith) who are led into the outlaw world, here by wounded badman Lee Marvin. Marvin played the sort of fading, over-the-hill Westerner prevalent in films of the seventies and eighties.

One interesting film that succeeded in combining the dying-of-the-West subgenre represented by *The Wild Bunch* with the lightly spoofing approach of *Butch Cassidy and the Sundance Kid* was Blake Edwards's *Wild Rovers*, released in 1971. One of the best Western films of the decade, it came up with a quirky quality all its own in its depiction of self-styled outlaws. As over-the-hill cowboy Ross Bodine (William Holden) and naive younger cowboy Frank Post (Ryan O'Neal) launch their adventure in bank robbing, we can sense the doom that awaits them at the end of the trail; although inexperienced, they are as fatally and irrevocably driven as Pike and his Bunch. (At one point, Ross remarks, "We're just doin' what was decided the moment we popped onto this earth.") Yet along the way, many of their experiences have the brash and eccentric comedy edge that followed Butch and Sundance on the road to their final destiny. As the two spend their booty in town, we can hear echoes of the earlier film in their joking attitude. "What do you think the poor folk are doin'?" one asks. "Without," the other replies.

Often the ties that linked Western men to each other were created out of a special need. Whereas sheriffs formed posses to rout the villains, and outlaws organized gangs to rob the banks and trains, men of disparate backgrounds sometimes found themselves thrust together in a common cause, combining their strengths and overcoming their weaknesses in order to triumph over disruptive forces. *High Noon* and its various clones of the fifties had advanced the reverse idea: that in the West (as in the mid-twentieth century), men often had to stand alone, betrayed by the cowardice and self-serving ambitions of others. For director Howard Hawks and others of his stripe, this was an unacceptable, even despicable concept, and he countered with Western films that turned oddly assorted men into effective fighting units. (Male bonding had been a recurring theme in earlier Hawks films, such as *Only Angels Have Wings*, 1939.)

Partially in answer to *High Noon*, he directed *Rio Bravo*, one of his most highly regarded Western films, in 1959. Maintaining that no respectable lawman would turn to townspeople for help and support—he valued his professionalism too much to resort to amateurs—Hawks presented an entirely different view of a beleaguered sheriff. Instead of Sheriff Will Kane standing proudly alone in the street and bitterly tossing his badge into the dust, *Rio Bravo* offered John T. Chance (John Wayne) who, when confronted by danger, forges a loyal, responsible, and trustworthy group of "deputies" out of an alcoholic has-been, a lame and toothless

Rio Bravo (Warner Bros., 1959). Stumpy (Walter Brennan) and Sheriff John T. Chance (John Wayne) prepare to defend themselves against the villains. The movie distilled director Howard Hawks's view on men in groups and the bond that links them together whenever danger threatens.

Wild Rovers (MGM, 1971). William Holden starred as aging cowboy Ross Bodine in Blake Edwards's odd but compelling Western. Bodine's attempt to rob a bank in league with young Frank Post (Ryan O'Neal) ultimately spells his doom.

old man, and a callow boy. The high-minded integrity of Carl Foreman's parabolic screenplay for *High Noon* is traded for Jules Furthman and Leigh Brackett's straightforward script that emphasizes male bonding.

Leisurely paced and staged on more indoor sets than the usual large-scale Western, *Rio Bravo* also concentrates on character relationships to an extent rare in the genre. The story is simple: to rout the villains, Sheriff Chance finds that he must rely on not the "well-meaning amateurs" in his town but on three unlikely men with varying attitudes: Dude (Dean Martin), a hard-drinking deputy who would like to end the humiliation and rejection he faces every day of his sorry life; Stumpy (Walter Brennan), a cantankerous old veteran willing to assert his sense of pride and loyalty; and young Colorado (Ricky Nelson), eager to prove that he is quick on the draw. Also on hand is Feathers (Angie Dickinson), a sharp-edged dance-hall girl who can hold her own with the men but who recognizes that her place lies outside their bonded circle. Feathers's relationship with Chance, made up of equal parts of admiration, amusement, and sexual attraction, recalls other man-woman relationships in Hawks's movies.

The core of *Rio Bravo* lies in the way in which the men Chance must rely on, especially Dude, recover (or in Colorado's case, discover) their manhood and integrity under great pressure. John Chance, of course, is long past the need to prove his manhood and integrity, and he assumes none of Will Kane's moral stance. Asked how a man becomes a sheriff, he replies, "Just lazy. Tired of selling his gun all over. Decides to sell it in one place." Primarily, it is Dude who must regain his status. From a beaten-down wreck who is cajoled into recovering a coin thrown into a spittoon, he becomes the catalyst that turns a desperate situation into a triumph.

The events that lead to his transformation reflect the strong ties that exist between Chance and Dude, one willing to risk his life with a man he once trusted, the other hoping to justify that trust. There are moments that are surprisingly moving: Chance telling a newly confident Dude, "I guess they'll let you in the front door from now on," or later returning Dude's guns in an honest acknowledgement of his faith. Most effective is the scene in which Dude, after losing his confidence again and turning in his deputy's badge, decides, with shaking hands, to pour his drink back into the bottle. Although *Rio Bravo* closes with the requisite shoot-out (staged, incidentally, with more roughhouse humor than usual), the movie gains its special resonance, and its place with Western fans, from scenes like these.

Rio Bravo may not be the classic Western film it is considered by many critics—it meanders too often and it lacks the visual splendor of the great Westerns—but John T. Chance has the stature of a classic Western lawman. Free of the symbolic weight with which Will Kane is invested, he is one of Howard Hawks's definitive figures, a man who lives by self-imposed rules of honor and friendship.

The central concept of *Rio Bravo*—the ill-assorted group of men who unite against a common enemy—appealed so strongly to Howard Hawks that he used it twice more in loose remakes of the original film. In each case, the group consisted of a steady, well-seasoned hero (always John Wayne), a sidekick with human failings, a gruff old man used partly for comic relief, and a handsome juvenile. In each case as well, women are admitted into the circle, not as decorative damsels decrying the violence but as scrappy participants in the action. In *El Dorado* (1967), which most closely approached *Rio Bravo* in plot line, characters, and theme, an aging gunfighter (John Wayne), fearing for the safety of his old friend, an alcoholic sheriff (Robert Mitchum), joins him in fighting for the homesteaders against a greedy cattle baron (Ed Asner). Roles played in *Rio Bravo* by Walter Brennan, Ricky Nelson, and Angie Dickinson were taken respectively by Arthur Hunnicutt, James Caan, and Charlene Holt. Leigh Brackett's screenplay, from a novel by Harry Brown, stressed easy ribaldry more than its predecessor and also lingered too long on the heroes' infirmities. However, Hawks managed to stage a nighttime street gunfight that, as in *Rio Bravo*, generated excitement, as figures move quickly and stealthily from place to place in the darkness, finally converging in a gloom-ridden church. In the end, the

Rio Bravo *(Warner Bros., 1959). Colorado (Ricky Nelson) and Sheriff John T. Chance (John Wayne) shoot it out with the villains in Howard Hawks's highly regarded Western. The film contains one of the purest examples of a common Western phenomenon: men with different backgrounds and aspirations banding together to fight in a common cause.*

Rio Lobo *(National General, 1970). Colonel Cord McNally (John Wayne) engages in a gun battle with the enemy. Like John Ford's later Westerns, this final film from director Howard Hawks had a darker, more melancholy tone than the other films in his trilogy (*Rio Bravo *and* El Dorado*).*

chain forged by this motley group has withstood a test of strength.

Rio Lobo (1970), the third film in Hawks's trilogy, and his last film as well, repeated the familiar ingredients of the other two. Once again wildly disparate types join together to confront a common enemy, and once again their closeness and camaraderie, joined with their worn but still appreciable skills, carry them through the rough periods to a kind of battered triumph. In *Rio Lobo*, Colonel McNally (John Wayne), a former Union officer, searches for the traitors who informed on a crucial shipment of gold and caused the death of a young man he looked on as a son. He discovers that the traitors are part of a gang terrorizing a town on behalf of a greedy land baron. Together with a young girl (Jennifer O'Neill) and a former Confederate captain (Jorge Rivero), now a friend, McNally gets his revenge and saves the town.

Although *Rio Lobo* bears a resemblance to *Rio Bravo*, especially in the climactic situation of the group trying to

hold on to its prisoner in a besieged jail house, the films are markedly different in other, crucial ways. *Rio Lobo* is essentially an old man's film, lacking the spirit and the energy of the earlier effort. Heavy and weary in the saddle, John Wayne tries but fails to summon up a measure of his usual relaxed strength. Most significantly, however, *Rio Lobo* pushes the *Rio Bravo* formula into darker and more disturbing areas ill-suited to Hawks's style and attitude. The principal women are far from the stoic "pals" of many of Hawks's films; this time they are forced to share some of the pain and suffering usually endured by the men alone. (One, the corrupt sheriff's mistress, is brutally disfigured.) *Rio Lobo* seems to indicate that Hawks, aware of the new revisionist trend in Westerns inspired by the "spaghetti" Westerns from Italy and by *The Wild Bunch*, was trying to incorporate it into his work, but his heart was clearly not in it.

As the sixties waned and the seventies got under way, Hawks's beleaguered lawman, joining with an oddly matched group to defeat the common enemy, appeared to have overstayed his welcome. On the whole, audiences tended to mock the venerable attitudes and traditions of the old-line Westerns; they seemed indifferent to the lawmen who went about their jobs with solemn efficiency, preferring their sheriffs and marshals with tongues planted firmly in their cheeks. Films

such as *Waterhole No. 3* (1967), *Support Your Local Sheriff* (1969), and *Support Your Local Gunfighter* (1971) poked fun at the Western conventions. Mel Brooks brought his irreverence and borscht-belt *shtick* to the genre in *Blazing Saddles* (1974), the decade's most successful Western. In a nonstop barrage of outrageous and often hilariously tasteless verbal and sight gags, Brooks parodied the familiar traditions of the Western, concentrating on a resourceful black man (Cleavon Little), who, in cahoots with a has-been gunslinger (Gene Wilder), manages to eliminate the corrupt elements in a Western town. The movie included uproarious burlesques on standard Western types: the Dietrich-like saloon singer (Madeline Kahn), the hulking, dim-witted cowboy (Alex Karras), the "respectable" townspeople, and others.

As the eighties took over, moviemakers were ready to return to the Hawksian theme of men bonded in a common cause, although the cynical and skeptical nature of the times evoked a new sensibility on the theme. The result was Lawrence Kasdan's *Silverado* (1985), a partially successful attempt to combine both the present and the past in its view of men together in the West. The screenplay by Kasdan and his brother Mark focuses on a group of men who have nothing in common except their past history in Western films: the loner with the secret past (Kevin Kline), the slow-speaking, quick-drawing gunslinger (Scott Glenn) and his trigger-

Blazing Saddles *(Warner Bros., 1974). The once-legendary, now-alcoholic Waco Kid (Gene Wilder) shares a toast with Bart (Cleavon Little), the newly appointed sheriff* (BELOW). *Mel Brooks's freewheeling parody of the Western genre contained a nonstop barrage of gags, many tasteless as well as outrageously funny.* ABOVE *Madeline Kahn's parody of Marlene Dietrich's Teutonic Frenchy in* Destry Rides Again—*"One wed wose?"—proved one of the movie's highlights.*

Silverado (Columbia, 1985). In Lawrence Kasdan's new-age Western, four unlikely partners (ABOVE; from left: Kevin Costner, Scott Glenn, Kevin Kline, and Danny Glover) head for the town of Silverado to exact revenge against a nasty family of outlaws. BELOW   Kevin Kline (right) starred as the gun-totin' drifter Paden. Kasdan's film took the familiar situations of classic Westerns and gave them a flippant, contemporary spin.

Cowboys pose for a group portrait. Like the men in Silverado, cowboys in the true West depended on each other for companionship and for support and strength in times of trouble. On long, difficult cattle drives, they would often gather around the campfire, singing favorite tunes or telling jokes and tall tales.

happy younger brother (Kevin Costner). The only relatively new addition is Danny Glover as a black man battling frontier racism. As they band together on their way to Silverado and wipe out an evil family of outlaws, they become involved in themes and situations that have stood the test of time since the days of William S. Hart: standard Western concepts—the conflict between rancher and homesteader, the shifting loyalties on both sides of the law—are trotted out and refurbished, and the obligatory shoot-outs and chases seem almost nonstop.

Yet *Silverado* is no mere anthology of Western clichés. From the first scene, in which Glenn discovers a bearded Kline in the desert, wandering about aimlessly in his long johns, the movie winks at the Western film conventions it re-creates, injecting them with dollops of irreverent humor. Director and coauthor Kasdan clearly hopes to make the audience smile with recognition at the familiar, timeworn ideas and characters and then laugh at their foolishness. Most particularly, the screenplay carries the Western concept of male bonding to the edge of parody, then adroitly manages to keep from falling off the edge. With the exception of Glover, the members of the hard-riding fraternity resemble amusing clones of past movie Westerners, yet their loyalty to each other in times of danger and crisis is genuine.

Virtually every scene is filtered through a modern sensibility—nostalgia speckled with satire. A jail breakout turns into slapstick farce, and the large-scale climactic scene crowds so much into its running time (a shoot-out, a stampede, and so on) that it hovers between homage and spoof. Most perversely, Kasdan cast stock Western characters with the least likely players: British comedian John Cleese as a sheriff, diminutive actress Linda Hunt as a wise barmaid (her precise, cultured diction is laughably out of place), urban wiseguy Jeff Goldblum as a gambler, among others. *Silverado* disconcerts as it entertains.

If male bonding in Westerns sometimes took a curious turn—stoic sheriffs shooting alongside grizzled old men, a black gunslinger riding with an aimless drifter—it also grew out of relationships that seemed inevitable on the lonely plains. For many young Westerners, orphaned by violence or torn away from their families by events beyond their control, the presence of a mentor or father-figure became reassuring; on the other hand, the older man needed to play the mentor, to have some sort of progeny. Many Western films, especially in the forties and fifties, turned on the theme of the surrogate son, struggling to emulate and then surpass the efforts of the father who has adopted him. Time and again the story concerned the fraying of the links between them through deceit, betrayal, or simple misunderstanding. Perhaps the classic example of this theme is Howard Hawks's *Red River*, in

which a cattle baron (John Wayne) raises a surrogate son (Montgomery Clift) and then becomes his implacable enemy when the younger man usurps his authority.

Two worthy if uneven fifties films, *Run for Cover* (1955) and *The Tin Star* (1957), also deal with the tribulations and occasional rewards of surrogate parenthood. In Nicholas Ray's *Run for Cover*, James Cagney, looking no more comfortable in Western garb than he did sixteen years earlier in *The Oklahoma Kid*, played Matt Dow, a leathery Westerner with a mysterious past, who befriends a wild young hellion named Davey (John Derek). When the two are mistaken for bank robbers and Davey is critically wounded, the remorseful townspeople make Matt their sheriff and Davey his deputy. Anxious to turn Davey into the son he lost years ago, Matt blinds himself to the boy's faults, leading to Davey's rebellion, his turning to crime, and his ultimate death at Matt's hand.

Although played at too leisurely a pace, with a number of sluggish stretches, *Run for Cover* succeeds in its final scenes in expressing the complex relationship of two men, one bitter at finding his trust betrayed, the other straining to be released from the confines of duty and obligation. "There's no more good in you than there is in a rattlesnake," Matt shouts just before he shoots Davey. But when the towns-people give him the reward money, he flings it at their feet, "with Davey's compliments!" As in many other Westerns, Matt cannot violate the uncompromising code of the West

Run for Cover *(Paramount, 1955). As Sheriff Matt Dow, James Cagney* (OPPOSITE) *starred in his first Western in sixteen years—his second ever—and probably with good reason: despite his usual vigorous acting, he seemed ill at ease in cow-boy garb.* BELOW *The outlaw named Morgan (Ernest Borgnine) and Davey Bishop (John Derek) face a final gun-fight with Matt, whose gun can be seen. Nicholas Ray's film centered on the relationship of Sheriff Dow and Davey, his weakling surrogate son.*

that demands the punishment of evil whatever the cost; he can only express his own moral revulsion at having to carry it out against someone he loves, suggesting that the price may be too high.

Young Anthony Perkins fared much better as an inexpe-rienced sheriff who learns how to handle himself from an ex-sheriff turned bounty hunter in Anthony Mann's *The Tin Star*. As Ben Owens, the newly arrived lawman in a wild town, Perkins is taught the Western code by surrogate father Morg (Henry Fonda), an ex-sheriff who once had a home and family but who now rides the trails in search of outlaws. Morg teaches Ben the basic rules: "A decent man doesn't want to kill a man, but if you have to shoot, shoot to kill!" "A gun's only a tool. . . . It's harder to learn men." In the final showdown, Ben must confront the villainous Bogardus (Neville Brand) by himself—Morg has helped him all he can and all the townspeople desert him—and he becomes a man to be trusted, respected, and feared. Buoyed by the promise of a new life with a young widow and her son, Morg leaves

The Tin Star (Paramount, 1957). One of the classic Western situations (ABOVE): *villainous Bogardus (Neville Brand) confronts untried sheriff Ben Owens (Anthony Perkins). Henry Fonda starred as Morg* (LEFT), *a seasoned bounty hunter and ex-sheriff, who teaches Ben the code of the West. Fonda's sturdy American presence and quiet sincerity made him a particularly apt performer in Western films.*

town with one last aphorism for Ben, "A man can't run away from his job." Despite the obvious echoes of *Shane* and *High Noon, The Tin Star* works best on its own terms as a study of two contrasting men whose lives are intertwined. Fonda and Perkins invest their roles with a sincerity and sensitivity that make their father-son relationship entirely credible.

Surrogate sons of various stripe continued to turn up in Westerns during the sixties and seventies. In *One-Eyed Jacks,* Marlon Brando directed himself as a vengeance-driven outlaw who seeks out the father figure (significantly known as "Dad") who betrayed him in the past. Burt Kennedy's *Young Billy Young* (1969) involved Robert Mitchum as Ben Kane, a lawman who takes a trigger-happy young gunslinger (Robert Walker) under his wing because he reminds him of his murdered son. During the film's course, he forces a reluctant Billy to walk a straight and narrow path, dispatches his son's killer, and cleans up the town of Lordsburg. John Wayne took on the role of guardian to four orphaned boys in Mark Rydell's *The Cowboys*, in which their inevitable coming of age focused on the violent revenge the boys perpetrate against the dastardly villain who murdered their "father."

Perhaps the oddest surrogate father-and-son relationship in Western films grew out of the legend that developed

around a young man born Henry McCarty but also known as William H. Bonney. By the time he was in his late teens, he had acquired nationwide infamy as the remorseless killer called Billy the Kid. According to all reports, young Billy was taken under the wing of a rancher named John H. Tunstall, whom he regarded as his father. During the violent Lincoln County War, in which Tunstall and others fought against

Billy the Kid (MGM, 1930). Outlaw Billy (John, later Johnny Mack Brown) and his men hold the townsfolk at bay. Surprisingly, for all the many outlaws in silent Westerns, this King Vidor film marked the first time Billy the Kid was depicted on the screen.

the corrupt officials who controlled New Mexico Territory, Tunstall was murdered. Billy vowed revenge on his killers; apparently, he had little compunction about shooting his enemies, and reports of his quick trigger finger and cold stare circulated widely. Betrayed by Lew Wallace, the territory's governor (and author of *Ben Hur*), who had promised him amnesty in exchange for information about statewide corruption, Billy was imprisoned and sentenced to hang. He broke out of jail several times before being shot dead by Sheriff Pat Garrett in July 1881 at the age of twenty-one.

Although the saga of Billy the Kid would seem ripe for mythologizing, it was not until the sound era that his life and activities became the stuff of screen fiction. As early as 1906, a play called *Billy the Kid* had dramatized his exploits, blaming all of Billy's troubles on an evil father, and in 1926 a novel by Walter Noble Burns entitled *The Saga of Billy the Kid* offered a wildly romantic version of Billy's brief life and career. King Vidor, in 1930, was the first to turn Burns's book into a movie, and Billy the Kid into a Western hero. *Billy the Kid* blithely ignored history by giving Billy's story a happy ending; John (later Johnny) Mack Brown played the outlaw as a darkly handsome rebel who is permitted to escape with

his girl by Sheriff Pat Garrett (Wallace Beery). A decade later, under David Miller's direction, history was corrected in a 1941 Technicolor remake, also called *Billy the Kid*, in which Billy (Robert Taylor) expires at the hand of Sheriff Garrett, here called Jim Sherwood (Brian Donlevy). In this version, Billy deliberately allows the sheriff to draw first.

In these films and the films that followed, Billy the Kid's transformation from amoral killer to troubled rebel was made complete. In most every case, at least part of the narrative dealt with the Kid's relationship with Pat Garrett. Garrett becomes the unhappy surrogate father to a wild son or the sorrowful surrogate older brother to an unruly sibling he must shoot dead out of duty. At the end of Miller's *Billy the Kid*, the sheriff even carries off Billy's body in his arms as if he were some fallen Shakespearean hero.

Billy the Kid's bonding with Pat Garrett received its oddest treatment in Howard Hughes's notorious and controversial Western *The Outlaw*. Filmed in 1940–41, the movie was intended to launch the career of Hughes's buxom discovery Jane Russell. (Early in the filming, Howard Hawks left the production, and a furious Hughes had taken over the director's chair.) The completed film went into limited release in 1943 after many arguments with the censors over Russell's steamy love scenes with Jack Buetel (as Billy). Hughes suddenly withdrew the film from circulation, re-releasing it in 1947 with a new and vulgar advertising campaign that asked, "How would you like to tussle with Russell?"

For all the brouhaha, *The Outlaw* turned out to be an offbeat though surprisingly tame and even tacky Western, in which the focus is not on Billy's torrid romance with the tempestuous Rio (Russell) but rather on his relationship with Sheriff Pat Garrett (Thomas Mitchell) and the ubiquitous Doc Holliday (Walter Huston). The friendship and shifting loyalties of these men, and Billy and Doc's contention over a strawberry roan, are given much more footage than any

amorous entanglements of the ostensible hero and heroine. In fact, at one point in the film, Billy offers Doc a choice of either Rio or the roan, and Doc chooses the roan!

The strong bonding of the three male characters—their hints of jealousy, their mutual hatred and distrust of women (Doc: "They're all alike." Billy: "You can't trust 'em")—gives the movie a distinctly odd flavor that reaches its peak in the climax. After many battles and reconciliations, Doc finally confronts Billy, who refuses to draw. Doc fires at him, nicking him in the hand and then both ears. A touched and happy Doc realizes that Billy truly values his friendship, whereupon

Pat Garrett, coming upon this tender scene like a jealous lover, shoots Doc dead. Afterward, he expresses his regret at coming between Doc and Billy. A stranger triangle never existed in Western films. (In later years, the theme of male bonding would become increasingly prevalent in Westerns, but with only a flicker of the homoerotic or misogynistic overtones of *The Outlaw*.)

Versions of Billy the Kid's short life continued to surface in the fifties, usually treating him as a hotheaded young man forced into outlawry by circumstances. Unquestionably, the most unconventional portrait of Billy came from Arthur Penn

The Outlaw *(United Artists, 1943). The romance of Billy the Kid (Jack Buetel) and Rio (Jane Russell) took several odd turns in Howard Hughes's controversial Western. The brouhaha over the movie was due mainly to the couple's heated love scenes (*LEFT*) and the display of Russell's cleavage. A poster for the movie (*BELOW*) clearly indicates that Jane Russell's bust measurements were considered the film's principal attraction.*

*Pat Garrett and Billy the Kid (MGM, 1973). James Coburn played Sheriff Pat Garrett, here hanging out at the saloon with Richard Jaeckel, in Sam Peckinpah's melancholy Western (*OPPOSITE, ABOVE*). The true Garrett shot Billy the Kid on the night of June 14, 1881, to the general rejoicing of the press. Only one year later, however, Garrett himself started the glorification process by signing his name to an Authentic Life of Billy the Kid, which was almost entirely fabricated. In Peckinpah's movie, folksinger Bob Dylan played Billy's monosyllabic sidekick Alias (*OPPOSITE, BELOW*).*

in his first feature film, *The Left-Handed Gun* (1958). From a screenplay by Leslie Stevens (adapted from Gore Vidal's television play "The Death of Billy the Kid"), Penn fashioned a Billy unlike any other: an illiterate and alternately brooding and playful young man who comes to believe the lurid stories about him in the nation's press. As played by Paul Newman in his most intense Actors Studio style (he had also starred in the television film), Billy is a Dead End Kid out West, a rebel with a cause: he exacts revenge on the men who killed John Tunstall, the rancher who befriended him. Pat Garrett (John Dehner), again a kind of surrogate father to Billy, tracks him down and shoots him. Penn filmed the story in self-consciously arty fashion, even resorting to a dab or two of religious symbolism: Billy is revered in print as a Christ-like "figure of glory," and he is betrayed by an overwrought, Judas-like Eastern drummer (Hurd Hatfield). J. Peverell

Marley's austere black-and-white photography emphasized suddenly rapid motion, tight close-ups, and odd camera angles.

By the sixties, many American filmmakers were relegating the Western to their Italian counterparts, who had begun to produce their feverish, violent "spaghetti" Westerns, the most influential of them directed by Sergio Leone and starring American actor Clint Eastwood. Although some Westerns were being made in the old tradition, others presented either spoofs of the genre (*Cat Ballou* in 1965 was the best example) or melancholy reflections on the passing of the Old West, such as *Ride the High Country* (1962) and *Will Penny* (1968). By the end of the decade, a rising generation weaned on Vietnam was unable to accept the standard, long-established heroic conventions of the Western as sanctified by the "establishment." Many of the relatively sparse Westerns of the late sixties and early seventies took either a tongue-in-cheek attitude or a hard-edged and sometimes bitterly ironic approach to the Western saga.

Although Billy the Kid was not immune to this prevalent approach—Stan Dragoti's *Dirty Little Billy* (1972) portrayed him as a nasty, retarded psychopath—the most interesting and, in many ways, most successful version of the Billy the Kid legend appeared in Sam Peckinpah's *Pat Garrett and Billy the Kid*. Released in 1973 to a mixture of controversy and acclaim, the film opted for a mournful, elegiac view of the subject rather than the parodistic or harshly debunking view. The movie depicted Billy (Kris Kristofferson) as an aimless drifter who moves into crime as if by chance and Pat Garrett (James Coburn) as a disillusioned man who serves the law only to retain his freedom. *Pat Garrett and Billy the Kid* is an autumnal film in which bursts of violent action, Peckinpah-style, cannot relieve the overall sadness.

Rudolph Wurlitzer's screenplay traces, in flashback, the events leading to the final, fatal confrontation of Billy and Pat Garrett in 1881. This Billy, although softened by Kris Kristofferson's low-key appeal as an actor, is a cold-blooded killer out of step with the changing times, while Pat Garrett is a cynic with no real regard for his sheriff's badge. ("It's just a way of staying alive.") Both resent and despise the "civilizing" influences represented by the sleek, callous businessmen who want to put "a fence around the country." Their paths cross as Garrett stalks Billy, but neither can win, and in the film's best scene, Garrett shoots Billy, then bitterly fires at his own reflection, filled with self-loathing for selling out and sadness for having to kill someone who, for all his lawlessness, shares his contempt for the changing times. Punctuated by Bob Dylan's ballads—he also played a role as Billy's sidekick Alias—*Pat Garrett and Billy the Kid* has unusual

The Left-Handed Gun (Warner Bros., 1958). While being held a prisoner, Billy the Kid (Paul Newman, right) brags about the fanciful pulp magazine stories that are turning him into a national hero. Arthur Penn's film offered a Billy unlike any other: a neurotic adolescent who resembled a rebel of the 1950s.

strength and texture. It even manages to survive the changes insisted on by the studio, which cut sixteen minutes and deleted a vital prologue and epilogue.

The most recent reincarnation of Billy the Kid appeared in Christopher Cain's 1988 Western *Young Guns*, which was less interested in reinterpreting his story than in assigning juicy roles to a number of popular young actors. In a role that suggested other rebels he had played, Emilio Estevez brought a tense edge to William Bonney, who starts to believe the newspaper reports about his bold exploits. Increasingly out of control, this Billy the Kid leads his friends into a bloody vendetta against the killers of their protector, rancher John Tunstall (Terence Stamp). Clearly aiming at a young audience, the movie not only included a drug-oriented scene (Billy's gang gets high on peyote) but also gives a contemporary spin to some plot elements: Doc (Kiefer Sutherland) has an interracial romance with a Chinese girl (Alice Carter) that, unlike previous interracial romances in Westerns, ends happily, and the mystical Navaho-Mexican Chavez (Lou Diamond Phillips), burdened with the harrowing memory of his family's massacre, survives the fracas to become a beacon for his martyred race ("I have to make my people live again"). Billy, of course, is doomed to a violent end; by the climactic shoot-out, he has become completely unhinged, a far cry from the romanticized outlaw of earlier films. *Young Guns II*, which dealt with Pat Garrett's hunt for Billy, was released in 1990.

Whether it has been the outlaw gang riding together against the society that threatens to displace them, or men banding together to defy the forces of anarchy and disorder, or two men from opposing worlds locked in an uneasy alliance, men of the Western genre have constantly found some degree of communion with each other. As a wedge against loneliness or fear, as a source of united strength, they have often forged a chain difficult to sever. Whether this bonding has represented an affirmation of loyalty and trust or a last desperate attempt to stand together before slipping into oblivion, it has formed the core of many memorable Western movies.

The Vanishing American (Paramount, 1925). Richard Dix (right) played the noble Nophaie, whose efforts on behalf of his people end in tragedy. The movie is notable for its long pro-logue, which sketches American Indian life over the centuries.

Savage or Saint?

"We are asked to remember much. The white man is asked to remember nothing. The white man's words are lies."

—An Indian chieftain in *Cheyenne Autumn* (Warner Bros., 1964)

EVER SINCE COLUMBUS and scores of Europeans descended on the New World, looting and burning villages and killing or kidnapping hundreds of men, women, and children, the story of our treatment of the Indians has stained the fabric of American history with shame and sorrow. Incidents of cruelty and treachery, tales riddled with lies and blunders recur continually. In 1838 a band of Cherokees, forced into camps by the discovery of gold, began a long trek back to Indian country in which one of every four died from cold, hunger, or disease. Increasingly angered by the white man's cheating and false promises, the Santee Sioux Indians, in the summer of 1862, launched a bitter war led by Chief Little Crow; less than a year later, the last remnants of the tribe had been destroyed, and Little Crow was shot trying to steal horses. In 1864 the Navahos, starved and beaten into a ragged, emaciated fragment of their former glory, began the Long Walk to Fort Sumner, enduring freezing weather, hunger, dysentery, and the jeers of soldiers and civilians. Scores of Apache Indians were brutally massacred at Camp Grant in 1871.

The record is grim. On the other hand, not even the most ardent champion of Indian rights could deny the savagery of Indian tribes intimidated by many years of white deceit and cruelty. Stories of Indian retaliation or unprovoked attacks on helpless settlers horrify with their details of torture and mutilation. Although some of the Indian chiefs, such as the imposing, intelligent Cochise, may have made cautious attempts at peace with the whites, others, burning with a flame fanned by years of blatant treachery, attacked the enemy with terrifying ferocity.

Whether victims or aggressors, American Indians have, on the whole, been badly treated in films, at least until the fifties. In the silent years, among the scores of quickly made movies, they usually appeared as a swarm of colorfully clad figures on horseback, attacking pioneers in their covered wagons or ambushing unwary riders. Films starring William S. Hart, Tom Mix, and other Western heroes frequently turned Indians into plot devices rather than characters or used them in humiliating ways. In *The Rainbow Trail* (1925), Mix throttles a passing "redskin," then dresses in the Indian's jacket and feathers and smears his face with the Indian's war paint to fool the tribe. Many a film such as *Pioneer Trails* (1923) or *The Flaming Forest* (1926) suggested that one stalwart hero could outwit and outmaneuver any number of primitive Indians. Others presented degrading views of "friendly" Indians, tattered remnants of a once proud people, selling their beads or blankets at army outposts.

Although most Westerns during the silent years relied on Indians for easy villainy, not all the movies were unsympathetic or indifferent; in fact, a surprising number of silent films treated Indians with at least a modicum of compassion and understanding. (In the years before World War I, there were Indian actors and even an Indian director, named James Young Deer.) While many of D. W. Griffith's early Westerns featured shrieking, barbaric savages, he occasionally mustered indignation at white treatment of the Indians. *The Bat-*

tle at Elderbush Gulch (1913) showed Indians aroused to fury only when the chief's son is slain in cold blood, and *The Massacre* (1915) depicted Indians as hapless victims of an unprovoked cavalry raid. Producer-director Thomas Ince also touched on the Indian's plight in some of his efforts; *The Indian Massacre* (1912), re-released in 1913 as *The Heart of an Indian*, coaxed tears from its audiences with a story of two mothers, one a white pioneer woman whose infant is kidnapped by Indians, the other an Indian squaw grieving for her dead child who is given the kidnapped baby by her husband. Moved by the white woman's plight, the squaw returns the baby. ("The stone heart melts before a mother's grief.") Ironically, "the white man's vengeance" still causes the Indian village to be destroyed.

Although most of William S. Hart's Westerns centered on his character's transformation as bad man into good man, some of them involved him sympathetically with Indian themes. In *The Captive God* (1916), he played a boy raised by Tehuan Indians who is given authority over the tribe when he grows to manhood. Captured by his enemy, the Aztec

Indians, he becomes amorously entangled with the daughter of Aztec chief Montezuma; eventually, he returns to his own people. *The Dawn Maker* (1916) cast him as half-breed Joe Elk, who works to uplift his people and meets a sacrificial death after falling hopelessly in love with a white girl. At other times, Hart used Indians conventionally as marauding savages in such films as *Wagon Tracks* (1919) and *White Oak* (1921).

Despite fluctuating interest in the genre, Westerns continued to appear throughout the twenties, and a number of them featured Indians or Indian-related themes, handled in a standard manner, without a sense of history. One 1925 film, however, brought an unusual viewpoint to the screen's treatment of Indians. George B. Seitz's *The Vanishing American* placed its Zane Grey story of a sacrificial Indian leader against the background of American Indian history, giving it a perspective that no previous film had attempted. A long prologue, directed as a second unit by the producer Lucien Hubbard, dramatized the progression of American Indian life, moving from the Basket Makers and the Slab House People to the Cliff Dwellers, "an indolent, harmless people drowning in the dust of centuries," and finally to the nearly total subjugation of the Navaho Indians three centuries later. Promises from the white establishment reek of hypocrisy:

Redskin (Paramount, 1929). Following his role in The Vanishing American, *Richard Dix (center) played Wing Foot, a Navaho Indian who triumphs over the white man's hostility.*

Geronimo *(Paramount, 1940). Chief Thundercloud (not really a chief) played the title role in this ordinary but surprisingly successful Western that epitomized Hollywood's condescending, single-minded attitude toward Indians in the thirties and forties.*

Indian Chief Broken Arm in the 1880s. By this time, most of the chiefs and their tribes, weakened by years of war and deprivation, had been moved onto reservations. The most elusive chief was Geronimo, who refused to surrender until September 1886. He and his people finally settled at Fort Sill, Oklahoma, and in 1903, a subdued Geronimo was taken to the Saint Louis World's Fair, where he sold pictures of himself for twenty-five cents each.

"We will help you to live as white men live. We will teach you to farm, to turn the desert into green fields." Yet the start of the twentieth century finds the Indians living meagerly on inadequate reservations.

The narrative of *The Vanishing American* takes up the story at this point, focusing on Nophaie (Richard Dix), descendant of the old warriors, who dreams of peace and prosperity for his people. Sadly, however, he finds only treachery at the hands of unscrupulous Indian agent Henry Booker (Noah Beery). Nophaie's only support comes from a handful of local residents, most notably schoolteacher Marian Warner (Lois Wilson), whom he loves. Hoping that the advent of World War I will change matters for the Indians, Nophaie joins the army and becomes a hero in battle. When he returns, he finds that Booker has taken over the land and driven virtually all of his people into bitter exile. In despair, Nophaie tries to avoid the inevitable conflict, only to fail. Booker is killed in the fracas, and he himself is mortally wounded. His body is carried off in state.

The melodramatic content of *The Vanishing American* leads to some overstated sequences, which, coupled with the overplaying of the leads, makes for some difficult going. Also, many of the titles strain in their efforts to sound "Indian" in flavor ("The Indian Love Moon cast its spell over the hearts of the primitive desert children"). Nevertheless, the film manages to convey at least an idea of the hopeless circumstances under which Indians lived. Nophaie's decision to fight for a country that has rejected him and his people has a plaintive sincerity ("Maybe if we fight. . . . Maybe if we die . . . our country will deal fairly with our people"), and his final moments as he summons the clan heads around him bring his story to an affecting close ("Through a veil . . . I seem to see our people . . . coming . . . home").

Several years after *The Vanishing American*, Richard Dix played another Indian in Victor Schertzinger's *Redskin* (1929). Here he was Wing Foot, an intelligent Navaho brave who surmounts ignorance and prejudice to win oil-rich land for his people and the love of a young Pueblo girl.

Throughout the thirties and forties, Western films continued to use Indians as their most convenient and conventional villains. When the Indian became the central figure in a rare film, the result was solemn sentiment, as in Henry King's 1936 version of Helen Hunt Jackson's novel *Ramona* (filmed twice before), in which Don Ameche and Loretta Young appeared as rather unlikely ill-fated Indian lovers.

More often, he was depicted as a fiercely driven savage, used as an excuse to show brutal attacks on frightened pioneers or unwary soldiers. Paul H. Sloane's *Geronimo* (1940) portrayed the Indian chieftain as a revenge-minded primitive who meets an ignominious end. Chief Thundercloud, a full-blooded Indian who was not really a chieftain, played Geronimo in this routine remake of *The Lives of a Bengal Lancer*

Broken Arrow (Fox, 1950). *Despite his enlightened attitude toward the Apaches, scout Tom Jeffords (James Stewart) is about to run into trouble with an Apache brave. Stewart's role in this film began his long series of appearances in Westerns.*

(1935), which transferred the locale of the story from India to the American West.

There were exceptions, of course, most notably a 1932 film entitled *End of the Trail*, directed by D. Ross Lederman. The plot was familiar: an army officer (cowboy star Tim McCoy) is wrongly convicted of selling arms to the Indians and must restore his good name. Remarkably for its time, the film pleads the Indians' cause with fervor and conviction. McCoy, who insists that the government "has never kept a single treaty" with the Indians, not only goes to live in an Indian village but also angrily accuses the army of "burning teepees, killing men, women, and children." He succeeds in preventing a massacre at the last minute and, after the real culprit confesses to selling arms, he is made an Indian agent. (Although an earlier version had him killed at the end, the studio insisted on his "recovery.") In another long-forgotten thirties Western, Alan Crosland's *Massacre* (1934), Richard Barthelmess played a Sioux chieftain who stops corrupt officials from victimizing his tribe.

In the forties, Cecil B. DeMille revealed a special penchant for demeaning Indians: in *North West Mounted Police* (1940), the Indians are comically awed and terrified by a player piano, and in *Unconquered* (1947), they behave like ill-tempered children under the thumb of a stern chieftain played, surprisingly, by Boris Karloff. When Indians were not being used en masse for attacks against forts, encampments, or towns, they became objects for inducing sudden fright (an Indian warrior looms up abruptly in *Western Union*, filling the entire frame) or for comic relief, as in *My Little Chickadee* (1940), *The Paleface* (1948), and many other movies. Occasionally, the weapon used against the Indian was humiliation: in *They Died with Their Boots On* (1941), Custer takes Indian leader Crazy Horse prisoner and locks him up for sixty days. "Maybe he'll be a good boy," he tells nobody in particular.

By the late forties, it was clear that a distinct change in the screen's treatment of Indians was long overdue. The postwar years had seen a significant shift in subject matter; with war themes no longer relevant, filmmakers were turning to America's homegrown social problems, bringing a touch of Hollywood-style boldness to such topics as anti-Semitism (*Gentleman's Agreement*, 1947), alcoholism (*The Lost Weekend*, 1945), mental illness (*The Snake Pit*, 1948), and racial intolerance (*Home of the Brave*, 1949). In this socially conscious climate, it was inevitable that the American Indian would be scrutinized in a new and much more sympathetic light. A major breakthrough came in 1950 with the release of Delmer Daves's *Broken Arrow*.

Although some distance from the documented truth, and less important as a Western film than as a sensitive (per-

North West Mounted Police *(Paramount, 1940). Paulette Goddard and Robert Preston play doomed lovers in Cecil B. DeMille's sprawling Technicolor adventure. As a fiery half-breed vixen named Louvette, passionately in love with a white man, Goddard could hardly be expected to survive the film, and, indeed, she dies with her lover.*

Devil's Doorway *(MGM, 1950). At the limit of his endurance, Shoshone brave Broken Lance (Robert Taylor) attacks his nemesis, Verne Coolan (Louis Calhern). Anthony Mann's Western—his first—was made before* Broken Arrow *but was held for release until Fox's movie had proven the popularity of a strongly pro-Indian film.*

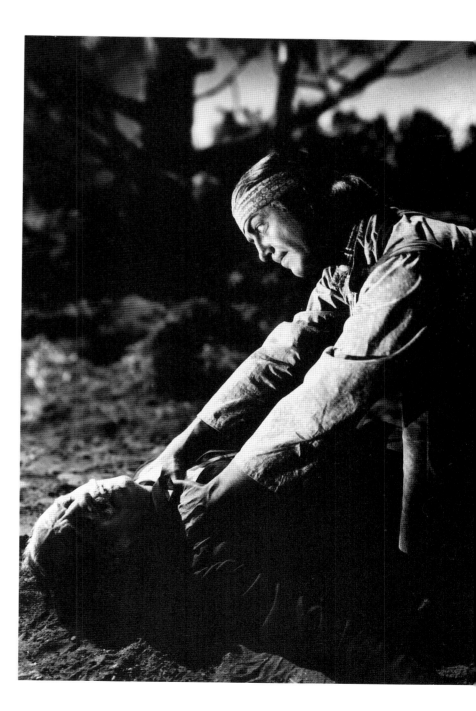

haps even overreverent) statement of the Indians' point of view, *Broken Arrow* portrayed the Apaches and their leader Cochise (Jeff Chandler) as proud, dignified people whose last, desperate attacks on the whites were in retaliation for the pillaging of their land. Much footage is given to Apache customs and lore and to Cochise's willingness to rise above his hatred and anger in a search for peace. James Stewart starred as Tom Jeffords, a scout and prospector who is "sick and tired of all this killin'!" (a line usually relegated to the womenfolk). His efforts to establish a just, lasting peace between Apaches and whites leads him to marry Cochise's lovely daughter Sonseeahray (Debra Paget). When she is killed in an ambush by renegade whites, Cochise still refuses to resume war, and Jeffords, his fury abated by Cochise's stoic acceptance, returns to the white man's world.

Admirably, *Broken Arrow* takes us far from the screaming savages of earlier years; for all their war paint and war

Broken Arrow *(Fox, 1950). Scout Tom Jeffords (James Stewart) meets with the Apaches in an effort to make peace between them and the whites in the Arizona of 1870. Delmer Daves's breakthrough film rejected the conventional cinematic view of Indians as bloodthirsty savages and presented them as a noble, deeply wronged people.*

cries, these Apaches are entirely worthy of our sympathy and respect. The film, however, cannot escape a patronizing air—how beautiful are the primitive ways of these simple people—and many of the Indians, especially the hapless Sonseeahray, are somewhat less than believable in their designer Western clothing. Still, *Broken Arrow* boasts exceptionally beautiful photography by Ernest Palmer and a dependable performance by James Stewart in one of the first of his series of portrayals of hard-bitten Westerners throughout the fifties. Jeff Chandler's performance as the noble Cochise, consisting mainly of a solemn demeanor and a sonorous voice, won him an Academy Award nomination and sparked his sadly brief career.

Anthony Mann's *Devil's Doorway* followed close on the heels of *Broken Arrow* as another key, although less influential, film of 1950. Robert Taylor starred as a Shoshone brave all too symbolically called Broken Lance, although known to the whites as Lance Poole. Cited as a hero during the Civil War, Lance returns to Wyoming to find his father's land (and that of all his fellow tribesmen) coveted by sheepherders who have been stirred up by Indian-hating lawyer Verne Coolan (Louis Calhern). Angrily insisting that he is part of the land, Lance refuses any compromise suggested by sympathetic lawyer Orrie Masters (Paula Raymond). Inevitably, the trouble escalates until a violent and bloody battle ensues between the Indians and the sheepherders. Desperately, Lance tries to prevent a massacre of his people; ultimately, he is fatally shot. As he dies, the Indian women and children are led off to the reservation.

Although Taylor gives a characteristically inexpressive performance as the besieged Indian, *Devil's Doorway* benefits from Anthony Mann's strong, forceful direction, especially in the climactic battle scenes. Most effective is the sequence in which the Indians first move against the sheepmen, blowing up their wagons with explosives and terrifying the sheep. Later in the fifties, in such Westerns as *Bend of the River* (1952) and *The Far Country* (1955), Mann used the newly complex persona of James Stewart to explore his recur-

Indians gather in Glacier National Park in Montana. In earlier times, the rivers of the sparsely populated Montana Territory were avenues of travel for many Indian tribes, including the Blackfoot, the Sioux, the Shoshone, and the Cheyenne. For many years, they blocked the passage of white men across its wilderness of forest and grass.

rent theme of a man seeking to establish his identity in a hostile world. In these films the protagonist succeeded despite adversity. In *Devil's Doorway*, however, since the hero is an Indian, he must perish to make a point about the plight of his race.

Viewed through rose-colored glasses, the Indian leaders of history served as the heroes of more than one fifties Western. The brutal and arrogant savages of earlier films were transformed into proud, strong, quietly suffering men forced to battle white men against their will. The noble Cochise, played by Jeff Chandler in *Broken Arrow*, returned briefly as the dying chieftain who bequeaths his rule to his offspring in Douglas Sirk's *Taza, Son of Cochise* (1954). In Sidney Salkow's *Sitting Bull* (1954), the title character, played by J. Carrol Naish, pauses long enough in his ceaseless struggle to petition General Grant for the life of his friend Parrish (Dale Robertson), who is being court-martialed for befriending the Indians and trying to prevent the massacre of Little Bighorn. George Sherman's *Chief Crazy Horse* (1955) at least restored a measure of dignity to the Indian chief who was acknowledged to be brave and skillful and who was revered by the Sioux as their greatest leader. As played by Victor Mature, he

is seen as a visionary inspired by an ancient prediction that a member of his tribe will ultimately triumph against the white man. Departing from history, the movie depicts his murder at the hand of a treacherous renegade half-caste named Little Big Man (Ray Danton) rather than in the prison where he was sent when a rumor began that he was planning another revolt.

Throughout the fifties, in such films as George Sherman's *Tomahawk* (1951) or Charles Marquis Warren's *Arrowhead* (1953), the American Indian was raised to virtual sainthood, or if he was somewhat less than saintly, then he was shown to be at least a victim of cruel injustice. The newly exalted state of the Indian in films became most evident when popular stars were assigned to play Indian roles or, as in the case of Charlton Heston in George Marshall's *The Savage*

(1952), were charged with playing white men raised as Indians. Heston was cast as James Glenn, Jr., who, as a boy, is the sole survivor of an Indian raid. Raised by the Sioux, he is renamed Warbonnet and hailed as the loyal son of Chief Yellow Eagle. Inevitably the question arises: Will he side with his Indian family when war threatens, or will he revert to his status as a white man? The decision is made for him when his beloved "sister" Luta (Joan Taylor) is murdered by the men of Indian-hating Captain Vaugant (Richard Rober). ("From this day forth, let no man call me white!") However, his compassion and decency will not permit him to lead the

Chief Crazy Horse *(Universal, 1955). Victor Mature starred as the strong, defiant chieftain* (RIGHT *and* BELOW) *who wants to organize the tribes against the white man, and Suzan Ball appeared as his wife, Black Shawl* (RIGHT)*. The historical Crazy Horse, revered as a brave leader, was imprisoned in September 1877 when a false rumor was spread that he was planning a revolt. Soon afterward, he was stabbed to death in a scuffle, and it is still argued whether the fatal wound was inflicted by his own knife or by a prison guard's bayonet.*

The Savage (*Paramount, 1952*). *Charlton Heston, as the loyalty-torn adopted Sioux Warbonnet, poses with Indian maiden Luta (Joan Taylor) in George Marshall's Indian Western. The movie's best feature was its location photography in the Dakota Black Hills.*

OPPOSITE, ABOVE Apache (*United Artists, 1954*). *Apache warrior Masai (Burt Lancaster, right), standing alone against the white man's injustice, struggles with Al Sieber (John McIntire). The movie's flaws weakened its sincere attempt to state the case for the embattled Indians.*

OPPOSITE, BELOW Flaming Star (*Fox, 1960*). *In a role originally written for Marlon Brando, Elvis Presley played a half-breed torn between the opposing worlds of the whites and the Kiowas. Fighting beside him are John McIntire and Steve Forrest.*

white settlers and soldiers into a trap, and he is condemned by his tribe as a traitor, despite his eloquent plea that "all whites are not killers." His life is spared at the last moment, and although he must part from his Sioux family forever, he vows to return someday. The theme of divided white and Indian loyalties surfaced periodically in such films as *The Searchers, Two Rode Together,* and *Little Big Man.* Here, it receives a rather perfunctory treatment, aided not at all by Heston's sincere but stolid performance as Warbonnet.

Robert Aldrich's *Apache* (1954) fared somewhat better, although it, too, had severe shortcomings. In this film Burt Lancaster played Masai, pointedly described as "the last Apache warrior." Refusing to surrender with Geronimo in 1886, he decides to stand alone, a one-man army against injustice. Naninle (Jean Peters), a strong-minded Indian maiden who follows him with a fierce and unyielding devotion, tries to end his pattern of destruction ("There is nothing in you but hate!"); nothing, however, can allay his anger. Ultimately, his love for Naninle and the imminent birth of their baby dissuade him from violence, and he throws down his gun.

Although beautifully photographed by Ernest Laszlo

and competently directed by Aldrich (minus some of the director's usual force and energy), *Apache* suffers from a verbose, often awkward screenplay by James R. Webb in which, not for the first or last time, an attempt to duplicate Indian speech makes the principal characters sound more foolish than dignified. The ludicrous ending, forced on Aldrich by the producers, also detracts from the overall impact. The original screenplay called for Masai to be shot in the back by Federal troops. Aldrich was asked to film a new ending in which Masai survives and surrenders. At first he refused, but when Lancaster himself agreed, he had no alternative, and the entire point of the film vanished in a blur of false optimism.

When Elvis Presley appeared in Don Siegel's *Flaming Star* in 1960, the concept of the American Indian as a proud, noble, severely wronged warrior had entered the mainstream so completely that his portrayal of an ill-fated young half-breed torn between his mother's world of the Kiowas and the white world of the settlers did not faze his legion of fans. At the same time, a new note was added to the Indian Western. While many fifties films had portrayed Indians in broad terms as victims of white greed and treachery, some sixties Westerns took on a more sociological patina by depicting specific acts of racial bigotry against Indians, in the same way that postwar films of the late forties and early fifties had focused on acts of prejudice against Jews and blacks.

Several prominent examples come to mind. In John Huston's often majestic *The Unforgiven* (1960), Audrey Hepburn plays a young Indian maiden adopted by a ranch family who becomes the object of virulent hatred by her

Two Rode Together *(Columbia, 1961). Guthrie McCabe (James Stewart), the hard-drinking, mercenary marshal given the job of ransoming captive white children from the Comanches, confronts cavalry officer Lieutenant Jim Gray (Richard Widmark). Although John Ford's somber and bitter Western is markedly uneven, it contains several powerful scenes of rampant bigotry.*

adopted brother (Audie Murphy) when her Indian background becomes known. A larger conflict emerges when her Indian family insists on her return. John Ford's dark-hued *Two Rode Together* (1961) climaxes with a brutal incident: a young white boy who has reverted to savagery after long imprisonment by the Comanches is lynched by settlers when he kills the woman who tries to tame him. Far removed from Ford's much more hopeful *The Searchers* (there are no welcoming arms for the victim), *Two Rode Together* reflects the director's increasingly dark view of civilization in general and the treatment of Indians in particular.

This view reached fruition three years later in Ford's epic Western *Cheyenne Autumn* (1964), which, in dealing with a specific tragic event, offered the decade's most blistering indictment of America's abuse of Indians. Until this point, Ford had concentrated in his Westerns largely on the traditional values embodied by the pioneers—the settlers, the ranchers, and the cowboys who populated the plains. He had painted the Indians as little more than a hostile or threatening presence, attacking those who would invade their land. In *Cheyenne Autumn*, they became a visible, sorrowful reprimand to years of indifference, neglect, and treachery. The film was Ford's effort, made in the face of many production obstacles and his own flagging energy, to set the record straight. Speaking about the film to Peter Bogdanovich, he said, "Let's face it, we've treated them very badly—it's a blot on our shield; we've cheated and robbed, killed, murdered, massacred, and everything else, but they kill one white man and God, out come the troops" (Bogdanovich, *John Ford*, p. 104).

Cochiti Indians perform a war dance. The ceremonial dance, held after winning a battle, lasted for days. Warriors danced to the beat of drums while they shook their rattles, waved the scalps they had taken, and boasted of their bravery.

Cheyenne Autumn (Warner Bros., 1964). The Cheyenne Indians await the arrival of the soldiers. Whereas previous John Ford Westerns had treated Indians as a savage and dangerous force to be confronted on the journey westward, this film harshly condemned America's genocide of the Indian nations.

Cheyenne Autumn *(Warner Bros., 1964). In an autumnal setting (*LEFT*), Army troops ride to deal with the recalcitrant Cheyennes. John Ford's melancholy Western generated sympathy for the plight of nearly three hundred Cheyennes undergoing the ordeal of a 1,500-mile trek to their sacred ancestral grounds. Deborah Wright (Carroll Baker), a Quaker schoolteacher, gives her sympathy and support to the Cheyennes on their long and painful journey (*BELOW*). The subplot of Deborah's romance with a cavalry officer (played by Richard Widmark) intruded on the Indians' tragic story, diluting its impact. The Cheyennes (*OPPOSITE*) meet with government officials. Director John Ford considered the film an act of expiation toward the Indians. He said, "Let's face it, we've treated them very badly—it's a blot on our shield. . . ." (Peter Bogdanovich,* John Ford, *p. 104).*

Hombre *(Fox, 1967). Paul Newman (foreground) starred as John Russell, a taciturn, cynical white man raised as an Indian, who ultimately—and ironically—gives up his life for an Indian-hating woman. Martin Ritt's harsh film about man's prejudices and frailties benefited from James Wong Howe's fine photography.*

James R. Webb's screenplay, suggested but not truly based on Mari Sandoz's novel, has a historical basis: the painful and devastating trek of nearly three hundred Cheyenne Indians (the survivors of a tribe of one thousand) who, in 1878, decided to return to their ancestral lands in the Dakota mountains from an Oklahoma reservation. Decimated by bitter cold and starvation, harassed and attacked by American troops, the Cheyennes faced almost total annihilation over their fifteen-hundred-mile journey, with only a pitiful few surviving the ordeal. *Cheyenne Autumn* records the event through the eyes of Captain Archer (Richard Widmark), who passes from prejudice ("War is a Cheyenne's life. He's fierce

and he's smart and he's meaner than sin") to compassion and a genuine desire to help the Indians, whatever the risk to his career. While other characters figure importantly in the story, especially a sympathetic Quaker teacher (Carroll Baker), the film's beating heart remains the Cheyennes themselves, portrayed with a minimum of false movie-imposed dignity by such actors as Ricardo Montalban, Dolores Del Rio, and Sal Mineo. (Their dialogue is delivered in the Indian language, with subtitles.)

Cheyenne Autumn contains a number of virtues, including William Clothier's stunning color photography and John Ford's characteristic ability to orchestrate scenes of imposing grandeur without sacrificing detail. (The views of the desolate band of Cheyennes snaking across the plains speak more eloquently than any amount of dialogue.) On the other hand, the film suffers from overlength, too many side issues left vaguely unresolved, and an odd, disconcerting comic sequence set in Dodge City in which James Stewart as Wyatt Earp and Arthur Kennedy as Doc Holliday participate in

Tell Them Willie Boy Is Here (Universal, 1969). After killing his girlfriend's father in self-defense, young Indian Willie Boy (Robert Blake) flees from the law. Abraham Polonsky's film was only partially successful in conveying the plight of the Indian in a hostile society.

satirizing the way Indians are usually treated in the movies. Most interesting, however, is the degree to which *Cheyenne Autumn* reveals John Ford's altered—and infinitely darker—view of the relationship between Indians and the military. Whereas *Fort Apache* asked us to look beyond the vainglorious, arrogant colonel (Henry Fonda) who led his men into ambush and salute the regiment he commanded, *Cheyenne Autumn* offers the spectacle of a loutish, drunken captain named Wessels (overplayed by Karl Malden), who precipitates the final bloody action against the Cheyennes. While *Fort Apache* appears to excuse military blunderers in the name of the larger picture ("Print the legend"), *Cheyenne Autumn* focuses without flinching on the blunderer who insists that he was only obeying orders ("Nothing I have done is personal") and who firmly believes that anarchy reigns whenever orders, however unpleasant, are disobeyed. The sight of Wessels staggering drunkenly among the dead bodies of the Cheyennes is the most haunting in the film.

In the waning years of the sixties, as people became angrier and more socially aware, the heroes of such movies as *Hombre* (1967) and *Tell Them Willie Boy Is Here* (1969), far from the romantically isolated figures fighting in vain against entrenched bigotry, as portrayed in the fifties, stood as bitterly realistic harbingers of their own preordained doom in an antagonistic society. Martin Ritt's darkly pessimistic *Hombre* starred Paul Newman as John Russell, a white man raised by Apaches who has learned not only to guard his own self-interest but also to live with the hatred his Indian heritage provokes in bigoted whites. Through fateful circumstances, Russell joins a motley group of largely contemptible people in a desert stagecoach ride (inevitably suggestive of John Ford's *Stagecoach*) that results in robbery, shoot-outs, and death for both the villains and Russell. Ironically, Russell gives up his life to save an Indian-hating woman (Barbara Rush) who has been left by the robbers to expire in the blazing desert sun. His act is more suicidal than sacrificial, appearing as a final gesture of hopelessness. "We all die," Russell says. "It's just a matter of when." Ritt's taut direction, Newman's tough-fibered performance, and James Wong Howe's spare, unfussy photography combined to make *Hombre* a compelling film.

Abraham Polonsky's *Tell Them Willie Boy Is Here*, a Western set in the early years of this century, is much less successful at dramatizing the plight of the outsider in a closed society. Heavily didactic and insistent in its themes and effects, the movie concerns Willie Boy (Robert Blake), a young Indian who becomes the object of a search after killing his girlfriend's father in self-defense. Joined by his girlfriend Lola (Katharine Ross), Willie Boy flees to avoid capture, but he is trapped and shot by a posse headed by Cooper (Robert Redford), the sympathetic, saddened sheriff. Lola also dies, in somewhat cloudy circumstances—she appears to have killed herself (offscreen) to keep Willie from slowing down in his flight from the law.

In addition to an unconvincing subplot involving Cooper and a liberal-minded doctor (Susan Clark), *Tell Them Willie Boy Is Here* is weakened by a rigid schematic structure that assigns each major character a point of view that can be expressed in pat little speeches. Inevitably, Willie

Tell Them Willie Boy Is Here *(Universal, 1969). Lola (Katharine Ross) and Willie Boy (Robert Blake) share an ill-fated romance in Abraham Polonsky's film (*OPPOSITE, ABOVE*). As the body of young Willie Boy is carried off the mountain (*OPPOSITE, BELOW*), his pursuer, Sheriff Cooper (Robert Redford, bottom), regrets having to shoot him ("I gave him a chance. He didn't want it. He had no bullets in his gun"). Dr. Arnold (Susan Clark) looks on sympathetically.*

Little Big Man *(National General, 1970). At the Battle of Little Bighorn, Jack Crabb (Dustin Hoffman) registers amazement as General Custer (Richard Mulligan) finally bites the dust. Arthur Penn's film depicted Custer as a raving lunatic.*

Boy gets more than one chance to sound the theme of racial bigotry ("What did any of us do? What was wrong with us? Nothin'! Nothin'! Only our color!"). When Willie is finally killed, Cooper makes the by now obligatory gesture of flinging down his hated gun and helping to carry Willie's body down the mountain. Polonsky's screenplay, like his direction, is sledgehammer heavy and unsubtle. (This was his first movie since 1951, when he was blacklisted for refusing to confirm or deny his membership in the Communist party.) The film ends with an Indian plea for understanding: "The people have got to see something. Tell them we're all out of souvenirs."

As the seventies began, filmmakers preferred to move beyond the specific injustices of *Hombre* and *Tell Them Willie Boy Is Here* and to use the callous and inhumane treat-

ment of Indians across the years as a symbol of more contemporary crimes against humanity. Several 1970 films, in fact, suggested a parallel between genocide in the days of the Old West and in the age of Vietnam. Arthur Penn advanced this view in his curious and undeniably brilliant Western *Little Big Man* (1970). Adapted by Calder Willingham from Thomas Berger's novel, this film astonishes with its audacious combination of knockabout comedy, absurdist satire, and shocking, documentary-like realism. Narrated by Jack Crabb (Dustin Hoffman), a 121-year-old man who claims to be the sole survivor of Custer's Last Stand, the story takes Jack through a series of adventures in which he shuttles back and forth from the white settler's world to the world of the Cheyenne Indians. At first his experiences have the comic edge of a picaresque novel: he is adopted by the Cheyennes after his family is massacred and turned into a brave called Little Big Man; he becomes the ward of a reverend's wife (Faye Dunaway) with more than pious feelings toward him; he acts as a shill for a traveling medicine man (Martin Balsam) who keeps losing parts of his body; and, for a brief period, he is known as a gunfighter

called the Soda Pop Kid. Along the way he meets a rather benign, weary "Wild Bill" Hickok (Jeff Corey) and a vainglorious, possibly demented George Armstrong Custer (Richard Mulligan).

At midpoint, however, it becomes clear that the film's primary intention is hardly comic. In a scene of undiluted horror, we witness the army's massacre of a Cheyenne camp, in which scores of Indians, including Jack's young wife, are brutally slain. After this sequence the film darkens, and although it veers back occasionally to comedy (Jack discovers the reverend's wife working in a brothel), the acrid smell of genocide lingers in the air. A second, even more brutal attack on the Cheyennes, this one led by a mad Custer against the peaceful Indian Nations, harrows the mind with images of terror and wanton destruction. Jack's failed attempt to murder Custer after the massacre ("I was a total failure as an Indian") sends him reeling into despair; his vindication comes only when the massed Indians destroy Custer and his men at Little Bighorn. In this bravura sequence, the film's bold and often disconcerting mixture of the real and the fantastic coheres to stunning effect. Against all reason, a now deranged Custer charges his men directly into an ambush, crying, "Take no prisoners!" As his soldiers die all around him, he is finally left a solitary figure, spinning in a circle and shouting madly into the air until he himself is killed.

Despite its distracting leaps from farce to tragedy, *Little Big Man* generally impresses, not only as a major advancement in the screen's treatment of the Indians but also in its use of an Indian actor as a major character. As Old Lodge

*Little Big Man (National General, 1970). Adopted by the Cheyennes, young Jack Crabb (Dustin Hoffman) becomes as ferocious a warrior as any member of the tribe (*OPPOSITE*).* BELOW *Crabb greets his adoptive grandfather, Old Lodge Skins (Chief Dan George). Arthur Penn's astonishing, ambitious film veered from raucous comedy to horrifying tragedy, mostly with success.*

Skins, Jack's wise, serene, albeit deeply sad adoptive grandfather, Chief Dan George gives a dignified performance in a role that, while it occasionally threatens to lapse into terminal quaintness ("My heart soars like a hawk"), more often conveys a reserve of strength and fortitude. The film's thesis permits no "bad" or less than nobly militant Indians, although one, in probably a first and last for a Western, behaves with strident effeminacy and chooses not to fight. Dustin Hoffman's appearance as the 121-year-old Crabb represents a triumph of the makeup artist's skill, and Hoffman gives an amusing and capable performance that deliberately plays against the horrors he witnesses and survives.

Another 1970 film followed the example of *Little Big Man* by suggesting that the brutal acts committed against Indians were closely related to the behavior of some American soldiers in Vietnam. In *Soldier Blue,* director Ralph Nelson re-created the Sand Creek Massacre of 1864 against the Cheyennes, assaulting the viewer's eyes with hacked and mutilated bodies, a sequence that clearly hinted at the My Lai massacre of 1967. The intended impact of the sequence, however, was weakened by the portrayal of the American

A Man Called Horse *(National General, 1970). Captured by the Sioux in the early nineteenth century, Lord John Morgan (Richard Harris) prepares to undergo the excruciating Sun Vow Ceremony, a test of his courage and endurance before being accepted into the tribe. The ritual shown in the film was never actually practiced in that extreme way by the Sioux or any Plains tribe, yet the film was praised by some critics for its unflinching realism.*

officer who orders the massacre as a wild-eyed lunatic whose anti-Indian phobia rages out of control. In another heavy-handed touch, the United States Army tramples on the American flag given to the Cheyenne chieftain by the government.

Occasionally, an Indian film of the period, while not denying the injustice perpetrated by white people, moved away from the sanctification of Indians since the fifties to suggest that Indians were as capable of brutal behavior as any other race. Elliot Silverstein's *A Man Called Horse* (1970) dealt with an English lord (Richard Harris) who is captured by the Sioux and is repeatedly abused and humiliated. Among other things, he is treated as a beast of burden by the old woman who claims him. Eventually, to prove his

courage, he is forced to endure the horrifying Sun Vow ceremony. The most grisly (and almost unwatchable) part of the ceremony came when Harris is suspended in midair from ropes inserted in his chest with hooks. Harris survives the ordeal and learns to respect his captors. He takes an Indian wife, who, in time-honored Hollywood fashion, is killed off for daring to cohabit with a white man. At later intervals, the actor appeared in two sequels, *The Return of a Man Called Horse* (1976) and *Triumphs of a Man Called Horse* (1983). The trilogy has been condemned by those who regard its depiction of primitive Indian rites as fraudulent.

Robert Aldrich's *Ulzana's Raid* (1972) took the thesis of films like *A Man Called Horse* one step further, affirming that if both whites and Indians were guilty of savage behavior, they should be dealt with harshly as equal aggressors. Weakness, the film suggests, only worsens the situation. The rampage of the bloodthirsty Ulzana is ended only through the efforts of the forthright old Indian fighter McIntosh (Burt Lancaster) and not by the naive and confused Lieutenant DeBuin (Bruce Davison). When DeBuin expresses horror

Ulzana's Raid (Universal, 1972). Burt Lancaster (RIGHT) starred as a weathered scout named McIntosh in Robert Aldrich's savage Western. Aided by Apache scout Ke-Ni-Tay (Jorge Luke; BELOW), McIntosh joins a callow young lieutenant (Bruce Davison) in tracking down the murderous Apache named Ulzana. Much of the explicit violence in Robert Aldrich's film was severely cut before its release.

at the soldiers' mutilation of a dead Indian, McIntosh says, "What bothers you, Lieutenant, is that you don't like to think of white men behaving like Indians. It confuses the issue."

Whether characterized as savages or saints, American Indians have seldom been shown as complex human beings with their own culture and lore, as well as their own sorrows, regrets, and achievements. Films in recent years have made an effort to modify or change the single-hued portrait of Indians, yet on the whole, they continue to portray them as exotic and rather shadowy figures shrouded in their private world of ritual and superstition. Their wars have long been fought and lost; their struggle for dignity never seems to end.

Destry Rides Again *(Universal, 1939). In George Marshall's comedy Western, Marlene Dietrich changed her image from remote glamour queen to rowdy dance-hall queen and revitalized her career. Here, Frenchy finds herself both amused and fascinated by mild-mannered Tom Destry (James Stewart).*

The Distaff Side

IF INDIANS WERE TREATED as second-class citizens in scores of Westerns over the years, the same can certainly be said of women. In a genre where the traditional masculine virtues of rugged strength and unswerving determination dominated the scene, where the hard-riding action required man's muscle and sweat, women were usually relegated to the background. On the whole, they were either "good" (tenacious wives and mothers, demure sweethearts, prim schoolmarms) or, if not "bad," then no-better-than-they-should-be (dance-hall girls, Mexican señoritas, overly aggressive ranchers). When the "good" women worried, which was often, they worried about the safety of their men and families or the threat of Indians rather than the problems of building empires or founding dynasties. The "bad" women ended up dead or severely chastised. At least until the emergence of feminist ideas, women in Western movies revealed little shading or complexity.

Ironically, despite the cursory and demeaning way in which women were treated in Westerns, in reality they played an enormously important role in the settling of the West. Confronted with an ordeal of staggering proportions, faced with daily lives of privation, sickness, and lurking terrors, many perished. Those who survived drew on their tenacity and their ingenuity for the strength to overcome the countless calamities. Although many had been naive about the perils of pioneering, thinking of it as a rare chance to marry vigorous Western men and enjoy a great adventure, those that persevered came to represent stability in a hostile, unstable world,

in which they fought to create a semblance of order and routine. Often they struggled alone; a woman named Amelia Stewart Knight wrote in 1853, "The men and boys all had their hands full and I was obliged to take care of myself and little ones as best I could, there being no road except the one where the teams traveled." Many other pioneer women recorded their experiences in diaries, and their names have survived the years: Catherine Haun, Eliza Spaulding, Lydia Allen Rudd, and Jane Kellogg, to name only a few.

For the vast majority of these women, life was extraordinarily harsh and brutal. In addition to the myriad household or farm activities—cooking, sewing, tending the livestock—they were forced to cope with the seemingly endless heat, dirt, and dust. They lived in constant fear of hunger, disease, or accidents for which no medical help was available. Often they faced a lack of water, lost or straying cattle, desperately ill children, and a weariness deep in their bones. Dry winds, hailstorms, and sandstorms eroded their patience and even their sanity. To increase their misery, there was the constant threat of marauding Indians, deadly snakes, or predatory animals. Death was an almost daily occurrence. Lydia Allen Rudd wrote in her diary in 1852: "One young lady died last night and the other cannot live but a few hours longer, both sisters. Their Father an old feeble gray headed man told me that within two weeks he had buried his wife her brother two sons in law and his daughter died last night." A woman named Elizabeth Smith Geer, who traveled with her husband and seven children from Indiana to Oregon Territory in

With her daughter nearby, a frontier wife collects buffalo chips for fuel, around 1880. Although wives hoarded fuel against the onslaught of winter, a number of families either succumbed to—or barely survived—the destructive storms, the numbing cold, and the lack of food.

Pioneer women of several generations in Utah pose for the camera around 1875. Among their many tribulations, women of the frontier had to cope with the calamities of weather, which often included dry, blistering heat, blinding snowstorms, and driving rainstorms.

1847, entered this diary notation: "I have not told you half we suffered. I am not adequate to the task."

Although most of the Western women were wives and mothers, there were some independent-minded types who forged places for themselves without the help of men. A woman named Abigail Scott Duniway, inspired by her mother's sacrifices in the trek westward, rode from territory to territory preaching equal rights for women. Bethenia Owens-Adair, the first woman doctor, was almost tarred and feathered by townspeople for performing an autopsy on a male. Many single women with no special skills worked in the mining camps under primitive conditions, cooking, sewing, and washing for the miners in a determination to earn their own money.

While these women who struggled against terrible odds—and often lost—were the true backbone of the Western movement, they seldom played the most conspicuous roles in Western movies. Except for a rare film like Victor Seastrom's *The Wind* (1928), in which Lillian Gish starred as a pioneer wife driven to desperation and near madness by her isolation, they were usually shadowy figures, stoically suffering and enduring (and sometimes dying) as their men fought to cultivate and preserve the land. If they survive, as does Alice Brady in Henry King's *In Old Chicago* (1938), it is to see their sons become powerful men in burgeoning cities. If

they expire, as does Mildred Natwick in John Ford's *Three Godfathers* (1948), they place their progeny—a newborn infant—in the caring hands of three rambling cowpokes. Often, they are made to stand by helplessly weeping as members of their family engage in violent confrontations, sometimes with each other: Katharine Hepburn as Spencer Tracy's tear-streaked wife in Elia Kazan's *Sea of Grass* (1947) or Katy Jurado as Spencer Tracy's sorrowing Mexican wife in Edward Dmytryk's *Broken Lance* (1954).

In a cinematic world dominated by men, such women act as steadying influences providing warmth, comfort, and inspiration. They are seldom allowed to take a central role in the story's framework, and when they do, it is only through moral strength or force of will. Often those who have to strive the hardest are the most successful. When a mail-order bride arrives on the scene, we know that she will certainly overcome her lowly status and not only persevere but also triumph. Jan Troell's *Zandy's Bride* (1974) concerns a mail-order bride (Liv Ullmann) who is abused and humiliated by her rancher husband (Gene Hackman). Slowly, through endless patience and a kind of flinty humor, she succeeds in humanizing him, making him respect her feelings. In Richard Pearce's exquisite little film *Heartland* (1979), Conchata Ferrell travels with her daughter to Wyoming to become the housekeeper to Rip Torn's gruff Scottish rancher. With a quiet grace bolstered by beautiful images, *Heartland* traces the development of Ferrell as she first struggles to find her own identity, then marries the rancher. The events involving their survival through a bitter, sorrowful winter give a rounded picture of frontier life and the frontier woman's role.

While these pioneer women demonstrated exceptional fortitude, the military wives added an extra note of stoic nobility. Required to sustain lives of constant fear and uncertainty, they were also expected to keep their emotions in check and provide unswerving support for their husbands' combat activities. Few are allowed to voice the lament of "Buffalo Bill" Cody's wife in Cecil B. DeMille's *The Plainsman* (1936): "When will it ever stop? This killin' and killin'." As General Custer's wife in Raoul Walsh's *They Died with*

Zandy's Bride (Warner Bros., 1974). Gruff rancher Zandy (Gene Hackman) poses with his mail-order bride Catherine (Liv Ullmann) and their offspring (ABOVE) and grapples with a bear (BELOW). Jan Troell's film recorded the painstaking process by which Catherine, through her fortitude and intrinsic warmth, transforms Zandy from an abusive to a mellow and loving husband.

Their Boots On (1941), Olivia de Havilland provides an exemplary model for a military wife when she allows herself to faint only after Custer has left her on what she knows in her heart will be his last mission. Other military wives of iron will and determination include Anna Lee in John Ford's *Fort Apache* (1948), resolutely standing by her captain husband (George O'Brien), or Mildred Natwick as wife to the same George O'Brien in Ford's *She Wore a Yellow Ribbon* (1949), watching proudly as the troops march off to battle or bringing warmth and sympathy to the children who have survived an Indian massacre. Only Maureen O'Hara, as the estranged wife of Colonel Kirby Yorke (John Wayne) in Ford's *Rio Grande* (1950), defies the pattern—she wants nothing to do with his military glory and attempts to retrieve their son from the cavalry. ("What makes soldiers great is hateful to me," she tells her son.) Of course, she changes her attitude by the film's end.

On the whole, the Western wife and mother behaved herself under all circumstances, lending dignity and fortitude to Western films. Although her role may have been largely supportive, at least she was a seasoned veteran of the Western

wars. Usually the dispensing of girlish innocence was left to demure young heroines who waited in the wings while their stalwart men enacted their rituals of bitter conflict and revenge. If she was the resident schoolmarm, dainty and proper, or the rancher's daughter, spirited in jodhpurs while longing for gingham and lace, her purpose remained generally decorative. On the other hand, if she was a refined, Eastern-bred woman who craved domesticity, she represented the threat of "civilizing" influences to the free-living, hard-riding Westerner, who preferred the company of men. In *Honky Tonk* (1941), for example, Clark Gable plays a virile rascal who is domesticated (and, for a time, emasculated) by beribboned Lana Turner, an arrival from the East who is joining her con man father. Their relationship is given a few soap-

Heartland (*Wilderness Women Productions/Filmhaus, 1979). In turn-of-the-century Wyoming, Elinore (Conchata Ferrell, seated) marries rancher Clyde (Rip Torn, at her left). In the wedding party: Grandma (Lilia Skala), Jerrine (Megan Folsom), and Jack (Barry Primus). The film was based on the true experiences of Elinore Stewart, who described her frontier life in a series of letters.*

Honky Tonk *(MGM, 1941). Con man Candy Johnson (Clark Gable) courts and marries Bostonian Elizabeth Cotton (Lana Turner). The studio gave a glossy production to the familiar story of the Western rascal tamed by the Eastern lady.*

operatic twists (after they marry he neglects her, and she nearly dies from a miscarriage); more often, however, the theme of the cowboy-tamed-by-the-genteel-girl was treated not seriously but with song and dance, in such musicals as *The Harvey Girls* (1946) and *Seven Brides for Seven Brothers* (1954), or in comic terms, in such modern-day Western films as *The Cowboy and the Lady* (1938), *A Lady Takes a Chance* (1943), and *Never a Dull Moment* (1950).

Sometimes, when the heroine married, she assumed an additional role as the spokesperson for reason and anti-violence. In *Jesse James* (1939), wife Zee hurls the vision of a harsh future at her outlaw husband: "You won't be a hero forever. You'll get like a wolf—with an appetite for shootin' and robbin'!" In *The Gunfighter* (1950), when Jimmy Ringo pleads to return to his family, his wife, worn down by years of terror and uncertainty, can only say, "Too late." These women seek shelter from the storm raging outside their walls, and

they resent intrusions. "Damn you for bringing pain into this house!" widow Lauren Bacall cries to dying gunfighter John Wayne in *The Shootist* (1976).

Demure heroine or careworn wife, the Western woman almost invariably survived the gunplay that echoed all around her, and if she didn't always win the survivor, there was more than a good chance that he would be returning to her in the near future. This was not the case, however, when the heroine, no matter how sweetly virginal, was other than Caucasian. As if meting out punishment for any hint of miscegenation or act of racial intermarriage, young Indian women or women of Spanish or Mexican descent frequently ended up in a pine box before the film's conclusion. A half-breed such as Paulette Goddard's fiery Louvette in Cecil B. DeMille's *North West Mounted Police* (1940) or Chihuahua (Linda Darnell), the Mexican saloon girl who loves Doc Holliday in John Ford's *My Darling Clementine* (1946), has no chance for survival—Louvette dies with her Mountie lover and Chihuahua expires of a bullet wound. The Indian wives of, respectively, James Stewart in *Broken Arrow* (1950) and Clark Gable in *Across the Wide Missouri* (1951) suffer untimely deaths, and Jean Peters in *Apache* (1954) is spared only because her husband (Burt Lancaster) is an Apache warrior who agrees to end his battle with the white man. Even in an enlightened contemporary Western such as *Tell Them Willie Boy Is Here*, an Indian maiden's chances of staying alive are slim—Lola (Katharine Ross) apparently commits suicide when she fears she is holding up the flight of her renegade Indian lover (Robert Blake). Here she is not paying the price for racial "impurity" but making the kind of grand sacrificial gesture that is often given to nonwhite maidens in movies.

While young Indian girls are leaping into their graves, their white counterparts are usually standing their ground, waiting patiently for their men to return from dangerous duty or giving voice to their abhorrence of war and violence. In most cases, the young Western heroine exudes gentility, although, curiously, she becomes less genteel when she is somebody's daughter. The annals of Western movie history

are studded with the spunky, impertinent offspring of ranchers, railroad men, and other Western tycoons. Clad in trousers and ready and eager to ride along with the men, they ultimately surrender to domesticity and marriage. Examples abound: Barbara Stanwyck's feisty Mollie Monahan in *Union Pacific* (1939), Olivia de Havilland's tomboyish "Kit" Carson Halliday in *Dodge City* (1939), Anne Baxter's belligerent Mike in *Yellow Sky* (1948), and many others.

If the garden-variety Western heroine was merely a cactus flower blooming in the desert—pretty but not especially interesting—they were certainly equaled by the wildflowers and weeds. As prevalent as the schoolmarms and the ranchers' daughters were the brash, rowdy dance-hall girls and saloon singers who populated the frontier towns of Western movies. These girls, looking for a good time, were sisters to the girls in the brothels, but only a raucous comedienne like Mae West could get away with expressing the frankly carnal aspects of the characters, as she did so eloquently in Edward Cline's hilarious, ramshackle *My Little Chickadee* (1940). Usually the movies treated these ladies as hearty, good-natured dames who hovered around the card tables or sidled up to the bars for free drinks and some harmless bear hugs. Few of them resembled the coarse, promiscuous

My Little Chickadee *(Universal, 1940). Mae West meets the Wild West in this ramshackle but often riotous farce costarring the inimitable W. C. Fields. Here, Flower Belle gets a disapproving glance from fellow traveler Mrs. Gideon (Margaret Hamilton).*

Arizona (Columbia, 1940). The independent-minded owner of a struggling freight line, Phoebe Titus (Jean Arthur) draws a bead on villainous Lazarus Ward (Porter Hall). With this film, director Wesley Ruggles attempted unsuccessfully to match the epic-size sweep of his 1931 Western, Cimarron.

women who actually filled the hurdy-gurdy houses and parlor houses of the West, where miners and cowboys had a roaring good time while losing their hard-earned money.

On the whole, the movie "bad girls" had bad luck. If they began as mistresses to the villains, they often ended up in league with the hero, suffering pain and sometimes death for their change of heart. In *Destry Rides Again* (1939), Marlene Dietrich's Frenchy stops a bullet meant for the amiable, drawling hero (James Stewart), as does Shelley Winters in Louis King's inferior 1951 remake, *Frenchie*. If they survived, the dance-hall "hostesses" could count on losing their men to purer women, with their devotion unreciprocated. Claire Trevor, frequently cast in these "fancy lady" roles, has a soft spot for outlaw Glenn Ford in *The Desperadoes* (1943) and fairly pines for drifter Kirk Douglas in *Man without a Star* (1955).

While the ladies of the saloons and dance halls retained a certain tenacity in the face of abuse, they were still tied to—

and defined by—their men. The truly independent-minded woman, the tough dame who had the take-charge qualities usually associated with men, surfaced only occasionally in Western movies of the thirties and forties. Conspicuous examples include Jean Arthur's feisty Phoebe Titus in Wesley Ruggles's sprawling 1940 Western *Arizona* and Veronica Lake's predatory blonde in Andre de Toth's 1947 film *Ramrod*. It was not until the fifties, when women were used to assuming stronger roles in society at large, that the powerful woman emerged fully in the Western, challenging the men who were used to either "good" or "bad" women who accepted their low estate. These women usually had men in their lives, and in the venerable Hollywood tradition, they would, more often than not, surrender to their more "feminine" impulses. Nevertheless, they were a new breed, giving as good as they got and seldom surrendering until at least some of their terms were met.

For the most part, many of the tough Western ladies of the fifties were played by mature actresses who had already sharpened their teeth in man-devouring roles as much as two decades earlier. In *Rancho Notorious*, Fritz Lang's curious 1952 Western, Marlene Dietrich played a woman who runs a hideout for outlaws and who falls fatally in love with a

A photograph of the true "Calamity Jane," actually named Martha Jane Cannary. In truth, "Calam" was a crack marks-woman but also a rough-mannered and decidedly unattractive alcoholic. She died in poverty and obscurity.

Rancho Notorious (RKO, 1952). Outlaw Frenchy Fairmont (Mel Ferrer) and Altar Keane (Marlene Dietrich), mistress of a notorious hideout for outlaws, form two sides of a romantic triangle in Fritz Lang's distinctly odd Western. Many years later, Lang indicated that Dietrich resented the screenplay's implication that the character of Altar was past her prime; she also insisted on contradicting his ideas about directing and lighting.

Cattle Queen of Montana *(RKO, 1954). The eloquently named Sierra Nevada Jones (Barbara Stanwyck) struggles to hold on to her father's ranch, with the help of gunman (and secret government agent) Farrell (Ronald Reagan). In the fifties, Stanwyck played a number of feisty and sometimes devious ladies in Western movies.*

revenge-obsessed man (Arthur Kennedy). Barbara Stanwyck, the gritty heroine of many Depression dramas, transferred her commanding, don't-tangle-with-me style to the Western plains in a series of fifties films, including *The Violent Men* (1955), *Cattle Queen of Montana* (1954), *The Maverick Queen* (1956), and *Forty Guns* (1957). Directed feverishly and unevenly by Rudolph Maté, *The Violent Men*, in which Stanwyck played the scheming, cheating wife of a rancher (Edward G. Robinson), gave more footage to its sexual entanglements than to its Western action, while *Cattle Queen of Montana* and *The Maverick Queen* offered little more than Stanwyck playing variations of her boss-lady-of-the-plains. In *The Maverick Queen*, as the owner and proprietor of a saloon whose visitors include Butch Cassidy and the Sundance Kid, she dies in the arms of a Pinkerton agent (Barry Sullivan). In all of these films, like a female Samson, she is shorn of her considerable power by her involvement with men.

Samuel Fuller's *Forty Guns*, perhaps the best of Stanwyck's Westerns, has been either admired for its primitive vigor or derided for its overwrought hysteria. Stanwyck plays Jessica Drummond, the dangerous, whip-wielding boss of Cochise County, whose henchmen will kill or destroy on her behalf. Men, of course, are her undoing: first, a no-good younger brother (John Ericson) and then a marshal (Barry Sullivan) who was once a famous gunman. When her brother

The Maverick Queen (Republic, 1956). Saloon queen Kit Banion (Barbara Stanwyck) is involved with both the Sundance Kid (Scott Brady) and a Pinkerton agent (Barry Sullivan; ABOVE). Kit is the sort of tough Western lady who can say, "I did what I had to do to get where I am." She later expires in the arms of the Pinkerton agent (BELOW) who has posed as an outlaw. The movie was made in the short-lived wide-screen process called Naturama.

Forty Guns *(Fox, 1957). Barbara Stanwyck starred as Jessica Drummond in Samuel Fuller's Western as a ruthless woman who controls Cochise County with the aid of forty armed gunmen. With only a few of them for support* (BELOW), *she stands up to Sheriff Ned Logan (Dean Jagger), who is too weak to oppose her. However, she has a weak spot in her trigger-happy brother (John Ericson;* RIGHT), *who uses her as a shield against the law in the film's climax. Although Samuel Fuller's Western was largely dismissed in America, it was highly praised in Europe for its vigorous, if overly intense, style.*

Westward the Women *(MGM, 1951). Scout Robert Taylor rides across the land with the indisputably French Denise Darcel, one of the women traveling to their mail-order husbands in California. William Wellman's film was based on a story by Frank Capra.*

The King and Four Queens *(United Artists, 1956). Ma McDade (Jo Van Fleet) points her gun at Dan Kehoe (Clark Gable), the con man who is trying to bilk her widowed daughters out of their late husbands' money. Eventually, he realizes that he is the one who is being manipulated.*

OPPOSITE   Johnny Guitar *(Republic, 1954). Joan Crawford starred as the tough-minded, strong-willed saloon-casino owner named Vienna Jones. Nicholas Ray's bizarre Western has its ardent champions, who have read many meanings into its overwrought tale of the bitter rivalry between two strong women. Others have remained bewildered.*

murders the marshal's brother, there's hell to pay, despite the growing warm relationship between Jessica and the marshal. Jessica loses everything, but not without an ironic awareness that she is one of the last of a breed of tough, independent women. "This is the last stop," she tells the marshal. "The frontier is finished. There'll be no more towns to break—no more men to break." Astride her horse, leading her gunmen to the fray, Stanwyck's Jessica Drummond makes a striking contrast to the standard milky Western heroine.

Joan Crawford, Stanwyck's frequent thirties rival in feminine aggressiveness, also turned up on horseback in the fifties, starring in Nicholas Ray's distinctly odd Western *Johnny Guitar* (1954). Often praised and analyzed for its perfervid and sometimes almost surrealistic dialogue, this film has even been given a political subtext by some critics. Although its status as a cult film tends to obscure its deep-rooted absurdity, it remains a fascinating movie.

Basically, the film focuses on the conflict between two women: a strong-willed saloon-casino owner named Vienna Jones (Joan Crawford) and a neurotic rancher named Emma Small (Mercedes McCambridge) who loathes Vienna and longs to see her dead. Emma's unstated passion for the Dancin' Kid (Scott Brady), who is attracted to Vienna, fuels the conflict, while Vienna's former lover, Johnny Guitar (Sterling Hayden), stands by, waiting to become inevitably involved in the ensuing fracas. This hotbed of thwarted and rekindled passions and smoldering sexuality holds little room for conventional Western action, and a good deal of *Johnny Guitar* stays confined claustrophobically to Vienna's saloon. Despite its limited focus, the film manages to crowd in enough Freudian symbolism to keep analysts and some critics happy for weeks. For all its offbeat style, *Johnny Guitar* can best be considered a movie for those who find interest and deep significance in its reversal of traditional sex roles—as Danny Peary put it: "a male dancer and male guitarist vie for the love of a gun-toting woman" (*Cult Movies*, p. 174). Other hard-as-nails female gunslingers, riding beside or even leading men into shoot-outs, turned up quite often in the fifties.

The Lady from Cheyenne *(Universal, 1941). In 1869 Wyoming, Loretta Young fights for the women's suffrage movement. At her right is her chief adversary, gambler and racketeer Jim Cork (Edward Arnold). Hero Robert Preston (left) looks down at her with admiration.*

In addition to the outlaw queens and cattle queens who dominated many Westerns in that decade, there were many women who assumed power without benefit of guns or who behaved aggressively in man-woman relationships. In William Wellman's *Westward the Women* (1952), when a misogynistic scout (Robert Taylor) leads a wagon train of women to their mail-order husbands in California, it is the women who prove most courageous, taking the wagons over mountains and withstanding attacks by Indians. The scout is even tamed by a hot-tempered French girl (Denise Darcel). In Raoul Walsh's *The King and Four Queens* (1956), a con man (Clark Gable) is outsmarted and even humiliated by the mother and young widows of the outlaw gang he pretends to join. (His goal is to bilk them of a share of the money the outlaws had hidden before their capture.) Eventually, he settles down with the most comely of the widows (Eleanor Parker).

An occasional Western turned up the rare sort of woman who was not content merely to settle for a man or who sought achievement beyond needlepoint and apple pies. In Frank Lloyd's *The Lady from Cheyenne* (1941), Loretta Young played Annie Morgan, a determined young Quaker woman who fights for women's suffrage and ultimately wins the right to sit on a jury, where she can convict gamblers like Jim Cork (Edward Arnold). And in Mervyn LeRoy's *Strange Lady in Town* (1955), Greer Garson appeared as a doctor who arrives in Santa Fe in 1880 and proceeds to fight against social prejudice and male bigotry. She gets to treat Billy the Kid, Lew Wallace (governor of New Mexico and author of *Ben Hur*), and Indian chief Geronimo; she is also courted by a fellow doctor played by Dana Andrews.

Once in a great while, a Western heroine was permitted to be an independent-minded entrepreneur without sacrificing her femininity—in *The Big Country*, Julie Maragon (Jean Simmons) runs her own ranch efficiently and succeeds a rancher's frivolous daughter in the affections of hero Jim McKay (Gregory Peck). However, a single woman of questionable background must prove her worth the hard way. In Douglas Sirk's charming *Take Me to Town* (1953), saloon singer Vermillion O'Toole (Ann Sheridan) demonstrates that she can be a good wife and mother by performing various feats, including killing a bear and putting on a musical show to raise money for a church.

Capable women like Vermillion surfaced only sporadically in the sixties and seventies, and when they did, the film often had a comic emphasis. In Elliot Silverstein's funny but uneven Western spoof *Cat Ballou* (1965), schoolteacher Cat Ballou (Jane Fonda) becomes a gun-totin' outlaw after her father is murdered and perseveres in her thirst for revenge. The seemingly demure "little lady" (Joanne Woodward), in Fielder Cook's *A Big Hand for the Little Lady* (1966), turns out to be a key player in an elaborate con scheme manipulated by her husband (Henry Fonda) and others. And Doris Day, starring as a helpless widow in Andrew McLaglen's *The Ballad of Josie* (1967) transforms herself into an aggressive and successful sheep farmer, to the dismay of her fellow townsfolk. The seventies saw an occasional dominant woman: Katharine Hepburn as the feisty spinster in Stuart Millar's *Rooster Cogburn* (1975) and Conchata Ferrell in

A Big Hand for the Little Lady *(Warner Bros., 1966). Fielder Cook's clever comedy Western offered a few surprises at the climax of this card game with Kevin McCarthy, Jason Robards, and Joanne Woodward. Paul Ford watches in the background.*

Strange Lady in Town *(Warner Bros., 1955). Refined and genteel as ever, Greer Garson played Julia Winslow Garth, a doctor who arrives in New Mexico and accomplishes wonders in a short time. Dana Andrews (center) played the hotheaded Irish doctor who comes to love her.*

Cat Ballou *(Columbia, 1965). Cat Ballou (Jane Fonda) and friends look on (*ABOVE*) as Kid Sheleen (Lee Marvin) drinks himself into his usual stupor (*RIGHT*). In this raucous comedy, Fonda's schoolmarm is not the usual demure damsel; she fires a gun and robs a train with wide-eyed enthusiasm.*

OPPOSITE   A Big Hand for the Little Lady *(Warner Bros., 1966). This tender family tableau of father (Henry Fonda), wife (Joanne Woodward), and son (Gerald Michenaud) is not all that it seems to be. The forthright sincerity of Fonda's usual persona made his con game in this film all the more diverting.*

Richard Pearce's *Heartland* as a resilient frontier woman who achieves a measure of independence as she survives the rigors of winter.

In Western movie lore, if a man should by chance crave domesticity, he could either vigorously court the woman of his choice or resort to a mail-order bride. If he desired sexual recreation, he had his choice of the bold, gaudy saloon girls, or the dark-eyed Mexican girls, or the girls at the bawdy houses who surfaced in later, franker Westerns such as *The Cheyenne Social Club* (1970) and *McCabe and Mrs. Miller* (1971). For the careworn ranch wives and settlers' wives, however, there was no suggestion that sexual activity played a role in their precarious existence, or that their children had appeared from any source other than osmosis or divine intervention. When sex showed up in the Western, it sometimes palpitated with a passion that verged on the ludicrous. In *The Outlaw* (1943), that much buzzed-about Western from Howard Hughes, Jane Russell's enormous breasts seem to

overpower a rather woebegone Billy the Kid (Jack Buetel), and in King Vidor's *Duel in the Sun* (1947), Jennifer Jones as the tempestuous Pearl Chevez flared her nostrils and bared her teeth to indicate her uncontrollable lust for the no-good Lewt McCanles, and she writhed in his arms with a delirium that suggests a seizure rather than sexual fervor. Earlier, her mother (Tilly Losch) had performed a dance so wild and abandoned that it had inflamed her lover and led to their murder at the hands of her husband (Herbert Marshall).

Overt sexuality in the Western continued to appear from time to time, perhaps a mite subtler than the raw and feverish intensity that marked *Duel in the Sun*. (Could anything match the remarkable love-hate climax of that film in which Lewt and Pearl shoot each other and die in each other's arms?) King Vidor offered some of the same steamy passion he had brought to *Duel in the Sun* in *Man without a Star* (1955), in which a saddle tramp (Kirk Douglas) beds—and then defies—a wealthy rancher (Jeanne Crain), and then must fight the sadistic hoodlum (Richard Boone) she chooses to replace him. Douglas's scenes with Crain generated some surprising sexual heat considering the actress's longtime girl-next-door image. Even stronger in its sexual content was Delmer Daves's *Jubal* (1956), in which a ranch hand (Glenn Ford) is lusted after by his boss's (Ernest Borgnine) promiscuous wife (Valerie French). Violence ensues when, in an *Othello*-like plot twist, the foreman (Rod Steiger), one of the wife's rejected lovers, turns the rancher against his employee, with fatal results for the former. A sense of thwarted passions and barely controlled hysteria informs this overwrought but interesting Western.

The Cheyenne Social Club (National General, 1970). In a far cry from his Destry *days, James Stewart starred as a cowpoke who inherits a bawdy house. Henry Fonda played his friend and co-owner (*BELOW*), and Shirley Jones was one of the girls (*OPPOSITE*). Earlier Westerns could hardly hint at the very existence of brothels, which were not unknown in the Wild West.*

Films like *Jubal* and *Man without a Star* hinted that these frustrated women ranchers and ranchers' wives were not only seeking sexual release but also enjoyed the power over their men that their attraction bestowed. However, for Western women of a lower station, with no time for restlessness or boredom, sexuality was smothered by the endless drudgery of their lives. Occasionally, a suggestion of sexual feeling would rise to the surface. In Norman Foster's *Rachel and the Stranger* (1948), Loretta Young, as the bondswoman wife to a farmer (William Holden), responds to the attentions of the farmer's vagabond friend (Robert Mitchum), leading to Holden's new appreciation of the woman he bought only to cook for him and help raise his son. Similar feelings are aroused in the frontier wife played by Jean Arthur in *Shane*, in which her love for the mysterious blond gunslinger emerges in soft, smiling glances in his direction. It took years for a Western movie to acknowledge that such a relationship could ever be consummated—in Gary Nelson's *Molly and Lawless John* (1972), the sheriff's wife (Vera Miles) runs off with a young outlaw who seduces her, and Sidney Lumet's *Lovin' Molly* (1974), played by Blythe Danner, is lovin' indeed: over four decades, she sleeps repeatedly with the two men who have always loved her, although she is married to someone else.

Lovin' Molly *(Columbia, 1974). Molly (Blythe Danner) is embraced by one of the two important men in her life (Anthony Perkins). The film was based on a novel by Larry McMurtry, who disapproved of director Sidney Lumet's handling of the Texas background.*

OPPOSITE Rachel and the Stranger *(RKO, 1948). Farmer Big Davey Harvey (William Holden) and Rachel (Loretta Young), his bondswoman wife, ward off an attack by the Shawnees (*ABOVE*). By the film's end, he has come to love the woman he bought as more of a servant than a wife, seeing her blossom under the attention Jim Fairways (Robert Mitchum) pays to her (*BELOW*). Little Davey (Gary Gray) also falls under Jim's spell.*

If most Western movies had little concern with conveying a young woman's sexual feelings, except to hint at buried frustration, they showed even less interest in the needs of the elderly woman. Occasionally, a Western film permitted an older woman to emerge from the background (where she would appear as a bonneted blur) to play a larger role. When she did, it was usually as a source of deep-rooted strength and stability—in *The Man from Laramie* (1955), for example, Aline MacMahon plays the hearty ranch owner who befriends beleaguered James Stewart and comforts the broken cattle baron (Donald Crisp) when he loses his sons and his land.

Rarely did a Western film suggest that an elderly woman was less than saintly, and when it did, it was to involve her in a raucous senior romance (Marjorie Main coyly sparring with Wallace Beery) or to accuse her of long-ago indiscretions that marred or even crippled her life. In *Pursued* (1947), the illicit romance of Medora Callum (Judith Anderson) when young triggered the violent events that engulf her foster son (Robert Mitchum), and in *Duel in the Sun*, the youthful flight of Laura Belle McCanles (Lillian Gish) from her overbearing husband (Lionel Barrymore) has left a lifetime of scars and regrets. Even such benign Hollywood matriarchs as Beulah

Bondi and Jane Darwell were not always portraits of grandmotherly concern: Bondi was the mean-spirited mother of a quarreling brood in William Wellman's oppressive drama *Track of the Cat* (1954), and earlier, in Wellman's *The Ox-Bow Incident* (1943), Darwell played a cackling, obscene old harridan who prods a lynch mob into carrying out its nefarious deed. More often, however, these actresses were available to provide strength seasoned by age and wisdom. Darwell, in particular, brought dignity and tenacity to her roles in John Ford Westerns such as *My Darling Clementine* and *Wagonmaster*.

On the whole, the Western genre has not done well by women, treating them as weary matriarchs, demure maidens, or sullied wenches, with a trend in more recent decades toward aggressive *grande dames*. By concentrating on rugged men of action, with little time for romance or domesticity, Western films have neglected to portray the many facets or to capture the fierce intensity of the Western experience for women of all ages. To read the stories of the women who recorded their daily tribulations in the wilderness is to come upon a one-of-a-kind odyssey of courage and heartbreak that has never been adequately tapped for the screen.

Off the Beaten Trail

"We spend our time here between funerals and burials."

—a townsman to Clint Eastwood in *A Fistful of Dollars* (United Artists, 1964)

DURING THE COURSE of its long history, the Western has absorbed a variety of elements and themes into its basic structure. Western movies have accommodated raucous slapstick (from Buster Keaton to the Marx Brothers), songs (*The Harvey Girls, Annie Get Your Gun*, and others), an unmistakable suggestion of the supernatural (*Pale Rider*), and much more. There have been Westerns with an all-black cast (*Harlem on the Prairie*, 1937, was the first), and even one with a cast of midgets (*Terror of Tiny Town*, 1938). Billy the Kid grappled with Count Dracula in a film called (what else?) *Billy the Kid vs. Dracula* (1966), and Fox loosely remade its crime melodrama *Kiss of Death* as a peculiar Western called *The Fiend Who Walked the West* (1958). For a period of time in the late thirties, Germany produced a series of popular Western movies starting with *The Emperor of California (Der Kaiser von Kalifornien)* in 1936. Robert Aldrich's *The Frisco Kid* (1979) presented a Polish Orthodox rabbi as its hero.

A handful of Westerns have managed to stitch a message into their fabric without being overly blatant about it. By now it is generally agreed that Carl Foreman, in *High Noon*, intended to add an oblique comment on the self-serving cowardice and evasiveness of many people during the troubled McCarthy years to his narrative about a sheriff forced to stand alone. While keeping the familiar trappings of the epic Western in *The Big Country*, William Wyler, by way of the screenplay by James R. Webb, Sy Bartlett, and Robert Wilder, may have hinted at the hopeless futility of open warfare. (In the end, old Rufus Hannassey and Henry Terrill, like two enraged, bloated superpowers, have a fatal final encounter in the desert.) And in a more overt attempt to provoke thought, *The Outrage* (1964) used a Western framework to consider the multilayered nature of truth.

Derived from Akira Kurosawa's classic 1951 Japanese film *Rashomon*, *The Outrage* retained the basic story of an investigation into a crime in which a notorious outlaw had apparently waylaid a merchant and his wife in the forest, raped the wife, and then slain the merchant in a duel. In a series of flashbacks, the event is dramatized from each participant's point of view, along with that of a wood-gatherer who claims to have witnessed the crime. *The Outrage* transferred the story to the post–Civil War Southwest, turning the Japanese outlaw into Mexican bandit Juan Carrasco (Paul Newman, complete with bristling mustache, beard, and a large sombrero). In this version, Carrasco accosts a Confederate colonel (Laurence Harvey) and his beautiful wife (Claire Bloom) in a forest glade and then, under ambiguous circumstances, rapes the wife and kills the colonel. Once again, each participant relates his contrasting version of the event to the frontier judge, suggesting that truth is a relative matter in which "facts" are altered to serve—and flatter—the speaker. This cynical point of view is expressed bluntly by the old prospector (Edward G. Robinson), whose philosophy is, "Tell people what they want to hear."

Competently directed by Martin Ritt and strikingly photographed by the masterly James Wong Howe, *The Outrage* fascinates as an offbeat experiment in Western drama. The attempt to blend a philosophical point with conventional Western action falters more than once in Fay and Michael Kanin's screenplay (from the Kurosawa film and their own

1959 stage play), and Newman's key performance is overly broad. Still, there are scenes of surprising force, such as the wife's account of the incident. On the whole, however, the complex and enigmatic quality of the original film is seldom duplicated, and the conflicting stories, handled in styles that range from intensely serious to farcical, remain unfocused and little more than an uneasy contrivance.

Occasionally, a Western movie has dispensed with indirection and presented its message with blunt authority. One such film was William Wellman's stark cautionary tale *The Ox-Bow Incident* (1943). Produced two years earlier but kept on the shelf by nervous executives, the film took on the subject of mob violence without flinching from its ugly ramifications. Lamar Trotti's screenplay, adapted from Walter Van Tilburg Clark's novel, centered on the brutal lynching of three hapless men by an angry mob that believes them to be guilty of rustling and murdering a rancher. There is no protagonist, only a roving cowpoke (Henry Fonda) who observes the event without interference but with mounting aversion. Discovering that the rancher was never murdered—and then realizing that they have conspired in a monstrous

The Outrage (MGM, 1964). In Martin Ritt's curious Western remake of Akira Kurosawa's classic Rashomon, *Paul Newman (left) starred as a Mexican bandit whose fatal encounter with a Confederate colonel and his wife (Laurence Harvey and Claire Bloom) is related from several points of view. To prepare for his role as Juan Carrasco, Newman spent two weeks in Mexico, studying accents and voice qualities.*

PAGE 222 For a Few Dollars More *(United Artists, 1967). The Man with No Name (Clint Eastwood) stands poised and ready for action. The film repeated the formula that had made* A Fistful of Dollars *so successful.*

act—leaves the perpetrators shaken and remorseful.

Filmed with an obviously limited budget (the major outdoor setting, highlighted by an artfully designed hanging tree, is patently phony), *The Ox-Bow Incident* scores its points with little subtlety; most of the central figures involved in the story represent attitudes rather than rounded characters: the solitary voice of reason ("It'll be murder if you carry this through"); the religious zealot, worried about "man taking on the vengeance of the Lord"; and the ineffectual man of the law (a blustery but powerless judge). Some of the participants are given psychological underpinnings that make them more interesting, most notably a sadistic Confederate colonel who takes charge of the lynching party and who is disgusted

with his weak son (at the end, the colonel shoots himself) and a cackling old harridan whose bawdy manner conceals a cold heart. Although Henry Fonda is unable to contribute much more than the force of his presence as the leading icon of decency in American films, his sincerity helps to offset some of the falsity of the movie's key scene in which he reads the letter of one of the victims, written to his wife just before he is hanged by the mob. Despite its flaws, *The Ox-Bow Incident* can still jolt us when the camera moves across the remorseless faces of the lynchers or later, when the sheriff withers them with his contempt: "God better have mercy on ya. Ya won't get any from me!"

While *The Ox-Bow Incident* specifically deplored lynching and mob rule, other films sought to take at least an implicit stand against racial prejudice by dramatizing its consequences in Western settings. The most interesting of these films was John Ford's 1960 drama *Sergeant Rutledge*, which marked the beginning of his final and darkest period, culminating in *The Man Who Shot Liberty Valance* and *Cheyenne Autumn*. For many years, Ford had resented his reputation as a racist, and he wanted to express his true feelings in this

The Ox-Bow Incident (Fox, 1943). While the nooses hang ominously from the tree, the cowboys settle down for some pre-lynching supper. At the right is their self-appointed leader (Frank Conroy), a bogus Confederate colonel. William Wellman's film presented a grimly pessimistic view of the West that could hardly find favor with movie audiences.

film. Dealing with a black cavalryman (Woody Strode) on trial for raping and murdering a major's daughter, the movie took on a restricted, almost claustrophobic feeling, most unusual for a Ford Western, as it depicted the virulent hatred of Rutledge that permeates his trial. He finally rebels and tries to escape, only to return to save his comrades from an Apache attack. *Sergeant Rutledge* achieves a powerful moment when Rutledge explains why he gave up his liberty and returned to prison. His anguished face in close-up, he cries, "The Ninth Cavalry was my home, my real freedom, and my self-respect, and the way I was desertin' it, I wasn't nothin' but a swamp-runnin' nigger. And I ain't that! Do you hear me? I'm a *man!*"

Racism in the West (and, by implication, in America) also became an issue in other movies of the late sixties and early seventies, a period of social activism and upheaval across the country. Ralph Nelson's exceptionally violent *Duel at Diablo* (1966) mixed elements of prejudice into its standard cavalry-versus-Indians story, including among its characters a black ex-sergeant (Sidney Poitier), who dreams of owning a gambling casino, who is compelled to prove that courage knows no color; a woman (Bibi Andersson) whose illegitimate half-breed baby is wrecking her life with her hus-

band (Dennis Weaver); and a weary but implacable scout (James Garner) seeking revenge for the killing of his Indian wife. Racial intolerance also dominated Edwin Sherin's *Valdez Is Coming* (1971), in which Mexican constable Burt Lancaster (in dark makeup) is reviled and humiliated for seeking compensation money for an Apache woman whose black husband, a freedman, was brutally murdered. In touching all minority bases (black, Mexican, Indian), the movie diffused rather than expanded its impact.

OPPOSITE   Duel at Diablo *(United Artists, 1966). A battle rages in Ralph Nelson's blistering, exceptionally brutal Western that starred Sidney Poitier (holding reins) as a former army sergeant who dreams of owning his own casino.*

Sergeant Rutledge *(Warner Bros., 1960). Believing (erroneously) that Sergeant Rutledge (Woody Strode) has committed murder, Mary Beecher (Constance Towers) holds a gun on him. Later, she becomes one of his few defenders. John Ford's Western was rare in having a black actor as its central character.*

These various attempts to bring a contemporary patina to the Western had hardly any effect at the box office. One Western with no such aspirations, cheaply made in Italy by a little-known second-unit director and screenwriter named Sergio Leone, enjoyed enormous and unexpected popularity, strongly influencing the genre for a number of years and turning Clint Eastwood, until then only a modestly successful actor, into a major star. *A Fistful of Dollars,* produced in 1964 and released in America early in 1967, startled viewers by reversing the familiar mythology of the American Western, turning the Western wilderness into a parched, cheerless, and extraordinarily violent wasteland, a hallucinatory vision of John Ford's West. Although not the first Italian-made Western, *A Fistful of Dollars* established the pattern that was fol-

lowed in scores of films for the balance of the decade and into the next: a mysterious, laconic drifter, here the Man with No Name (Eastwood), rides into a trouble-ridden town and, in a nonstop whirlwind of bloodshed, destroys the forces of evil. (In this instance, with no motive other than profit, he hires himself out to two warring families, then sets one against the other.)

Actually more international than Italian (it was filmed in Spain, coproduced with Spain and West Germany, and derived its plot from Japanese director Akira Kurosawa's *Yojimbo*), *A Fistful of Dollars* achieved its effects by stringing together established Western clichés and then boldly heightening them with stylistic devices that included frequent close-ups, a clanging musical score by Ennio Morricone, and,

A Fistful of Dollars *(United Artists, 1967). The Man with No Name (Clint Eastwood) and Marisol (Marianne Koch) face a tense moment (*RIGHT*). The invincible Man in the poncho and wide-brimmed hat is certain to survive any contingency, even a gunfight (*BELOW*). The enormous success of Sergio Leone's "spaghetti" Western triggered a large number of similar Westerns featuring violent gunplay and explicit gore.*

Sabata *(United Artists, 1969). In this Italian Western, Lee Van Cleef (left) starred in the title role of the bounty hunter who hunts down and kills a band of robbers.*

above all, sequences of explicit mayhem and carnage. The film's story line is of much less importance than the tricks and devices by which the seemingly indestructible Man with No Name wipes out both warring factions. Although he dispenses death, he is no avenging angel, merely a catalyst in a town where death is already too familiar.

Only in the last sequence does the Man suggest the mystical, supernatural aspects of the character Eastwood would later play in such American Westerns as *Hang 'em High* and *Pale Rider*. To the amazement of the villainous Rojos family, the Man, thought to have vanished, suddenly appears out of a mist of smoke. Shot repeatedly, he continues to rise, so confounding his antagonists that they fail to act quickly enough and are shot dead in a burst of gunfire from the Man's pistol. (Actually, the Man had fashioned a metal shield for his chest before coming to the shoot-out.)

Widely attended and imitated, *A Fistful of Dollars* prompted two sequels by Leone, both featuring the Man with No Name in his by now trademarked slouch hat, serape, and unyielding gaze. *For a Few Dollars More* (1967) added American actor Lee Van Cleef, who, as the eccentric, weapons-obsessed Colonel Mortimer, joins the Man in destroying the evil Indio (Gian Maria Volonte). (Mortimer's motive is revenge for Indio's rape of his sister.) Once again Leone splattered the screen with explicit violence and filled it with huge close-ups of disreputable characters. *The Good, the Bad, and the Ugly* (1967) ended the three-film cycle with even more lurid—and more expensive—Western melodramatics as three men (Eastwood, Van Cleef, and new addition Eli Wallach) cross paths and double-cross each other in a search for buried gold during the Civil War. Characteristically, the money is discovered hidden in a coffin. The film's morally anarchic attitude, also present in the other movies, influenced later filmmakers in their revisionist views of Western history and culture.

The huge success of *A Fistful of Dollars* and its sequels started a flood of "spaghetti" Westerns that continued into the seventies. Italian directors who had cut their teeth on costume epics switched to making Westerns. While lacking Leone's bravura style, they emulated him in blood-spurting violence, set against an arid Western landscape. Some were

quite prolific; in the late sixties, Sergio Corbucci directed *Django* (1966), the first of a series of popular, very violent Westerns featuring an indestructible gunfighter hero, as well as such movies as *The Hellbenders* (1966), *Navajo Joe* (1966), *A Professional Gun* (1968), and *Companeros* (1970). Although other directors, such as Sergio Sollima and Tonino Valerii, turned up regularly in the credits, the audiences that enjoyed their movies looked only to the taciturn gunslinging heroes who emulated the Man with No Name, all bearing names such as Ringo, Shanghai Joe, Minnesota Clay, and Pecos.

Some of the directors, seeking to blur their nationality in the English-speaking market, anglicized their names—Luigi Vanzi became Vance Lewis for such films as *For a Dollar in the Teeth* (1966) and *Shoot First, Laugh Last* (1967), and Gianfranco Parolini turned into Frank Kramer for *Sabata* (1969) and *Return of Sabata* (1972). A series of comedy Westerns featuring a character named Trinity was directed by E. B. Clucher, born Enzo Barboni. Anglicizing names even extended to the stars—Trinity was played by an actor billed as Terence Hill but actually named Mario Girotti, and his dim-witted brother, billed in the credits as Bud Spencer, was played by actor Carlo Pedersoli. To increase the appeal of these films to American audiences, familiar if somewhat faded actors such as Jack Palance, Dan Duryea, John Ireland, Van Johnson, and even Burt Reynolds (in the years before his superstardom) were used in leading or supporting roles.

Once upon a Time in the West *(Paramount, 1969). In a startling reversal of his usual casting, Henry Fonda* (ABOVE; *arm outstretched) played the cold-blooded gunman who, in an early sequence, coolly murders a man and his two young children. The revenge-minded Man with a Harmonica (Charles Bronson) finally catches up with Frank* (OPPOSITE). PRECEDING PAGES *Sergio Leone's elaborate, influential Western was filled with such stylized moments. What it did not have were unequivocal heroes, thus subverting the traditional Western code.*

Grim and cynical, these Italian Westerns took place in a morally bankrupt universe, where there were no traditions, no sense of honor or progress, only a series of explosive encounters in which sudden death prevails. The land is not a precious possession to be fought for but an arid desert leading nowhere. Weapons are not merely designed to maintain—or disrupt—law and order in the West; they become fetishes with mysterious powers. The stalwart Westerner, duty-bound to save a town or a ranch, has turned into an anachronism—good can hardly flourish in an atmosphere where evil is all-pervasive. (Only toward the end of the cycle does knockabout comedy begin to replace the explicit violence.) In the Italian Westerns, blank indifference (nothing matters) and a chilling disregard for human life (nothing is sacred or invulnerable) replace commitment and the tenacious pursuit of a dream.

Nowhere is this attitude more evident than in an early sequence of Sergio Leone's most ambitious and expensive Western, *Once upon a Time in the West* (1969). As a man and his young children prepare to eat a meal outdoors in a tableau of sweet innocence, five men suddenly appear and shoot the man and his daughter in cold blood. Their leader turns out to be that familiar icon of American decency and integrity, Henry Fonda. One of the men asks what they should do with the son and mentions Fonda's name. Whereupon the portrayer of Abraham Lincoln smiles at the child, spits out tobacco, and calmly guns him down.

In keeping with this startling beginning, which deliberately goes against the audience's expectations, *Once upon a Time in the West* not only subverts the Hollywood Western tradition but also carries it to a baroque extreme. The plot brings together two basic Western themes: revenge and the impact of the railroads. A greedy railroad tycoon, bent on establishing his power before he dies, employs a cold-blooded gunman named Frank (Fonda) and his gang to get his way. Opposing him are a mysterious Man with a Harmonica (Charles Bronson), whose brother had been killed by Frank, a grizzled bandit named Cheyenne (Jason Robards), and the wife (Claudia Cardinale) of the man gunned down in the early scene. Around this not unfamiliar story, Leone constructed a grandiose epic that impresses as often as it infuriates. To Ennio Morricone's thumping music, Leone staged sequences that combine brutal violence with oddly beautiful panoramic landscapes (some of the film was shot in Monument Valley) and enormous close-ups of the principals. The result is a delirious Western that received harsh treatment in America in its severely truncated version; it later earned respectful attention when released years later in its original form.

Now that the Italian Western, after a few years of popularity in the late sixties, has entered film annals as more of a footnote than a permanent subgenre, one can speculate on the reasons for its existence. Some have advanced the idea that it was a shameless attempt by Italian filmmakers to apply the new movement toward realism in films, with its emphasis on violence and sadomasochism, to a popular American genre. Others have claimed that it may have been a genuine if oblique way of commenting on the wrenching social and political upheavals not only in Italy but around the globe.

It has even been said that the Italian Western, out of Old World jealousy of the achievements of America, deliberately destroyed the conventions of the Hollywood Western, replacing the righteous knight-on-horseback with the amoral Man with No Name.

In any event, American audiences, for a time, flocked to see the "spaghetti" Westerns. As the industry-imposed censorship regulations began to relax under the impact of a new generation of young, rebellious, antiestablishment views, it became increasingly possible to show explicit scenes of sex and violence—another swipe at convention. Wicked, corrupt behavior, at least up on the screen, challenged the old entrenched rules of what was permissible. In addition, the "spaghetti" Western took place in the sort of moral wasteland—a world without reason, order, or guilt—that many moviegoers found (and still find) titillating. Clint Eastwood's Man with No Name ruled supreme in this world, as would Eastwood's urban "Dirty" Harry Callahan in 1971. Both the Man and Harry bestowed the illusion of power in a powerless universe and a sense of control amid the chaos—and some audiences loved them for it.

On the whole, Western filmmakers who attempted to introduce new elements into the fixed pattern of the genre have not met with conspicuous success. Many purists, in fact, resent the revisionist Westerns that depict a West that John Ford—or, at least, the John Ford of *Stagecoach* and *She Wore a Yellow Ribbon*—would not recognize. No doubt the basic structure of the Western, if it returns at all, will continue to be bent and stretched. And no doubt there will be those who cry, "Come back, Shane!"

Decline and Fall

"I've had a hell of a good time."

—John Wayne in *The Shootist* (Paramount, 1976)

AS THE NINETEENTH CENTURY waned, the Old West began fading into history. Although people continued to seek their fortunes out West, one of the last massive treks had taken place in April 1889, when a detachment of troops led ten thousand settlers across the land commonly known as the Cherokee Strip. The dreams and the opportunities lived on, but most of the work had been accomplished. The wilderness had been conquered and turned into a flourishing domain. Enemies both natural and man-made had been overcome, at the cost of many lives. Instead of forbidding, barren wasteland, there were thriving towns connected by railroad tracks and telegraph wires. The future held high promise for the New West.

Nevertheless, the winning of the West left an incalculable number of scars. The once proud Indian tribes had been virtually destroyed by massacres, disease, broken promises, and whiskey. Greedy ranchers had swallowed up vast tracts of land, ultimately with the enthusiastic cooperation of the railroad magnates, and when their power declined, many of those who had worked for them, the cowboys and ranch hands, turned without hope to lives of shiftlessness and crime. Confronted with more strictly enforced laws, the gunfighter became either a ghost out of his time, waiting for a fatal testing of his prowess, or a caricature created for Wild West shows.

The dark last decades of the Old West had not often earned the attention of filmmakers. (After all, Ford, Hawks, and others had devoted a lifetime to creating a legendary country by that name.) Yet as the postwar revisionist attitude prevailed, a number of films began to examine the decline that inevitably followed an ascent to the heights, as well as the men and women who inhabited the far side of the Western dream. Surfacing intermittently in the postwar years and reaching a peak in the sixties and seventies, Westerns disposed to take a hard, unblinkered look at the ultimate fate of the West turned the genre in a different direction. They depicted a Western scene in the final stages of dissolution, often involving characters at the end of their tether, both poignant and despicable. A lamentation for the dying West also seemed to sound a death knell for the Western film, or at least the Western film as movie audiences remembered it.

One of the first major films to deal with the decline of the legendary Western hero was Henry King's austere drama *The Gunfighter* (1950). Gregory Peck played Jimmy Ringo, a celebrated but weary gunman whose reputation follows him wherever he goes. An anachronism waiting for an assassin's bullet, Jimmy comes into town to visit his estranged wife and son, to plead for one last chance to settle down. During the course of the afternoon, he sends the town into an uproar of fear and apprehension, and he is finally shot dead by the town's swaggering young bully. At his funeral, his wife identifies herself proudly as "Mrs. Ringo," while his son adds, "And his boy."

A spare yet moving film, *The Gunfighter* contains few standard Western trappings—there are no shoot-outs or elaborate action scenes. Instead, the William Bowers-William Sellers screenplay comments ruefully on a man out of his time; Ringo resembles the gangsters in films of the early forties *(High Sierra, The Big Shot)* who are unable to find a place in a changing world. Sadly, stoically, he must deal with

The Gunfighter *(Fox, 1950). Fading gunfighter Jimmy Ringo (Gregory Peck) stands poised with gun at the ready* (PAGE 234). *He withstands a challenge by young Eddie (Richard Jaeckel), who lies dead on the barroom floor* (LEFT), *only to be shot down by the town's brazen young bully. Peck's laconic, understated style suited the role of Ringo, a gunman burdened with an exalted reputation.*

The Man Who Shot Liberty Valance *(Paramount, 1962). Nasty Liberty Valance (Lee Marvin) knocks down Ranse Stoddard (James Stewart) and scatters his law books* (RIGHT). *Later* (BELOW), *Tom Doniphon (John Wayne, right) intervenes with the vicious Valance on behalf of Ranse as Reese (Lee Van Cleef, left) looks on. Wishing to keep the film tightly focused on the drama, director John Ford eschewed the more expansive style he usually favored for a constricted style using an unusually large number of close-ups.*

Ride the High Country *(MGM, 1962). Icons of the Western genre, Randolph Scott and Joel McCrea played aging cowhands who seek one final moment of glory. Sam Peckinpah's affecting film eulogized men of their stripe and expressed sadness for their passing.*

choly film that lacks Ford's customary vigor and his palpable pleasure in the Western landscape, it was not well received by either the mainstream critics or the public. Many other critics found it an evocative extension of Ford's art, and it remains one of the director's most personal statements.

The Man Who Shot Liberty Valance contrasts the Old West with the New West, the untamed wilderness against the flourishing garden. James Stewart plays Ransom ("Ranse") Stoddard, a worthy United States senator who has returned to the town of Shinbone for the funeral of his old friend Tom Doniphon (John Wayne). His sadly reflective wife, Hallie (Vera Miles), has accompanied him. ("Place has sure changed.") Ranse decides that it is time to tell his story to the newspaper editor (Carleton Young), and we flash back to the day he arrives in Shinbone as a hopeful young lawyer from the East. He learns that the town has been in the terrified thrall of the evil Liberty Valance (Lee Marvin), who works in league with the neighboring cattle barons. Tom Doniphon's guns and forceful presence have kept the shaky peace, but Ranse, despite Valance's brutality toward him, favors legal action without gunplay. His chief ally is Dutton Peabody (Edmond O'Brien), the bibulous newspaper editor. When it seems that Ranse has changed his stance and finally gunned down Valance, he becomes a hero, a nationally famous figure.

Soon after, Tom reveals that it was he, not Ranse, who killed Valance. In remaining silent, he surrendered his life, his identity, and his girl, Hallie. After Ranse finishes his story, the editor decides that his paper will continue to publish the legendary version. Surprised, Ranse asks, "You're not going to use this story?" "No, sir," the editor answers. "This is the West, sir. When the legend becomes fact, print the legend."

The film's screenplay was written by Willis Goldbeck and James Warner Bellah, from a story by Dorothy M. Johnson, but the viewpoint is clearly Ford's. He acknowledges the virtues of Ranse's "civilized" point of view, which include his plans for irrigating the land, his zealous belief in education (in one marvelous scene, he teaches the basics of reading to children and illiterate adults), and his refusal to use a gun. Yet Ford is also urging us to remember the cost to men like Tom Doniphon, the kind of man who was needed to rid the West of men like Liberty Valance. He is asking us to consider the price of turning the wilderness into a garden. Going

those who challenge him, and when he lies dying, he tells his assassin, "I want you to go on being a big tough gunman. I want you to see how it is to live like a big tough gunnie!" Although Gregory Peck's stately reserve never allows him to appear fully at ease in a Western, his understated style of acting makes him a worthy choice to play a low-key but not-to-be-trifled-with gunfighter.

While *The Gunfighter* won respectful reviews, it failed to spark any other Western films in the same somber, end-of-an-era vein. By the skeptical sixties, however, audiences appeared ready to accept a more realistic, less mythic view of Western traditions and a franker assessment of the Old West in decline. The most active Western filmmakers could not help being influenced by this changing attitude, and John Ford was no exception. Affected as well, if not more so, by his own deepening sadness at the encroachment of old age, Ford directed *The Man Who Shot Liberty Valance* (1962), one of his darkest views of the Western experience. A melan-

The Professionals *(Columbia, 1966). In Richard Brooks's rousing, fast-paced Western adventure, Burt Lancaster played one of the mercenaries hired by a wealthy businessman to rescue his kidnapped young wife from a Mexican bandit.*

from the law of the gunslinger (Tom says, "Out here a man solves his own problems") to the law inscribed in books for one and all is unquestionably a civilized advance. However, Ford suggests that there is also a loss in individualism and, more important, in honor and heroism.

A curious entry in the Ford filmography, *The Man Who Shot Liberty Valance* has a constricted feel to it—there are few action sequences and hardly any outdoor scenes. The film's perfunctory air contrasts sharply with the meticulous detail of Ford's best Westerns. The actors all perform acceptably within their familiar characterizations; while the Ford regulars, including Andy Devine, John Carradine, John Qualen, and O. Z. Whitehead, remain a constant pleasure to watch, they had been given more challenging roles in the past. Yet in the final analysis, this movie contains deeper insights than many of Ford's more polished efforts, and it lingers in the mind.

The Man Who Shot Liberty Valance not only reflected John Ford's increasingly somber view of society and his disillusion with a changing world but also pointed the way for Western films in which the valiant heroes of the past confronted the realities of aging and death with stoic calm. As they grew older, the familiar Western stars used their lined, weather-beaten faces as visual records of hard-won experience. If the story required it, they could still show their mettle in a gunfight, and astride their horses, they could still suggest strength and moral authority. By now, however, their concern for the heroine was more paternal than romantic, and their eyes reflected a longing for more adventurous days.

A key film in this vein was released the same year as *The Man Who Shot Liberty Valance.* Sam Peckinpah's *Ride the High Country* (1962) was only the director's second film after some years as a television director and writer, but it displayed a skill and an assurance that would culminate seven years later with his masterwork, *The Wild Bunch. Ride the High Country* served as a fitting coda to the careers of Randolph Scott—this was, in fact, his last film—and Joel McCrea, two actors who had performed yeoman duty in the genre for over three decades, Scott in scores of films highlighted by a series of small, tightly constructed Westerns directed by Budd Boetticher in the fifties and McCrea in many large- and small-scale Westerns for various studios.

Scott and McCrea play aging cowhands who have seen better days. When we first meet Gil Westrum (Scott), he is working as a carnival barker, wearing a wig and false beard. His spirit revives when he comes upon his old friend Steve Judd (McCrea), who has been hired to deliver a shipment of gold to the bank, reawakening in Gil the familiar "hankerin' for a little old-time excitement." He joins Steve and a young cowboy named Heck Longtree (Ronald Starr), with the intention of convincing them to steal the gold. However, the trail leads them in an unexpected direction. By rescuing Elsa, an innocent girl (Mariette Hartley), from the brutal miner she has agreed to marry, the three men make dangerous enemies of the miner and his equally vicious brothers. Gil and Steve recover a brief moment of their old glory in a shoot-out with the villains, but Steve is mortally wounded.

Peckinpah's penchant for graphic violence would emerge in later films. In *Ride the High Country*, the tone is rueful and autumnal, reflecting a West very much like its heroes: badly frayed around the edges but still capable of bursts of gunplay and rowdiness. One of the film's best scenes is the marriage of Elsa and the miner, a raucous affair presided over by a tipsy judge, with the local madam and girls as attendants to the bewildered bride. Lucien Ballard's characteristically superb photography captures the film's mood, giving appropriate attention, without undue emphasis, to the worn, proudly lived-in faces of the stars.

The flavorsome original screenplay by N. B. Stone, Jr., fleshes out the characters of Gil and Steve with more subtlety than usual. Steve is the more complex of the two, a rigid, even puritanical man who has finally learned to have some respect for himself, and who longs to expiate his sins of the past. ("All I want is to enter my house justified.") When he learns of Gil's plan to steal the gold, he is appalled at the betrayal of simple trust. "You were my friend," he tells Gil, and the line reverberates with bitter disappointment. Gil is more easygoing, more devious (a change of the usual persona for Scott), but he confesses to Steve, "I don't sleep so good anymore." Their final scene is one of the most memorable in the genre. The dying Steve asks Gil to leave and to make sure that nobody is around. "I don't want them to see this. I'll go it alone," he tells Gil. After exchanging a curt farewell ("So long, partner." "I'll see you later"), Steve takes one last, lingering look at the hills and sinks slowly out of the frame.

Throughout the sixties, the theme of the aging Westerner living off past glories or dying alone and unremembered continued to surface. A band of weary, cynical mercenaries, barely surviving in a world where the good guys and the bad guys can no longer be differentiated, appears in Richard Brooks's pounding Western *The Professionals* (1966). Burt Lancaster, Robert Ryan, Lee Marvin, and Woody Strode played professional fighters who are hired by a wealthy businessman to rescue his young bride (Claudia Cardinale) from the clutches of a notorious Mexican bandit (Jack Palance). When they discover that the bride prefers the bandit, they reverse themselves and turn on their employer. The year is 1916, and only remnants of the old Western code still apply. Prospects are as bleak as the landscape, and yet the mercenaries manage to survive the turbulent events that follow in their path. Despite the aura of a fading West, *The Professionals* is anything but elegiac—Brooks keeps the action moving at a thunderous pace, and the actors perform with brashness and agility.

A different sort of aging Westerner turned up in Tom Gries's *Will Penny* (1968). No rough-and-ready gunman with many notches on his belt, Will (Charlton Heston) is merely a lonely, illiterate cowhand nearing fifty, which makes him almost elderly in a land where lives are often brief. Early in the film, he has the misfortune to tangle with a family of nasty

The Professionals (Columbia, 1966). Lee Marvin, Claudia Cardinale, and Burt Lancaster starred in Richard Brooks's boisterous, nonstop adventure. Behind all the action, the film evoked a deep sense of the West in decline.

rawhiders led by a self-styled preacher named Quint (Donald Pleasence). (The Western genre is overrun with evil, Bible-spouting patriarchs and their homicidal offspring.) Badly wounded and left for dead, Will is taken in and nursed by Catherine Allen (Joan Hackett), a tenacious woman with a small son who is traveling to meet her husband in California. In a situation that strongly resembles *Shane*, Will acts as mentor to the boy while falling discreetly in love with Catherine. When they are attacked by the returning rawhiders, Will, now imbued with some of his old strength, succeeds in breaking away, then returns to rescue Catherine and the boy. In the tradition of *Shane*, they part sadly, and Will is once again the homeless wanderer. He has, however, achieved a measure of peace and contentment and is willing to accept his fate as a man drifting through life.

Another drifting cowpoke, one with a past more checkered than Will Penny's but as dubious a future, was embodied by Lee Marvin in *Monte Walsh* (1970). (Until his Academy Award–winning double role in *Cat Ballou* in 1965, Marvin had been largely typecast as a surly villain.) Monte Walsh is a man at the end of his rope: dispossessed by the invisible Eastern capitalists who have taken over the ranches, he has lost his identity but not his Westerner's code of honor. His friends have also fallen on hard times—one commits suicide by riding his horse down the side of a canyon; another, Shorty (Mitch Ryan), becomes a killer almost inadvertently. When Shorty murders Monte's best friend, Chet (Jack Palance, in an uncharacteristically gentle role), Monte must exact justice. In a showdown scene that would probably mortify the earlier Western heroes, Shorty refuses to draw on Monte out of shame for what he has become, and Monte shoots him dead. Alone after the death of his longtime mistress (French actress Jeanne Moreau), Monte rides through the barren Western landscape with only his horse for company.

Loosely written and episodic, the screenplay for *Monte Walsh* (by Lukas Heller and David Z. Goodman, from Jack Schaeffer's novel) never coheres into a unified film; still, it contains moments that aptly illustrate the life of the cowboy and its perilously changing state. An early scene captures the excitement of rounding up mustangs; on the other hand, in

Will Penny (*Paramount, 1968*). *In Tom Gries's quietly effective Western, Charlton Heston played a lonely, aging cowboy who becomes attached to a woman and her small son (Jon Francis). This exceptional film received little backing from the studio and scant attention from the press.*

craggy face contained the residue of a violent, dangerous life, while his slow, drawling speech and dignified manner suggested a man who had come to terms with his past. The role provided Wayne with a fitting close to his work in Westerns.

The screenplay, by Miles Hood Swarthout and Scott Hale, based on Swarthout's novel, begins with Books arriving in Carson City in 1901, where he finds a bustling town with all the signs of encroaching "civilization"—clanging trolley cars, thriving businesses, and so on. When a doctor (James Stewart) diagnoses that he is suffering from terminal cancer, Books settles in the town, arranging to board with the widowed Mrs. Rogers (Lauren Bacall, somewhat too sophisticated for the role) and her teenage son Gillam (Ron Howard). Although his presence in the town generates fear and excitement, along with much cruelty and insensitivity, he sets about putting his life in order. After initial resentment, Mrs. Rogers comes to admire him, and he teaches the awed Gillam to fire a gun, cautioning him to use it only when he has no other choice. Finally, he deliberately arranges a shootout with three men who have reason to hate him. He shoots them all, only to be felled by a bartender. Young Gillam shoots the bartender, then flings the gun away in tears. In one harrowing encounter, he has moved from innocence to the

an extended sequence, we see the emptiness of Monte's existence as he moves from one menial task to another. Monte is bitterly aware of his plight. When a fussy money man from the East takes credit for Western progress, Monte exclaims, "You damned accountants! *We* did it!" And he rejects the notion of joining a Wild West show as a "legendary" gunman: "I ain't spittin' on my whole life!" he tells the show's owner. Most moving is his farewell to his mistress, the "Countess," who has died of tuberculosis. Their relationship, although without commitment, has been loving, and as he gazes at her body in the coffin, he cuts off a lock of her hair. Skillfully handled by cinematographer William A. Fraker in his first assignment as a director, *Monte Walsh* offers more genuine feeling about the decline of the West than many more perfect films.

Perhaps the definitive portrait of the aging cowboy out of step in a changing world was etched by the screen's principal Western star, John Wayne, in his last film, *The Shootist* (1976). After a long career of playing strong, hardened Westerners, Wayne was the ideal choice for the role of J. B. Books, a legendary gunman whose credo is "I won't be wronged. I won't be insulted. And I won't be laid a hand on." His lined,

Monte Walsh (*Cinema Center Films, 1970*). *Jack Palance and Lee Marvin (in the title role) play down-on-their-luck cowboys who have lost their way in the world. Monte Walsh earns one moment of regained pride when he tames a wild stallion.*

The Shootist *(Paramount, 1976). Legendary gunman J. B. Books (John Wayne) instructs young Gillam Rogers (Ron Howard) in marksmanship. In contrast with the shining blond Western knight of* Shane *(1953), who also taught marksmanship to the film's young boy, Joey Starrett, Books is a dying man, bewildered and saddened by the changing Western world.*

gunfighter's code of expedient action. The screenplay never questions the dubious validity of this code, nor asks why Books needs to kill three men who have committed no serious crime in order to achieve a glorious death.

Efficiently directed by Don Siegel, *The Shootist* contains the familiar ingredients of the passing-of-the-West subgenre: burnished, autumnal photography (this time by Bruce Surtees), overreliance on the end-of-an-era details (a headline proclaiming the death of Queen Victoria, an Oldsmobile driven by one of the villains). The film also has a source of strength that sets it above the others: the richly observed if idealized character of J. B. Books and John Wayne's assured, mellow embodiment of this character. Books represents a pure vision of all the gunfighters who have ever shot their way into Western legend. He is convinced that every notch in his gun belt was justified ("I don't believe I ever killed a man that didn't deserve it"). And when he is asked to fabricate

stories about his "glorious" past, he angrily retorts, "I'll not be remembered for a pack of lies!" (Amusingly, he is not above a bit of historical debunking—"Bat Masterson was always full of sheep dip.") Books may be too good to be true, but as played by Wayne, here heavy and weary in the saddle, he has undeniable stature. At several points, character and actor become intertwined beyond the obvious fact that both were dying of cancer. The movie begins with tinted clips from old Wayne Westerns, and when Books tells the doctor, "I've had a hell of a good time," we can clearly hear Wayne himself expressing the same sentiment.

By the time J. B. Books died, the vast open ranges were being replaced by sprawling cities emblazoned with lights that obscured the stars, once a canopy for the cowboys. Eventually, Western towns that did not develop into cities became the arid, ghost-haunted places seen in such films as *The Last Picture Show* (1971). The cowmen, the ranchers, and the sheepherders who had once struggled to hold on to their precious part of the land grew old and watched, baffled, as the entrepreneurs and developers took over. For the Westerners old enough to recall the formative West yet too young to settle for wood-whittling on the porch, life could be especially difficult. In the sixties, a number of movies picked up on the theme of the displaced cowboy in the modern world.

One film that brought familiar Western themes and the concept of a dying West into contemporary times was John Huston's controversial *The Misfits* (1961). The story of this trouble-ridden production has been amply related; the resulting film received generally harsh treatment by the critics and indifference from the public, despite the presence of an imposing cast headed by Clark Gable and Marilyn Monroe in their last roles. Nonetheless, *The Misfits* warrants serious

The Misfits (United Artists, 1961). In their last film, Clark Gable played aging cowboy Gay Langland and Marilyn Monroe was Roslyn (LEFT), *the guileless divorcée whom Gay calls "the saddest girl I ever met." Rosyln looks on* (BELOW) *as vagrant rodeo rider Perce Howland (Montgomery Clift), Gay, and mechanic Guido (Eli Wallach) tie up the wild horse they have captured.* OPPOSITE *In this unusual color still, Gay struggles with the wild horse. Both cowboy and horse are misfits in the world, doomed to eventual extinction.*

Lonely Are the Brave *(Universal-International, 1962). To get into prison so that he can help his jailed friend, cowboy Jack Burns (Kirk Douglas) deliberately provokes a bar fight* (LEFT). RIGHT *Jack visits his friend's wife, Gerri (Gena Rowlands). David Miller's movie leaned too heavily on its symbols of a changing latter-day West, but its story of a man out of step with his time was often effective.*

consideration as a deeply flawed but compassionate, oddly affecting portrait of the New West as a repository of regrets and lost hopes, a place where nonconformity cannot be tolerated. On the one hand, Arthur Miller's screenplay skirts and sometimes tumbles over into pretentiousness; on the other, the movie often strikes a true and honest note.

The people who come together to form their own isolated society epitomize the sad, bitter end of the Western dream. The rugged, independent cowboy has become Gay Langland (Gable), an aging drifter who organizes a motley group of men to round up "misfit" horses to be sold for dog food. The daring broncobuster is now Perce Howland (Montgomery Clift), a battered, mother-ridden rodeo performer on the skids. The demure heroine who deplored "all the shootin' and killin'" in countless Westerns takes the ample form of Marilyn Monroe as Roslyn, a guileless, neurotic divorcée who hysterically averts the slaughter of the wild horses in the film's climactic sequence. In the modern West, these characters are no less misfits than the horses, and the screenplay combines with Huston's erratic direction to emphasize their lost and lonely status. Although too much of their dialogue is strained and cryptic, they acquire a kind of rough-hewn nobility by the film's end.

A year after *The Misfits*, the displaced modern cowboy became the central concern of another contemporary Western, David Miller's *Lonely Are the Brave* (1962). Playing in a somewhat less hypertense style than usual, Kirk Douglas starred as Jack Burns, an amiable, drifting cowpoke who still rides his horse in a world of fast-traveling automobiles. To

help a jailed friend, he gets himself thrown into prison on a charge of disorderly conduct. When conditions become unbearable, he escapes, and he is pursued by a posse headed by a compassionate sheriff (Walter Matthau). On the verge of a successful getaway, Jack and his horse are struck down by a truck on the highway. The crippled horse is shot, and Jack is taken away in an ambulance.

Under Miller's sympathetic if somewhat overinsistent direction, *Lonely Are the Brave* offers a convincing portrait of a man unable to accept the society in which circumstances have placed him. Jack Burns is bemused by the cluttered cities and highways—"A Westerner likes open places," he tells the wife of his friend (Gena Rowlands). Later, he returns to her after his escape but refuses her help. "I'm a loner," he says. "A loner is a born cripple." Frequently, cinematographer Philip Lathrop gives us shots of Jack riding alone in the desert, almost as if he were the last cowboy on earth.

Although *Lonely Are the Brave* attempts serious commentary, Dalton Trumbo's screenplay works too hard at its effects and symbols to truly succeed. In the film's first scene, Jack, on horseback, arrives at the highway, and we can plainly see an auto graveyard behind him. (Everything dies eventually, even the cars.) It is scarcely a surprise that when he comes to prison, the guard in charge is a sadistic bully, played at full viciousness by George Kennedy. And lest we miss the import of the story, the script has sheriff Matthau remark to his deputies, "I think we're chasing a ghost." By the time of the movie's closing scene, the heavy hand of the filmmaker has become even more destructive than the truck.

Other films displayed a lighter touch toward the cowboy out of his time. Burt Kennedy's amiable if rather uneventful comedy *The Rounders* (1965) cast Glenn Ford and Henry Fonda as seedy, drifting broncobusters who make various

The Rounders (MGM, 1965). Burt Kennedy wrote and directed this genial, rambling Western comedy about Howdy (Henry Fonda) and Ben (Glenn Ford), two down-on-their-luck cowboys trying to make some money any way they can.

A group of cowboys working on the range around 1920. Contrary to movie Western lore, few cowboys actually wore six-shooters strapped around their waists, and when they did wear guns, they were not expected to shoot at other human beings. Sometimes, a cowboy would strap on a six-shooter as a flaunted badge of distinction, to impress his girlfriend.

The Rounders *(MGM, 1965). Fists fly and furniture collapses in this Western melee, one of the standard features of the genre. Burt Kennedy's contemporary Western starred Henry Fonda and Glenn Ford as cowboys forever on the verge of settling down.*

futile attempts to earn a dollar. (They enter a wild horse in a rodeo only to have the horse demolish a barn.) Fonda's relaxed if muddled cowboy meshed nicely with Ford's more volatile character. In Stuart Rosenberg's *Pocket Money* (1972), Paul Newman and Lee Marvin also played amiable losers in the contemporary West, Newman as a Texas cowboy whose schemes go all wrong and Marvin as his boozy pal. Terry Malick's screenplay was richly flavored with cowboy jargon. Sydney Pollack's *The Electric Horseman* (1979) starred Robert Redford as a modern-day cowboy who steals a million-dollar horse to save it from commercial exploitation and Jane Fonda as a television reporter who helps (and falls in love with) him.

The Electric Horseman *(Columbia, 1979). Television reporter Hallie (Jane Fonda) pursues over-the-hill rodeo rider Sonny (Robert Redford) in search of a story and finds romance in Sydney Pollack's contemporary Western.*

The main street of a town in Arizona. During Arizona's forma-tive years as a territory, towns like this were the sites of rampant lawlessness, and in the wilderness outside of the towns, United States soldiers engaged in cruel, intermittent warfare with the Apache Indians.

OPPOSITE   McCabe and Mrs. Miller *(Warner Bros., 1971). Two misguided entrepreneurs in turn-of-the-century Washing-ton State: the ever-hopeful McCabe (Warren Beatty) and his business partner and local madam, Mrs. Miller (Julie Christie). Robert Altman's film provoked either angry dismissal or all-out enthusiasm.*

While the cowboys and gunslingers were playing out their lives in a different—and bewildering—landscape, oth-ers, like the tinhorn gambler McCabe in Robert Altman's *McCabe and Mrs. Miller* (1971), expired almost incidentally, with at least a passing awareness of the profound changes in Western life but without the ability or even common sense to deal with them. Here was no weary cowboy or gunslinger but a grubby, self-deluding, would-be entrepreneur who, in turn-of-the-century Washington State, fatally underestimates his enemies and dies in the snow. As played by Warren Beatty, McCabe exemplifies the cocksure Westerner with an exag-gerated sense of his own importance and ability. Determined to make it big in the burgeoning world of business, he enters into partnership with a drugged and wraithlike Mrs. Miller (Julie Christie), who operates a combination gambling casino and bordello. When a syndicate tries to take over their profit-able venture, McCabe resists, heedless of the danger, until hired killers shoot him dead in a confrontation. Mrs. Miller, who had become his mistress as well as partner, sinks even deeper into an opium-induced daze.

McCabe and Mrs. Miller *(Warner Bros., 1971). Robert Altman's unusual Western used Vilmos Zsigmond's low-key photography to advantage, giving a depressingly realistic look to the town of Presbyterian Church* (ABOVE), *where McCabe* (Warren Beatty; OPPOSITE) *lives and dies. Robert Altman's eccentric Western had many champions.*

Both vilified and praised by the critics, *McCabe and Mrs. Miller* can lay genuine claim to originality and boldness, if not to success at the box office. Altman's Western town, ironically called Presbyterian Church, resembles no other town in Western annals—we see no ordered assemblage of humble houses and shops but a cluttered, dangerous pigsty of a town where wretched people (and not one character is even vaguely likable) live out their wretched existences. This is no celebration of the Fordian or Hawksian West, no golden vision of the frontier, although it should be noted that Altman intrudes an ambiguous note of hope at the end: as McCabe lies dying, the oblivious townsfolk celebrate the saving of their church from a fire. In striving to give audiences a sense of life as it was lived at the time, Altman pulls out all of his familiar stylistic tricks—overlapping dialogue, a busy zoom lens, and sudden jumps in editing, combining them with

Vilmos Zsigmond's muted camerawork and Leonard Cohen's songs to create an environment so real that one can almost smell the stench of a West in decay.

Another enterprising Westerner in a changing world appears in Sam Peckinpah's diverting movie *The Ballad of Cable Hogue* (1970), a much lighter tale. Jason Robards plays Cable, an irascible drifter who is deserted by two shifty partners in the desert. Four days later, he discovers water and decides to build the only water station and stagecoach stop in the area. It prospers, and Cable becomes an entrepreneur who runs his business in his own way. He also becomes involved with Hildy (Stella Stevens), a whore with the proverbial heart of gold, whom he truly loves, and with a lecherous preacher named Joshua (David Warner). Cable, however, is a creature of the past, not the changing present, and he is run down and killed by an automobile that he tries to stop as

if it were a horse. Clearly, the individualistic spirit of the West dies with him.

Uncharacteristically amiable and gentle for Sam Peckinpah, *The Ballad of Cable Hogue* can never quite make up its mind whether it wants to be a shaggy-dog story, a romantic comedy, or a rueful drama about the demise of men like Cable. Yet the film's untidy, unpredictable style is actually the source of much of its charm. Whether brusquely shooting his first customer because the hapless man failed to pay his dime or nailing his dinner plates to a table because it makes them easier to wash, Robards creates an endearing anachronism in Cable Hogue. Like McCabe, Cable falls in love with a whore. Their relationship, however, is not mutually destructive, as was McCabe's with Mrs. Miller; their flippant romance has a touching underside of genuine caring and concern.

The Ballad of Cable Hogue *(Warner Bros., 1970). Self-styled codger Cable Hogue (Jason Robards) shares a meal with Hildy (Stella Stevens), the prostitute he has come to love. Watching them at the window is the lecherous preacher Joshua (David Warner). Sam Peckinpah's movie was an entertaining if uncertain mixture of eccentric comedy, ironic drama, and unlikely romance.*

While films such as *McCabe and Mrs. Miller* and *The Ballad of Cable Hogue* marked a West in decay and disarray, Arthur Penn's film *The Missouri Breaks* (1976) went one step further, portraying a West not only dying but also turned upside down. As he had in *Bonnie and Clyde* and other films, Penn deliberately reversed our expectations. In this determinedly unconventional Western, the forces of law and order are represented by an increasingly mad cattle baron who hangs rustlers without a trial and by a grotesque, cold-blooded "regulator" who assumes many guises to stalk and trap his prey. The lawless faction, on the other hand, is represented by a rustler who enjoys becoming a committed landowner. Rather than tall-in-the-saddle cowboys, the men who work for him are a scruffy lot and the last of their breed. Even the heroine is not the demure maiden decrying the violence but a bored, sex-starved girl who flings herself boldly at the rustler-turned-rancher. All these role reversals make *The Missouri Breaks* an unusual, if far from impressive Western.

Thomas McGuane's screenplay focuses largely on two characters: Tom Logan (Jack Nicholson), the rustler chief who finds unexpected pleasure in the land, and Lee Clayton (Marlon Brando in one of his oddest roles), the gunman hired by the cattle baron to wipe out the men who are stealing his horses and cattle. Clayton, a fat, cold-eyed killer with long, blond hair and a soft Irish brogue, tracks down and shoots Logan's cronies, one by one, until he meets sudden death at Logan's hand. Played out against Western backgrounds beautifully photographed by Michael Butler, the story fascinates with its unblinkered look at a crumbling West. ("You're almost the last of your kind, old man," Clayton tells Logan's friend Cal, just before he kills him.) Yet as it progresses, *The Missouri Breaks* goes fatally awry. Logan's amorous relationship with Jane Paxton (Kathleen Lloyd), the cattle baron's daughter, becomes tedious despite her sexual

bluntness; more seriously, the series of scenes in which Clayton shoots his prey, catching each victim in a compromising or embarrassing position, must surely generate a queasy, apprehensive feeling in viewers. (This may account for the film's exceptionally hostile reception.) Unlike in *The Wild Bunch*, the shootings are not mirrors of a disordered universe but random bloodlettings uncomfortably allied with the pornography of violence.

In the real West, the sort of men represented by McCabe, Cable Hogue, and Lee Clayton continued to die off as the decades passed, and as the West faded into legend, the cowboys and gunfighters epitomized by Will Penny and J. B. Books died off with them. The traditional conflict persisted: ranchers still fought homesteaders to hold onto their land—and to hold off the encroachment of civilization, which they feared would sap their power. At the end of the nineteenth century, strongly entrenched ranchers faced a new breed of pioneer: a flood of immigrants from Europe that engulfed the territory, seeking to plant roots in their newly adopted nation. In the early 1890s, violent and bloody conflict broke out between the ranchers and immigrants in Johnson County, Wyoming. A massacre of immigrants was barely averted as the Stock Growers Association hired mercenaries to kill and terrorize the people they considered thieves and anarchists.

The Johnson County Wars, as the series of incidents came to be known, became the subject of Michael Cimino's massive and controversial Western film *Heaven's Gate* (1980). The extraordinary story of the making of this film has been recounted in exhaustive detail in Steven Bach's book *Final Cut* (Morrow, 1985), while the finished film, either in its original or considerably shortened version, stands as an epic that fairly boggles the mind in its excess and incoherence. Paradoxically, no other Western drama has been more successful in conveying the turbulence and rousing spirit of the Western pioneer world or the physical look of its towns and people. *Heaven's Gate* may be a lumbering giant of a movie, but no giant ever looked so stunningly and impressively real. The sets and costumes warrant the highest praise, and Vilmos Zsigmond's photography bathes the screen with a burnished splendor.

Fatally, however, Michael Cimino's screenplay, compounded by his self-indulgent direction, sinks the film with its muddled plot and characterizations. Basically, the story appears to concern Jim Averill (Kris Kristofferson), a wealthy Bostonian who, inexplicably, becomes marshal of Johnson County twenty years after graduating from Harvard. (The elaborate opening sequence, filmed at Oxford, depicts the Harvard graduation ceremony.) Out West, Averill becomes embroiled in the fierce conflict between the Stock Growers

OPPOSITE   The Ballad of Cable Hogue *(Warner Bros., 1970).*
Ornery, down-and-out drifter Cable Hogue (Jason Robards,
left), who later reveals a surprising gift for entrepreneurship,
flees from the mocking children. Sam Peckinpah's oddball
movie mixed several styles and moods in its fable about the
decline of the old-time Westerner.

The Missouri Breaks *(United Artists, 1976). Marlon Brando*
played Lee Clayton, the decidedly weird "regulator" hired by a
rancher to rid himself of a rustling gang led by Tom Logan
(Jack Nicholson). Arthur Penn's extremely violent, unpleasant
Western was admired by some; many others considered it a film
of wretched excess.

Heaven's Gate *(United Artists, 1980). Mr. Eggleston (Brad*
*Dourif) passionately addresses the Polish immigrants (*OPPOSITE,
BELOW*), who are under savage attack by the powerful Stock*
Growers Association. Bartender John H. Bridges (Jeff
Bridges, right) looks on. Michael Cimino's epic drew fire
from critics and the public, despite such virtues as Vilmos
Zsigmond's burnished photography, evident in the scene in
which the immigrant homesteaders gather at their church
*(*BELOW*). Although a shorter, trimmer version of Michael*
Cimino's gargantuan film was released in April 1981, the result
*was not appreciably better. (*The New York Times *reviewer*
said, in the issue of April 24, 1981, that it went from "an
unqualified disaster" to "a muddled compromise.")

Association, led by a rancher named Canton (Sam Waterston), and European immigrant homesteaders. He also becomes involved in a triangular relationship with a madam named Ella Watson (Isabelle Huppert) and Nate Champion (Christopher Walken), a former friend who works for the cattle barons. In the ensuing open warfare, only Averill survives.

Embedded in the lavish sequences of pioneer celebrations and tumultuous clashes between immigrants and mercenaries lies a basically trite, hollow story. Many of the actions and motivations of principal characters are indecipherable, disorienting the viewer. The actors work hard but in vain to establish genuine characters, and not even such commendable performers as John Hurt (as a troubled, alcoholic cattle baron) and Jeff Bridges (as a sympathetic bartender) can rise above the confusion. Most seriously, *Heaven's Gate* fails to achieve its overall purpose of depicting the decline of the American West through unrestrained greed and lust for power. The viewer is left with a memory of several impressively staged scenes, especially the ferocious decisive battle between the opposing forces, and a melancholy sense of the movie that might have been.

One movie that successfully showed the passing of the baton from the Old West, with its code of honor, to the new West of greed and indifference was *Hud* (1963). To make its point economically, the film depicted three generations of a modern-day Western family. In an exemplary, Oscar-winning performance, Melvyn Douglas played Homer Bannon, a worn but still feisty old man whose many years as a Texas rancher have instilled in him a sense of pride in conquering the wilderness and an abiding love for the land. His son, Hud (Paul Newman), however, is a new breed of Western man: unprincipled, insensitive, and mean-spirited. Their conflict in the film hinges on the ranch's cattle, inflicted with hoof-and-mouth disease. Hud would like to sell them quickly in another state, while Homer insists on the painful task of destroying them. The bitter dispute—and Hud's loutish behavior toward the housekeeper, Alma (Patricia Neal)—are observed by Hud's teenage nephew Lon (Brandon de Wilde), who, from idolizing his uncle, ends up loathing him. When Homer dies, Lon leaves the ranch forever, vowing never to return to an unrepentant, still cynical Hud.

Although the screenplay by Irving Ravetch and Harriet Frank, Jr., from Larry McMurtry's novel, is too obviously schematic in its view of three generations of Western men, *Hud*, as directed by Martin Ritt, has a harsh and stinging power. Newman, who was always adept at suggesting the corruption lurking beneath the movie-star handsomeness— the worm in the shiny apple—created an incisive portrait that contrasts vividly with Douglas's grizzled, honorable Homer. When his father insists that they must prevent a devastating epidemic, he brings conviction to his reply, "How many honest men you know? This country's run on epidemics." His comment on his father, "He's made of high principles," is etched in venom, and we believe it when Homer accuses him of icy indifference: "You don't give a damn! You don't care about people! You don't value nothing!"

The central scene—the shooting of the cattle—crystallizes the film's theme. The cattle are herded into a huge ditch as Homer's men, standing around the ditch's edge, are ordered to fire. The gunshots and the terrified bellowing of the cattle punctuate the air, and then there is silence. The

OPPOSITE   *The town of Westcott, in Custer County, Nebraska, around 1886. Two decades earlier, when the Union Pacific Railroad was built across the state, the already vigorous land boom became a rush. Cow towns such as Westcott sprang up around the state as shipping points on overland cattle trails.*

Heaven's Gate *(United Artists, 1980). Jim Averill (Kris Kristofferson) enjoys skating with Ella Watson (Isabelle Huppert) at the Heaven's Gate roller rink, an amusement arena attended by newly arrived settlers in Sweetwater, Wyoming.*

Hud *(Paramount, 1963). Cynical and arrogant Hud Bannon (Paul Newman) wrestles a pig in Martin Ritt's contemporary Western drama. Hud's credo: "You don't look out for yourself, the only hand you'll ever get is when they lower the box."*

OPPOSITE   The Shootist *(Paramount, 1976). John Wayne's valedictory. In Don Siegel's Western, he played J. B. Books, a legendary gunfighter who is dying of cancer. He leaves a legacy to the young son of his landlady, who learns that "there's more to bein' a man than handlin' a gun!"*

camera moves to Homer's face, which reflects a deep sorrow and despair. Lon moves to his grandfather's side and remarks, "It didn't take long." The old man says, "It don't take long to kill things. Not like it does to grow." Homer elects to shoot his two prize longhorns himself—we hear the shots ring out as Lon and Hud stand by. Although it carries too heavy a symbolic weight, the scene is both harrowing and moving, as

well as impressively photographed by James Wong Howe (as is the entire film).

Hud makes an interesting contrast with George Stevens's 1953 Western *Shane.* An idyllic tribute to the old—and, to some extent, mythical—values of individualism, perseverence, and courage in the face of adversity, *Shane* ended with young Joey's echoing cry, "Come back, Shane!" It was clearly meant as a plea for a vanished time when brave Western knights on white horses defeated the black-garbed forces of evil. Young Brandon de Wilde played the hero-worshiping Joey, and a decade later, in *Hud,* he played Lon, once again in the throes of hero worship. This time, however, his god proves false, and Lon returns to the values of his grandfather, the values of *Shane.* (He might be saying, "Come back, Homer!") Both *Hud* and *Shane,* and, of course, many other films in the genre, advance the notion that the rugged existence of pioneer life in the Old West strengthened character and fostered independent-mindedness. While this concept may have only a fleeting resemblance to reality, until the revisionist Westerns of the sixties and seventies, it was one that was popular with the Hollywood studios, which continued to cling to it.

Many of the Western purists who revere the mythic West of John Ford and Howard Hawks have condemned or dismissed the melancholy, often somber Westerns of the last few decades as pretentious folderol. Their gritty, realistic detail, their casual violence, and especially their mordant view of the Old West as a world in decline have not been much appreciated by those whose hearts reside in Monument Valley. Indeed, it has been suggested that such films have sounded the death knell for the Western genre.

Despite such dire rumblings, it could be said that the greedy, vicious men of *McCabe and Mrs. Miller* and *Heaven's Gate* or an amoral scoundrel like Hud Bannon represent a much-needed modification of the idealized West of Ford and Hawks, a view of the West without blinkers. It could also be said that the films in which they wend their doleful way connote the times in which they were created: the cynical, disillusioned sixties and seventies. Whatever the reasons for their appearance, they altered our view of Western history, and as such, they cannot be dismissed with a shrug of indifference.

Somewhere between the unquestioning loyalty and valor of John Ford's military Westerns and the warts-and-all materialism of Robert Altman's Western movies lies a Western film that recognizes the need to strike a balance between truth and legend. Lawrence Kasdan's *Silverado* made one move in that direction. Perhaps another Western, yet unseen, will go the rest of the way.

Coda

In recent years, the cinematic Western trails have become dustier than ever from lack of use. With the exception of the occasional Western made for television, especially the splendid *Lonesome Dove* (1989), the genre has been fading for some time.

Nobody, however, would claim that it has vanished forever, and if Western films are few and far between these days, the Western myth endures. In many foreign countries, the Western movie, with its portrayal of valor, indomitability, and often summary justice, is the very image of America, the mirror in which they see the reflection of our greatest virtues and worst excesses. In this country, as well, we have come to embrace the legend of the Old West and its strong, fearless, sometimes violence-prone people.

As the myth continues, so do the memories of moviegoers. They still listen to the sound of hoofbeats echoing through Monument Valley. The gunfighter and the sheriff never cease to confront each other in the final shoot-out, and the Indians still mount their fierce attacks on the wagon trains heading for golden Western lands. Western films may be in limbo, but the virtues of duty, resilience, and unswerving determination they celebrate remain indestructible. American icons such as John Wayne occupy a lasting place in film history.

This book has looked backward across seven decades of Westerns. It is conceivable that at some point in the future, the Western genre will flourish again. Until then, it has been gratifying to recall its past glories and accomplishments.

Acknowledgments

I am extremely grateful to the people who helped me carry out this project. Their help was at all times invaluable.

As always, I want to thank the good people at Abrams, especially for their patience. A deep bow to Margaret Kaplan, John Crowley, Dirk Luykx, Leta Bostelman, Barbara Lyons, and my creative editor, Lory Frankel, who have been more than generous to me over the years.

I should like to thank the people who helped me obtain the visual material: the indispensable Jerry Vermilye; Robert Cushman and the staff of the Margaret Herrick Library of the Academy of Motion Picture Arts and Sciences, Los Angeles; the staff of the Billy Rose Collection of the New York Public Library at Lincoln Center; and Leith Adams, archivist at the University of Southern California. I am also grateful to the people at MGM-UA, Warner Bros., 20th Century-Fox, Columbia Pictures, and Universal Pictures, who provided me with many photographs.

No book of mine is ever complete before I have acknowledged the loving support of my wife, Roxane. If my ride down those Western trails proved to be more than a little bumpy, she helped to make the journey smoother.

Selected Bibliography

Anderson, Lindsay. *About John Ford*. New York: McGraw-Hill, 1981.

Basinger, Jeanine. *Anthony Mann*. Boston: Twayne, 1979.

Baxter, John. *The Cinema of John Ford*. London: A. Zwemmer, 1971.

Bogdanovich, Peter. *John Ford*. Berkeley: University of California Press, 1968.

Brown, Dee. *Bury My Heart at Wounded Knee*. New York: Holt, Rinehart & Winston, 1970.

Brownlow, Kevin. *The War, the West, and the Wilderness*. New York: Alfred A. Knopf, 1979.

Calder, Jenni. *There Must Be a Lone Ranger: The American West in Film and in Reality*. New York: Taplinger, 1974.

Connell, Evan. *Son of the Morning Star*. San Francisco: North Point Press, 1984.

Everson, William K. *A Pictorial History of the Western Film*. New York: Citadel Press, 1969.

Fenin, George N., and William K. Everson. *The Western: From Silents to the Seventies*. New York: Grossman, 1973.

Frayling, Christopher. *Spaghetti Westerns*. London and Boston: Routledge & Kegan Paul, 1981.

French, Phillip. *Westerns: Aspects of a Movie Genre*. New York: Oxford University Press, 1977.

Friar, Ralph and Natasha. *The Only Good Indian: The Hollywood Gospel*. New York: Drama Book Specialists/Publishers, 1972.

Gallagher, Tay. *John Ford: The Man and His Films*. Berkeley: University of California Press, 1986.

Garfield, Brian: *Western Films: A Complete Guide*. New York: Rawson Associates, 1982.

Hardy, Phil. *The Western*. New York: William Morrow, 1983.

Hawgood, John A. *America's Western Frontiers*. New York: Alfred A. Knopf, 1967.

Horan, James D. *The Authentic Wild West: The Gunfighters*. New York: Crown Publishers, 1976.

———. *The Authentic Wild West: The Outlaws*. New York: Crown Publishers, 1977.

———. *The Great American West*. Rev. ed. New York: Crown Publishers, 1978.

Hyams, Jay. *The Life and Times of the Western Movie*. New York: Gallery Books, 1983.

Kitses, Jim. *Horizons West*. Bloomington: Indiana University Press, 1969.

Lavender, David. *The Great West*. New York: American Heritage Press, 1985.

McBride, Joseph. *Hawks on Hawks*. Berkeley: University of California Press, 1982.

———, ed. *Focus on Howard Hawks*. Englewood Cliffs, N.J.: Prentice-Hall, 1972.

McBride, Joseph, and Michael Wilmington. *John Ford*. New York: Da Capo Press, 1975.

Manchel, Frank. *Cameras West*. Englewood Cliffs, N.J.: Prentice-Hall, 1971.

Matthews, Leonard. *History of Western Movies*. New York: Crescent Books, 1984.

Parish, James Robert, and Michael R. Pitts. *The Great Western Pictures*. Metuchen, N.J.: Scarecrow Press, 1976.

Ross, Nancy Wilson. *Westward the Women*. Freeport, N.Y.: Books for Libraries Press, 1970.

Sarf, Wayne Michael. *God Bless You, Buffalo Bill: A Layman's Guide to History and the Western Film*. East Brunswick, N.J.: Associated University Presses and Cornwall Books, 1983.

Schlissel, Lillian. *Women's Diaries of the Westward Journey*. New York: Schocken Books, 1982.

Seydor, Paul. *Peckinpah: The Western Films*. Urbana: University of Illinois Press, 1980.

Silver, Charles. *The Western Film*. New York: Pyramid Publications, 1976.

Sinclair, Andrew. *John Ford: A Biography*. New York: Lorrimer, 1984.

Tuska, Jon. *The Filming of the West*. Garden City, N.Y.: Doubleday, 1976.

Walsh, Raoul. *Each Man in His Time*. New York: Farrar, Straus and Giroux, 1974.

Willis, Donald C. *The Films of Howard Hawks*. Metuchen, N.J.: Scarecrow Press, 1975.

Wood, Robin. *Howard Hawks*. London: British Film Institute, 1981.

Index

Italic page numbers refer to captions and illustrations. In film title entries, the director's name follows the release date. Entries for historical persons include references to fictionalized film portrayals.

A

Aaker, Lee, 128
Abernaki Indians, *40*
Abilene, Kansas, 68
Academy Awards (Oscars): for best actor, 100, 109, 113, 240; *98, 113;* for best musical score, 100; for best picture, 48; *49;* for best song, 100, 154; for best supporting actor, 105, 258; *105;* for cinematography, 82, 154; *126;* for film editing, 100; nominees, 134, 182; for special contributions, 27
Across the Wide Missouri (1951; Wellman), 41–43, 205–6; *42*
Actor's Life, An (Heston), 89
Adams, Julia, *54*
Agar, John, 81, 82; *83*
aging, 113, 158, 221, 239–42
Aldrich, Robert, 186, 198, 223; *199*
Al Jennings of Oklahoma (1951; Nazarro), 150
Allegheny Uprising (1939; Seiter), 43
Altman, Robert, 139–40, 251, 253–54, 260; *140, 251, 253*
Alvarez Kelly (1966; Dmytryk), 89
Ameche, Don, 178
Anderson, Gilbert "Broncho Billy" (Max Aronson), 26–27
Anderson, Judith, 73, 221; *73*
Andersson, Bibi, 226
Andrews, Dana, 121, 214; *215*
Andriot, Lucien, 47
Annie Get Your Gun (1950; Sidney), 56, 140, 223
Annie Oakley (1935; Stevens), 140
Apache (1954; Aldrich), 186, 206; *187*
Apache Indians, 61, 63, 79, 81, 128, 177, 181–82, 186, 193, 206, 226; *80–81, 136, 180, 182–83, 186, 199, 251*
Apfel, Oscar, 27
Arbuckle, Fatty, 35
Arizona, *251*
Arizona (1940; Ruggles), 207; *207*
Arnold, Edward, 214; *214*
Aronson, Max. *See* Anderson, Gilbert "Broncho Billy"
Arrowhead (1953; Warren), 184
Artcraft Productions, 29
Arthur, Jean, 130, 131, 137, 207, 219; *129, 137, 207*
Aryan, The (1916; Hart), 28
Asner, Ed, 162
At Gunpoint (1955; Werker), 100–101
August, Joseph, 29, 30
Authentic Life of Billy the Kid (Garrett), *172*
Autry, Gene, 91, 120, 128
Aztec Indians, 178

B

Bacall, Lauren, 205, 242
Bach, Steven, 255
Bacharach, Burt, 154
Bacon, Lloyd, 120; *120*

Bad Company (1972; Benton), 157–58; *158*
Badlands of Dakota (1941; Green), 138
Badman's Territory (1946; Whelan), 146
Bad Men of Missouri (1941; Enright), 148
Baggot, King, 30
Baker, Carroll, 55, 75, 192; *55, 75, 190*
Ball, Suzan, *185*
Ballad of Cable Hogue, The (1970; Peckinpah), 254–55; *254, 256*
Ballad of Josie, The (1967; McLaglen), 215
Ballard, Lucien, 155, 240
Balsam, Martin, 196
Bancroft, George, 97–98; *62, 63*
Bandit's Baby, The (1925; Hogan), 33
Bandolero! (1968; McLaglen), 113; *112*
Barbarosa (1982; Schepisi), 114–16; *115*
Barboni, Enzo (E. B. Clucher), 229
Bargain, The (1914; Ince), 28
Barnes, George, 26, 145; *25*
Barrymore, Lionel, 71, 72, 221
Barthelmess, Richard, 180
Bartlett, Sy, 223
Barton, James, 111; *111*
Battle at Elderbush Gulch, The (1913; Griffith), 27, 177–78
Baxter, Anne, 111, 206; *111*
Baxter, Warner, 109; *109*
Beach, Rex, 27
Beadle, Irwin, 15
Bean, Judge Roy, 105–7; *105, 106, 107, 108*
Beatty, Warren, 251; *250, 252*
Beery, Noah, 178
Beery, Wallace, 170, 221
Bellah, James Warner, 238
Bellamy, Madge, *36*
Belle Starr (1941; Cummings), 150; *150*
Bend of the River (1952; Mann), 54–55, 182; *54*
Ben Hur (play; Young), 28; (novel; Wallace), 170, 214
Bentley, Irene, 92
Benton, Robert, 157–58; *158*
Berenger, Tom, 155; *153*
Berger, Thomas, 196
Bickford, Charles, 75; *76*
Big Country, The (1958; Wyler), 75–77, 214, 223; *75–77*
Big Hand for the Little Lady, A (1966; Cook), 215; *215, 216*
bigotry, 78, 186, 193–95. *See also* racism
Big Shot, The (1942; Seiler), 235
Big Sky, The (1952; Hawks), 43; *43;* (novel; Guthrie), 43; *43*
Big Trail, The (1930; Walsh), 47; *46, 47*
Billy the Kid (William H. Bonney), 98, 157, 169–73, 174, 214, 218, 223; *169, 170, 172, 174*
Billy the Kid (1930; K. Vidor), 170; *169;* (1941; Miller), 98, 170; *170, 171;* (play), 170
Billy the Kid vs. Dracula (1966; Beaudine), 223
Biograph Studios, 27
Birdcage Theatre (Tombstone, Arizona), *93*
Bisset, Jacqueline, 107
Black Bart (1948; Sherman), 111
Blackfoot Indians, 43; *42, 184*
Black Hills, South Dakota, *186*
Blackjack Ketchum, Desperado (1956; Bellamy), 150
blacks, 223, 226; *226, 227*
Blake, Robert, 193, 206; *193, 194*
Blazing Saddles (1974; Brooks), 164; *164*
Bloom, Claire, 223; *224*

Bloom, Harold Jack, 134
Blue Streak Westerns, 37
Boetticher, Budd, 135, 136, 239; *135, 136*
Bogart, Humphrey, 111, 120; *120*
Bogdanovich, Peter, 81, 188
Bond, Ward, 39, 50, 111, 116; *44, 79, 94*
Bondi, Beulah, 221
bonding, male, 143–74
Bonney, William H. *See* Billy the Kid
Bonnie and Clyde (1967; Penn), 158, 255
Boone, Richard, 219
Borgnine, Ernest, 219; *167*
Bowers, William, 235
Boyd, Stephen, *123*
Boyd, William, 128
Brackett, Leigh, 161, 162
Brady, Alice, 202
Brady, Scott, 212; *210*
Brand, Neville, 167; *168*
Branding Broadway (1918; Hart), 29
Brando, Marlon, 125–26, 127, 168–69, 255; *127, 186, 257*
Bravados, The (1958; King), 122–23; *123*
Breed of Men (1919; Hart), 30
Brennan, Walter, 69, 93, 105, 106, 107, 161, 162; *105, 159*
Bridges, Jeff, 157, 258; *158, 256*
Brigham Young—Frontiersman (1940; Hathaway), 48–50; *49, 50*
Broken Arm, Chief, *179*
Broken Arrow (1950; Daves), 16, 180–82, 184, 205–6; *180, 181, 182–83*
Broken Lance (1954; Dmytryk), 73–75, 203; *74*
Broncho Billy and the Baby (1908; Anderson), 26–27
"Broncho Billy" Westerns, 27
Bronson, Charles, 138, 233; *233*
Brooks, Mel, 164; *164*
Brooks, Richard, 240; *239, 240*
Brown, Barry, 157; *158*
Brown, Harry, 162
Brown, Johnny (John) Mack, 170; *169*
Brown, Karl, 37
Bryden, Bill, 147
Brynner, Yul, 103; *157*
Buchanan, Edgar, 110
Buchanan Rides Again (1958; Boetticher), 136
Buetel, Jack, 170, 218; *172*
Buffalo Bill. *See* Cody, William Frederick "Buffalo Bill"
Buffalo Bill (1944; Wellman), 139, 140; *18–19, 21, 138, 139*
Buffalo Bill and the Indians or Sitting Bull's History Lesson (1976; Altman), 139–40; *140*
Bugles in the Afternoon (1952; Rowland), 140
Buntline, Ned (Edward Zane Carroll Judson), 15, 138
Burgess, Dorothy, 109; *109*
Burnett, W. R., 92, 111
Burns, Allan, 155
Burns, Walter Noble, 170
Burt, Frank, 121
Burt, Nellie, *147*
Busch, Niven, 73, 105
Busey, Gary, 114, 116; *115*
Butch and Sundance: The Early Days (1979; Lester), 154–55; *153*
Butch Cassidy and the Sundance Kid (1969; Hill), 107, 150–54, 155, 158; *151, 152, 153*
Butler, Frank, 140
Butler, Michael, 255

C

Caan, James, 162
Cabanne, Christy, 109
Cagney, James, 120, 143, 166; *120, 166*
Cahn, Edward L., 92
Cain, Christopher, 174
Calamity Jane (Martha Jane Cannary), 137; *136, 208*
Calhern, Louis, 182; *181*
California, 24, 59
Canadian Pacific (1949; Marin), 68
Canadian Pacific Railroad, 68
Cannary, Martha Jane. *See* Calamity Jane
Canyon de Chelly, Arizona, *41*
Capra, Frank, *212*
Captive God, The (1916; Hart), 178
Cardinale, Claudia, 233, 240; *241*
Carey, Harry, 35, 92, 109
Carey, Harry, Jr., 82, 84; *83*
Carey, Timothy, 127
Carradine, David, *149*
Carradine, John, 145, 239; *49, 62*
Carradine, Keith, 147; *149*
Carradine, Robert, 147; *149*
Carson, Robert, 110
Carter, Alice, 174
Cassidy, Butch (Robert LeRoy Parker), 150–55, 209; *151, 153*
Cassidy, "Hopalong" (William Boyd), 128
Cat Ballou (1965; Silverstein), 174, 214, 240; *217*
cattle drives, 68–69, 118–20; *69, 117*
Cattle Queen of Montana (1954; Dwan), 209; *209*
cattle stampede, *52–53*
cavalry, 78–87
Central Pacific Railroad, 37, 65, 68
Chandler, Jeff, 87, 181, 182, 184
Chaplin, Geraldine, 140
Chase, Borden, 69; *68*
Cherokee Indians, 123, 177; *48, 125*
Cherokee Strip land rush, 30, 235; *48, 49*
Cheyenne Autumn (1964; Ford), 177, 188–93, 225; *4–5, 189, 190, 191*; (novel; Sandoz), 192
Cheyenne Indians, 141, 188–93, 196–98; *184, 189, 190, 191, 196*
Cheyenne Social Club, The (1970; Kelly), 218; *218, 219*
Chief Crazy Horse (1955; Sherman), 184; *185*
Chisholm Trail, 39, 69
Christie, Julie, 251; *250*
"Chuckaswanna Swing," 54
Churchill, Berton, *62*
Churchill, Marguerite, *46*
Cimarron (1931; Ruggles), 30, 48; *49, 207;* (novel; Ferber), 48
Cimino, Michael, 255; *257, 259*
CinemaScope process, 73
Cinerama process, 55, 141
Civil War, 87–89; *87, 89*
Clanton gang, 92, 93, 95; *92, 93, 94*
Clark, Susan, 193; *194*
Clark, Walter Van Tilburg, 224
Cleese, John, 166
Clemens, Samuel L. *See* Mark Twain
Clift, Montgomery, 59, 69, 70, 166, 246; *68, 244*
Cline, Edward, 206
Clothier, William, 192
Clucher, E. B. *See* Barboni, Enzo
Cobb, Lee J., *135*
Coburn, James, 174; *173*
Cochise, 79, 177, 181, 182, 184
Cochiti Indians, *189*
Cody, William Frederick "Buffalo Bill," 15, 24, 61, 137, 138–40; *136, 138, 139, 140*
Coffeyville, Kansas, 148

Cohen, Leonard, 254
Colbert, Claudette, 43; *44*
Collins, Joan, 123
Colorado Territory (1949; Walsh), 111–12
Columbia Pictures, 110; *89*
Comanche Indians, 123, 188; *188*
Comanche Station (1960; Boetticher), 136
comedic Westerns, 107, 150–54, 158, 164, 205, 229
Companeros (1970; Corbucci), 229
Connell, Evan S., 140
Connors, Chuck, 75
Conroy, Frank, *225*
Conversion of Frosty Blake, The (1915; Hart), 28
Cooder, Ry, 147
Cook, Elisha, 131
Cook, Fielder, 215; *215*
Cooper, Gary, 37, 91, 98, 100, 102, 106, 128, 134, 137, 201; *97, 99, 100, 101, 105, 106, 135, 137*
Cooper, Jackie, 145; *142*
Corbucci, Sergio, 229
Corey, Jeff, 138, 196
Corey, Wendell, 73
Costner, Kevin, 166; *165*
Cotten, Joseph, 71, 87
Covered Wagon, The (1923; Cruze), 35–37, 39, 47, 60–61; *35;* (novel; Hough), 35–37
covered wagons. *See* wagon trains
Cowboy (1958; Daves), 118–20; *119*
Cowboy and the Lady, The (1938; Potter), 205
cowboys, 116–20, 143, 243–46; *34, 74, 117, 139, 165, 247*
Cowboys, The (1972; Rydell), 118, 169; *10–11, 119*
Crain, Jeanne, 218–19
Crawford, Joan, 212; *213*
Crazy Horse, Chief, 138, 180, 184; *185*
Cripple Creek Bar-Room (Edison), 15
Crisp, Donald, 121, 221
Crosby, Floyd, 98–100
Crosland, Alan, 180
Cruze, James, 35–37, 60; *35*
Culpepper Cattle Company, The (1972; Richards), 117–18; *116, 117, 118*
Cummings, Irving, 150
Curtis, Ken, 124
Curtiz, Michael, 91–92
Custer, General George Armstrong, 34, 81, 137, 140–41, 180, 196–97; *141, 195*
Custer of the West (1968; Siodmak); 140–141; *141*
Custer's Last Raid (1912; Ince), 28

D

Dallas (1950; Heisler), 138
Dalton, Bill, 148
Dalton, Bob, 148
Dalton brothers, 143, 148, 150
Dalton, Emmett, 148
Dalton, Frank, 148
Dalton, Grattan "Grat," 148
Daltons Ride Again, The (1945; Taylor), 148
dance-hall girls, 161, 206–7; *200*
Danner, Blythe, 219; *221*
Danton, Ray, 184
Darby, Kim, 113; *113*
Darcel, Denise, 214; *212*
Darnell, Linda, 48, 95, 205; *49, 94*
Darwell, Jane, 54, 221; *51*
Daves, Delmer, 101, 118, 129, 180, 219; *102, 182*
David, Hal, 154
Davison, Bruce, 198; *199*

Dawn Maker, The (1916; Hart), 178
Day, Doris, 215
death, 23, 46, 120, 201, 205–6, 239–40
Death of a Gunfighter (1969; Smithee), 103
"Death of Billy the Kid, The" (Vidal), 173
Dee, Frances, 60
de Havilland, Olivia, 140, 204, 206
Dehner, John, 173
Del Rio, Dolores, 192
DeMille, Cecil B., 27, 65–68, 137–38, 180, 203, 205; *65, 181*
Demon Rider, The (1925; Hurst), 34
Denver and the Rio Grande, The (1952; Haskin), 68
Derek, John, 166; *167*
Der Kaiser von Kalifornien. See *Emperor of California, The*
Dern, Bruce, 118
Deserter, The (1912; Ince), 28; *26*
desperadoes. *See* outlaws
Desperadoes, The (1943; C. Vidor), 110, 207
Destry Rides Again (1939; Marshall), 54, 59, 92, 97, 207; *164, 200*
de Toth, Andre, 207
Devil's Doorway (1950; Mann), 182, 184; *181*
Devil's Double, The (1916; Hart), 28
Devine, Andy, 92, 239; *62, 63*
de Wilde, Brandon, 130, 258, 260; *131*
Dickinson, Angie, 161, 162
Dietrich, Marlene, 207–9; *164, 200, 208*
dime novels, 15, 24, 138
Dino (1957; Carr), 147
Dirty Dingus Magee (1970; Kennedy), 157
Dirty Harry (1971; Siegel), 233
Dirty Little Billy (1972; Dragoti), 157, 174
Dix, Richard, 178; *49, 176, 178*
Django (1966; Corbucci), 229
Dmytryk, Edward, 73, 89, 102, 203; *103*
Doc (1971; Perry), 97
Dodge City (1939; Curtiz), 92, 206
Donlevy, Brian, 65, 98, 145, 170; *171*
Douglas, Kirk, 43, 97, 101, 207, 218–19, 246; *43, 96, 246*
Douglas, Melvyn, 258
Dourif, Brad, *256*
Downs, Cathy, 93
Dragoti, Stan, 174
Dru, Joanne, 69, 82; *83*
Drums along the Mohawk (1939; Ford), 43–45; *44, 45;* (novel; Edmonds), 43
Duel at Diablo (1966; Nelson), 226; *227*
Duel in the Sun (1947; K. Vidor), 71–72, 73, 78, 218, 221; *70, 71, 72*
Dunaway, Faye, 196
Duniway, Abigail Scott, 202
Dunn, Irene, *49*
Duryea, Dan, 111, 229; *121*
Duvall, Robert, 147; *147*
Dwan, Allan, 150
Dylan, Bob, 174; *173*

E

Each Man in His Own Time (Walsh), 46
Earp, James, 93
Earp, Morgan, *94*
Earp, Mrs. Wyatt, 92
Earp, Virgil, *94*
Earp, Wyatt, 15, 92–97, 192–93; *92, 94, 97*
Eastwood, Clint, 113, 131–33, 174, 223, 227, 229, 233; *115, 132, 133, 222, 228*

Edeson, Arthur, 47
Edison, Thomas, 15, 24, 25, 26
Edmonds, Walter D., 43
Edwards, Blake, 158; *161*
Edwards, Major John Newman, 144
Eisenhower, Dwight David, 16
El Dorado (1967; Hawks), 162–63; *163*
Eldridge, Charles, *63*
Electric Horseman, The (1979; Pollack), 249; *249*
Ellison, James, 137; *137*
Emperor of California, The (Der Kaiser von Kalifornien) (1936; Trenker), 223
End of the Trail (1932; Lederman), 180
Engel, Samuel G., 92
Ericson, John, 209; *211*
Escape from Fort Bravo (1953; Sturges), 87
Estevez, Emilio, 174

F

families, 15, 55, 69–70, 71–78, 120–28
Famous Players–Lasky, 29
Far Country, The (1955; Mann), 182
Fargo, William, 60
Farnum, Dustin, 27, 34
Farnum, William, 27
Farr, Felicia, *102*
Farrow, John, 128
father-daughter conflict, 72–73
father-son conflict, 69–70, 73–75, 166–74
Ferber, Edna, 48
Ferrell, Conchata, 203, 215–18; *204*
Ferrer, Mel, *208*
Fields, W. C., *206*
Fiend Who Walked the West, The (1958; Douglas), 223
Fight for Freedom, The (1908; Griffith), 27
Fighting Blood (1911; Griffith), 27
film noir, 111–12
Final Cut (Bach), 255
Fink, Harry Julian, 89
Firecreek (1968; McEveety), 103; *104*
Fistful of Dollars, A (1967; Leone), 223, 227–29; *224, 228*
Flaming Forest, The (1926; Barker), 177
Flaming Frontier, The (1926; Sedgwick), 34
Flaming Star (1960; Siegel), 186; *187*
Fleischer, Richard, 158
Flynn, Errol, 92, 140; *141*
Folsom, Megan, *204*
Fonda, Henry, 43–45, 79, 82, 92, 95, 102, 103, 133, 145, 167, 168, 193, 215, 224, 225, 233, 247–49; *44, 56, 79, 82, 94, 103, 104, 133, 142, 145, 168, 216, 219, 232, 233, 247, 248*
Fonda, Jane, 215, 249; *217, 249*
For a Dollar in the Teeth (1966; Lewis), 229
For a Few Dollars More (1967; Leone), 229; *222*
Ford, Bob, 144, 145, 146, 147
Ford, Charlie, 147
Ford, Francis, *51*
Ford, Glenn, 101, 110, 118, 207, 219, 247–49; *102, 119, 247, 248*
Ford, John, 15, 16, 21, 28, 33, 35, 37, 43, 48, 50–54, 55, 56, 61–62, 65, 78, 81–85, 87, 92, 93, 95, 97–98, 111, 123, 124, 157, 188, 192, 193, 203, 204, 205, 221, 225–26, 227, 233, 235, 238–39, 260; *21, 37, 44, 51, 63, 79, 81, 82, 84, 87, 89, 94, 110, 125, 126, 128, 163, 188, 189, 190, 226, 237*
Ford, Patrick, 50
Ford, Paul, *215*
Ford brothers, 147; *149*

Foreman, Carl, 161, 223
Forrest, Steve, *187*
Forsythe, John, 87
Fort Apache (1948; Ford), 78–82, 83, 193, 204; *79, 80–81, 82, 84*
Forty Guns (1957; Fuller), 209; *211*
Foster, Norman, 219
Fox studios. *See* 20th Century–Fox
Fraker, William A., 242
Francis, Jon, 242
Frank, Harriet, Jr., 258
French, Valerie, 219
French and Indian Wars, 40
Frenchie (1951; King), 207
Frisco Kid, The (1979; Aldrich), 223
frontier justice, 16, 102, 105. *See also* lawmen
Frontier Marshall (1934; Seiler), 92; (1939; Dwan), 92; *90, 92*
Frontiersman, The (1927; Barker), 34
frontier towns, 59; main streets, *148, 149, 251*
frontier women, 201–2; *202, 204*
Fuller, Samuel, 146, 209; *211*
Furies, The (1950; Mann), 72–73; *73*
Furthman, Jules, 161

G

Gable, Clark, 41, 204, 205, 214, 244, 246; *42, 205, 212, 244, 245*
Gaden, Alexander, *30*
gangster films, 109, 235
Gardner, Ava, 107
Garner, James, 97, 226
Garrett, Pat, 170–71, 173, 174; *170, 172*
Garson, Greer, 214; *215*
Geer, Elizabeth Smith, 201–2
genocide, 196; *189*
Gentlemen's Agreement (1947; Kazan), 180
George, Chief Dan, 114, 197; *197*
Geraghty, Carmelita, *33*
German Westerns, 223
Geronimo, 180, 186, 214; *63, 179*
Geronimo (1940; Sloane), 180; *179*
Gerstad, Harry, 100
Gibson, Althea, *88*
Gibson, Hoot, 33
Gillette, Ruth, 92
Gilmore, Virginia, 61
Girotti, Mario (Terence Hill), 229
Gish, Lillian, 27, 71, 72, 77, 78, 202, 221
Glacier National Park, Montana, *184*
Glenn, Scott, 164, 166; *165*
Glennon, Bert, 50, 61, 84, 140
Glover, Danny, 166; *165*
Goddard, Paulette, 205; *181*
Goddess of Sagebrush Gulch, The (1912; Griffith), 27
Goldbeck, Willis, 238
Goldblum, Jeff, 166
Goldman, William, 150
gold rush, 59
Goldwyn, Samuel, 105
Gone with the Wind (1939; Fleming), 71
Goodman, David Z., 240
Good, the Bad, and the Ugly, The (1967; Leone), 229
Go West (1940; Buzzell), 68
Grabill, J. C. H., *34*
Grandeur process, 47
Grand Teton National Park, Wyoming, 43, 131
Grant, Ulysses S., 56, 184
Gray, Coleen, 70

Gray, Gary, 220
Greaser's Gauntlet, The (1908; Griffith), 27
Great Missouri Raid, The (1950; Douglas), 146
Great Northfield, Minnesota Raid (1972; Kaufman), 147; *147, 148*
Great Train Robbery, The (1903; Porter), 15, 25–26, 68; *25*
Grey, Zane, 16, 24, 178
Gries, Tom, 240; *242*
Griffith, D. W., 26, 27, 28, 177–78
Griggs, Loyal, 131
Grimes, Gary, 117, 158; *116, 117, 118*
Guest, Christopher, 147; *149*
Guest, Nicholas, 147; *149*
Gunfight at the O.K. Corral (1957; Sturges), 91, 92, 95–97; *95, 96*
Gun Fighter, The (1916; Hart), 28
Gunfighter, The (1950; King), 205, 235–38; *234, 236*
Guthrie, A. B., Jr., 43, 130; *43*

H

Hackett, Joan, 240
Hackman, Gene, 203; *203*
Hale, Scott, 242
Hall, Conrad, 154
Hall, Porter, *207*
Hamill, Pete, 97
Hamilton, Margaret, *206*
Hang 'em High (1967; Post), 229
Hanging Tree, The (1959; Daves), 128
Hard-Boiled (1926; Blystone), 34
Harlan, Russell, 43, 69, 70; *68*
Harlem on the Prairie (1937; Newfield), 223
Harper's New Monthly Magazine, 136
Harris, Frank, 118–19; *119*
Harris, Richard, 89, 198; *198*
Hartley, Mariette, 239
Hart, William S., 23, 28–30, 31, 35, 60, 108, 120, 121, 132, 135, 137, 166, 177, 178; *22, 29, 30, 31, 33, 61*
Harvey, Laurence, 223; *224*
Harvey Girls, The (1946; Sidney), 68, 205, 223
Haskin, Byron, 68
Hatfield, Hurd, 173
Hathaway, Henry, 48, 55, 113
Haun, Catherine, 201
Hawks, Howard, 15, 43, 68, 70, 159, 161, 162–63, 164, 166, 170, 235, 260; *43, 68, 100, 159, 162, 163*
Haycox, Ernest, 61
Hayden, Sterling, 68, 212
Heartland (1979; Pearce), 203, 218; *204*
Heart of an Indian, The (1913; Ince), 178
Heaven's Gate (1980; Cimino), 255–58, 260; *256, 257, 259*
Heflin, Van, 101, 130; *102, 129*
Hellbenders, The (1966; Corbucci), 229
Hell Bent (1918; Ford), 35
Heller, Lukas, 240
Hellman, Sam, 145
Hell's Heroes (1930; Wyler), 110
Hell's Hinges (1916; Hart, Smith), 28–29, 35, 120, 132; *29*
Hepburn, Audrey, 77, 186; *78*
Hepburn, Katherine, 113, 203, 215; *114*
hermits, 134–36. *See also* loners
Heston, Charlton, 61, 75, 89, 184, 186, 240; *76, 89, 186, 242*
Hickok, James Butler "Wild Bill," 15, 24, 136–38, 196; *136, 137*
Highham, Charles, 127

High Noon (1952; Zinnemann), 21, 68, 98–101, 102–3, 159, 161, 168, 201, 223; *97, 98–99, 100, 101, 102*
"High Noon" (Tiomkin, Washington), 100
High Plains Drifter (1972; Eastwood), 131–132; *132*
High Sierra (1941; Walsh), 111, 235
Hill, George Roy, 150; *151*
Hill, Terence. *See* Girotti, Mario
Hill, Walter, 147, 148; *149*
Hillyer, Lambert, 29, 30
historical Westerns, 136–41. *See also entries for historical persons*
Hoch, Winton C., 82, 83, 111, 123; *126*
Hoffman, Dustin, 196, 197; *195, 196, 197*
Hogan, James, 68
Holden, William, 87, 89, 143, 155, 158, 219; *88, 154, 155, 160, 220*
Holliday, John H. "Doc," 92, 93, 95–97, 170–71, 174, 192–93, 205; *94, 97*
Holliman, Earl, 101
Hollywood, 27
Holt, Charlene, 162
Holt, Tim, *94*
Hombre (1967; Ritt), 193, 195; *192*
Home of the Brave (1949; Robson), 180
Hondo (1953; Farrow), 128; *128*
Honky Tonk (1941; Conway), 204–5; *205*
Hopper, Jerry, 61
Horse Soldiers, The (1959; Ford), 87; *8–9, 86–87, 88*
Hough, Emerson, 35–37
Hour of the Gun (1967; Sturges), 97
House of Strangers (play), 73
House Un-American Activities Committee (HUAC), 100
Howard, Ron, 158, 242; *243*
Howe, James Wong, 193, 223, 260; *192*
How Green Was My Valley (1941; Ford), 43
How the West Was Won (1963; Hathaway, Ford, Marshall), 55–56; *52–53, 55, 56–57, 89*
Hubbard, Lucien, 178
Hud (1963; Ritt), 258–60; *260*
Hughes, Howard, 170; *172*
Hunnicutt, Arthur, 162; *135*
Hunt, Linda, 166
Hunter, Jeffrey, 123, 147; *125, 126, 146*
Huppert, Isabelle, 258; *259*
Hurt, John, 258
Huston, John, 77, 78, 92, 106–7, 186, 244, 246; *107, 108*
Huston, Walter, 72, 92, 170; *73*
Hutton, Betty, 140

I

Ince, Thomas, 27–28, 29, 178; *27*
Inceville, 27
Indian Massacre, The (1912; Ince), 178
Indians, 16–21, 77–78, 79–81, 83, 177–99, 201, 205–6, 226; *45, 56–57, 139, 176, 178, 179, 180, 181, 182, 184, 185, 186, 188, 189, 190, 191, 193. See also entries for specific tribes*
Indians (play; Kopit), 139
Ingraham, Prentiss, 15
Innocents Abroad (Twain), 24
In Old Arizona (1929; Walsh), 109; *109*
In Old Chicago (1938; King), 202
interracial marriages and romances, 41–43, 174, 205
Ireland, John, 146, 229
Iron Horse, The (1924; Ford), 37, 65; *36*
Irwin Beadle and Co., 15
I Shot Jesse James (1949; Fuller), 146

Italian ("spaghetti") Westerns, 21, 103, 131, 133, 163, 174, 227–33; *132, 133, 157, 228, 229*
Ives, Burl, 75; *76*

J

Jack Slade (1953; Schuster), 150
Jackson, Helen Hunt, 178
Jaeckel, Richard, *173, 236*
Jagger, Dean, 48, 61; *211*
James, Frank, 143, 144, 145, 147; *142, 145, 146, 147*
James, Jesse, 15, 98, 143–47; *142, 144, 145, 146, 147*
James, Jesse Edward (Jesse James, Jr.), 144
James, Zee, 144, 205
James Boys in Missouri, The (1908), 144
James brothers, 15, 143–44, 145, 147; *149*
Jarman, Claude, Jr., 84
Jennings, Al, 150
Jeremiah Johnson (1972; Pollack), 127–28; *128, 129*
Jesse James (1927; Ingraham), 144; (1939; King), 98, 145, 147, 148, 205; *142, 144, 145*
Jesse James as the Outlaw (1921; Coates), 144
Jesse James at Bay (1941; Kane), 146
Jesse James under the Black Flag (1921; Coates), 144
Jesse James vs. the Daltons (1954; Castle), 146
Johnny Guitar (1954; Ray), 212; *213*
Johnson, Ben, 50, 83–84, 116; *21, 51, 156*
Johnson, Dorothy M., 238
Johnson, Nunnally, 145
Johnson, Van, 229
Johnson County Wars, 255
Jolson Story, The (1946; Green, Lewis), 110
Jones, Buck, 27, 34
Jones, Jennifer, 71, 218; *70, 72*
Jones, Shirley, *218*
Jordan, Dorothy, *124*
Jory, Victor, 68
Jubal (1956; Daves), 219
judges, 103–4
Judson, Edward Zane Carroll. *See* Buntline, Ned
Jurado, Katy, 73, 126, 203
Just Tony (1922; Reynolds), 31–33

K

Kahn, Madeline, 164; *164*
Kanin, Fay, 223–24
Kanin, Michael, 223–24
Kaquitts, Frank, 140
Karloff, Boris, 180
Karras, Alex, 164
Kasdan, Lawrence, 164–66, 260; *165*
Kasdan, Mark, 164, 166
Katt, William, 155; *153*
Kaufman, Philip, 113, 147, 148; *147*
Kazan, Elia, 203
Keach, James, 147; *149*
Keach, Stacy, 97, 107, 147; *149*
Keaton, Buster, 223
Keith, Ian, *46*
Kellogg, Jane, 201
Kelly, Grace, 98, 201; *101*
Kelly, Nancy, 145; *92*
Kennedy, Arthur, 54, 121, 140, 192–93, 209
Kennedy, Burt, 103, 136, 169, 247; *247, 248*
Kennedy, George, 247
Keno Bates—Liar (1915; Hart), 28
Ketchum, Blackjack, 150

Keyes, Evelyn, 110
Kid Curry, 150
kinetoscope, 15, 24
King, Brett, 146
King, Henry, 37, 98, 122, 145, 147, 178, 202, 235; *123, 144*
King, Louis, 207
King and Four Queens, The (1956; Walsh), 214; *212*
Kiowa Indians, 77, 78, 186; *78, 186*
Kiss of Death (1947; Hathaway), 223
Klein, Wally, 140
Kline, Kevin, 164, 166; *165*
Knight, Amelia Stewart, 201
Koch, Marianne, *228*
Kopit, Arthur, 139
Kovacs, Laszlo, 155
Kramer, Frank. *See* Parolini, Gianfranco
Kristofferson, Kris, 174, 255; *259*
Kubrick, Stanley, 126
Kurosawa, Akira, 155, 223, 227; *157, 224*
Kyne, Peter B., 27

L

Ladd, Alan, 129, 131; *129, 131*
Lady from Cheyenne, The (1941; Lloyd), 214; *214*
Lady Takes a Chance, A (1943; Seiter), 205
Lake, Stuart, 92; *92*
Lake, Veronica, 207
Lake Payette, Idaho, *38*
Lancaster, Burt, 77, 91, 97, 186, 198, 206, 226, 240; *78, 96, 187, 199, 239, 241*
Lang, Fritz, 61, 145, 207; *58, 142, 145, 208*
Langtry, Lillie, 105, 107
Last Outlaw, The (1936; Cabanne), 109–10
Last Picture Show, The (1971; Bogdanovich), 243
Last Trail, The (1927; Seiler), *33*
Last Train from Gun Hill (1959; Sturges), 68, 101–2
Laszlo, Ernest, 186
Lathrop, Philip, 246
Law and Order (1932; Cahn), 92
lawmen, 91–107, 109, 116
Lederman, D. Ross, 180
Lee, Anna, 204
Left-Handed Gun, The (1958; Penn), 173–74; *175*
Leigh, Janet, 134; *134*
LeMay, Alan, 77, 123
Lemmon, Jack, 118
Leone, Sergio, 131, 132, 174, 227, 229, 233; *133, 228, 232*
LeRoy, Mervin, 214
Lester, Richard, 155; *153*
Let Us Live (1939; Brahm), 145
Lewis, Jerry, *112*
Lewis, Vance. *See* Vanzi, Luigi
Life and Times of Judge Roy Bean, The (1972; Huston), 106–7; *107, 108*
Life of an American Fireman, The (1902; Porter), 25
Lincoln County War, 169–70
Little, Cleavon, 164; *164*
Little Bighorn, Battle of, 79, 140, 141, 196–97; *141, 195*
Little Big Man (1970; Penn), 138, 141, 186, 196–97; *195, 196, 197*; (novel; Berger), 196–197
Little Crow, Chief, 177
Little Train Robbery, The (1905; Edison), 26
Lives of a Bengal Lancer, The (1935; Hathaway), 180
Lloyd, Frank, 60, 214
Lloyd, Kathleen, 255
London, Julie, 134
Lonely Are the Brave (1962; Miller),

246–47; *246*
Lone Ranger, 128
loners, 91–141; cowboys, 116–20; hermits and isolationists, 120–36; judges, 103–7; outlaws, 107–16; sheriffs and marshals, 91–103
Lonesome Dove (1989; Wincer), 261
Lone Star Ranger, The (1923; Hillyer), 33
Longabaugh, Harry. *See* Sundance Kid
Long Riders, The (1980; Hill), 147–48, 150; *149*
Lord, Jack, *135*
Losch, Tilly, 218; *71*
Lost Weekend, The (1945; Wilder), 180
Lovin' Molly (1974; Lumet), 219; *221*
Lowe, Edmund, 109
Luke, Jorge, *199*
Lumet, Sidney, 219; *221*

M

M (1931; Lang), 61
McCabe and Mrs. Miller (1971; Altman), 218, 251–53, 254, 255, 260; *250, 252, 253*
McCall, Jack, 137
McCambridge, Mercedes, 212
McCarthy, Kevin, *215*
McCarty, Henry. *See* Billy the Kid
McClure, Doug, 77
McCoy, Tim, 34, 180
McCrea, Joel, 60, 65, 112, 117, 139, 239; *60, 138, 238*
MacDonald, Ian, 98; *100*
MacDonald, Joseph, 95; *111*
McDowell, Roddy, 107
McEveety, Vincent, 103
McGuane, Thomas, 255
McIntire, John, *187*
MacKenzie, Aeneas, 140
McLaglen, Andrew, 113, 215; *112*
McLaglen, Victor, 81, 83; *83*
MacLane, Barton, 61
MacMahon, Aline, 221
MacMurray, Fred, 100
McMurtry, Larry, 258; *221*
McNally, Stephen, 121; *121*
Maddow, Ben, 77
Magnificent Seven, The (1960; Sturges), 155; *157*
Main, Marjorie, 221
Major Dundee (1965; Peckinpah), 89; *89*
Malden, Karl, 55, 126, 193; *55*
male bonding, 143–74
Malick, Terry, 249
Malone, Dorothy, 101, 102
Man Called Horse, A (1970; Silverstein), 198; *6–7, 198*
Man from Laramie, The (1955; Mann), 121–22, 221; *122*
Mann, Anthony, 54, 72, 73, 121, 134, 167, 182–84; *54, 121, 122, 134, 135, 181*
Man of the West (1959; Mann), 134; *135*
Man Who Shot Liberty Valence, The (1962; Ford), 225, 238–39; *237*
Man without a Star (1955; K. Vidor), 207, 218–19
Marin, Edwin L., 68
Marked Men (1919; Ford), *110*
Marley, J. Peverell, 173–74
Marques, Maria Elena, 41; *42*
Marshall, George, 37, 55, 92, 97, 184; *186, 200*
Marshall, Herbert, 71, 218
marshals, 91. *See also* lawmen
Marsh, Mae, 27
Martin, Chris-Pin, 62
Martin, Dean, 113, 161; *112*

Martin, Dewey, 43
Marvin, Lee, 158, 238, 240, 249; *217, 237, 241, 242*
Marx Brothers, 68, 223
"M*A*S*H," 16
Massacre (1934; Crosland), 180
Massacre, The (1915; Griffith), 178
Maté, Rudolph, 209
Matthau, Walter, 246, 247
Mature, Victor, 93, 184; *94, 185*
Maverick Queen, The (1956; Kane), 209; *210*
Maynard, Ken, 34
Meek, Donald, *62*
Meeker, Ralph, 134
Mellor, William C., 134
men: bonding among, 143–74; loners, 91–141
Menjou, Adolphe, 43
Metropolis (1927; Lang), 61
MGM, 34, 55
Michenaud, Gerald, *216*
Miles, Vera, 124, 219, 238
military Westerns, 78–89; *79*
military wives, 84, 203–4; *84*
Milius, John, 106–7
Miljan, John, 137
Millar, Stuart, 215; *114*
Miller, Arthur, 246
Miller, David, 170, 246; *246*
Miller, Winston, 92
Miller brothers, *149*
Mineo, Sal, 192
Miracle Rider, The (1935; Schaeffer, Eason), 33
Misfits, The (1961; Huston), 244–46; *244, 245*
Missouri Breaks, The (1976; Penn), 255; *257*
Mr. Smith Goes to Washington (1939; Capra), 134
Mitchell, Millard, 134
Mitchell, Thomas, 170
Mitchum, Robert, 128, 162, 169, 219, 221; *220*
Mix, Tom, 27, 30–33, 177; *32, 33, 34*
Molly and Lawless John (1972; Nelson), 219
Money Corral, The (1919; Hillyer), 29–30
Monroe, Marilyn, 244, 246; *244*
Montalban, Ricardo, 192
Montana Belle (1952; Dwan), 150
Montana Territory, *184*
Monte Walsh (1970; Fraker), 240–42; *242*
Monument Valley (Utah-Arizona), 61, 62, 82–83, 124, 233, 260, 261; *63*
Moorehead, Agnes, 55; *55*
Moreau, Jeanne, 240
Morgan, Henry, 56
Mormons, 39, 48–54; *49, 50, 51*
Morricone, Ennio, 227, 233
Mowbray, Alan, 93; *93*
Mulligan, Richard, 196; *195*
Murphy, Audie, 77, 78, 186
Murray, Don, 138
musical Westerns, 205. *See also* songs
Mustang films, 37
Muybridge, Eadweard, 15
My Darling Clementine (1946; Ford), 92–95, 205, 221; *93, 94*
My Little Chickadee (1940; Cline), 180, 206; *206*
My Reminiscences as a Cowboy (Harris) 118; *119*

N

Naish, J. Carol, 184
Naked Spur, The (1953; Mann), 134; *134*
Naturama process, *210*
Natwick, Mildred, 203, 204; *83*

Navaho Indians, 174, 177, 178; *178*
Navajo Joe (1966; Corbucci), 229
Neal, Patricia, 258
Nebraska, *259*
Nelson, Gary, 219
Nelson, Ralph, 192, 226; *225*
Nelson, Ricky, 161, 162; *162*
Nelson, Willie, 114, 116; *115*
Nevada Territory, 24
Never a Dull Moment (1950; Marshall), 205
Newman, David, 158
Newman, Paul, 107, 139, 150, 173, 193, 223, 224, 249, 258; *107, 108, 140, 151, 152, 175, 192, 224, 260*
New Mexico Territory, 39, 170
New York Motion Picture Company, 28
New York Times, 137; *257*
Nichols, Dudley, 43, 61
Nichols, Colonel George Ward, 136, 137; *136*
Nicholson, Jack, 255; *257*
Nicol, Alex, 121
Northfield, Minnesota, 147
North of Hudson Bay (1923; Ford), 31–33
North West Mounted Police (1940; DeMille), 180, 205; *181*
Northwest Passage (1940; K. Vidor), 39–41; *38, 40*; (novel; Roberts), 39–40
Northwest Territory, 41
Nugent, Frank S., 50, 81, 82, 123

O

Oakley, Annie, 24, 140
Oates, Warren, *156*
O'Brien, Edmond, 68, 238
O'Brien, George, 92, 204; *36, 83*
O'Hara, Maureen, 84, 204; *84*
O.K. Corral (Tombstone, Arizona), 92; *92*
Oklahoma, 48; *49. See also* Cherokee Strip land rush
Oklahoma Kid, The (1939; Bacon), 120, 166; *120*
Oklahoma land rush, 48
Old West: dying of, 155, 158, 235, 243, 255; evolution of, 23; lure of, 39; military presence in, 78; role of women in, 201–2; romanticization of, 24
Olson, Moroni, *49*
Once upon a Time in the West (1969; Leone), 133, 233; *133, 230–31, 232, 233*
O'Neal, Ryan, 158; *161*
One-Eyed Jacks (1961; Brando), 125–27, 168–69; *127*
O'Neill, Jennifer, 163
Only Angels Have Wings (1939; Hawks), 159
"On the Atchison, Topeka and the Santa Fe," 68
On the Night Stage (1914; Ince), 28
Oregon Trail, 39, 47
Oscars. *See* Academy Awards
Outlaw, The (1943; Hughes), 170–71, 218; *172*
Outlaw Josey Wales, The (1976; Eastwood), 113–14; *115*
outlaws: bonding among, 143–58; as loners, 107–16
Outrage, The (1964; Ritt), 223–24; *224*
Owens-Adair, Bethenia, 202
Ox-Bow Incident, The (1943; Wellman), 221, 224–25; *225*; (novel; Clark), 224

P

Page, Geraldine, 128
Paget, Debra, 181
Palance, Jack, 22, 131, 240; *242*

Paleface, The (1948; McLeod), 180
Pale Rider (1985; Eastwood), 131, 132–33, 223, 229; *133*
Palmer, Ernest, 182
Paramount Pictures, 29, 35
Parker, Eleanor, 87, 214
Parker, Robert LeRoy. *See* Cassidy, Butch
Parks, Larry, 110–11
Parolini, Gianfranco (Frank Kramer), 229
Parrish, Robert, 128
Pat Garrett and Billy the Kid (1973; Peckinpah), 174; *173*
Pearce, John, *147*
Pearce, Richard, 203, 218
Peary, Danny, 212
Peck, Gregory, 56, 71, 75, 111, 122–23, 214, 235, 238; *70, 75, 76, 77, 111, 123, 234, 236*
Peckinpah, Sam, 89, 147, 155, 174, 239, 254; *89, 155, 156, 172, 238, 255, 257*
Pedersoli, Carlo (Bud Spencer), 229
Pellicer, Pina, 126; *127*
Penn, Arthur, 138, 141, 171–73, 196, 255; *174, 195, 197, 257*
Peppard, George, 56
Perkins, Anthony, 107, 167, 168; *168, 221*
Perry, Frank, 97
Peters, Jean, 73, 186, 206
Phillips, Lou Diamond, 174
Piazza, Ben, 128
Pickford, Mary, 27
Pinkerton Detective Agency, 143, 147; *146*
Pioneer Trails (1923; Smith), 177
Place, Etta, 150, 151–54
Plainsman, The (1936; DeMille), 137–38, 203; *137*; (1966; Rich), 138
Planer, Franz, 75
Pleasance, Donald, 240
Pocket Money (1972; Rosenberg), 249
Poitier, Sidney, 226; *226*
Pollack, Sydney, 127, 249; *128, 249*
Pollard, Michael J., 157
Polonsky, Abraham, 193, 195; *193, 194*
Pony Express, 60–61
Pony Express (1925; Cruze), 60; (1953; Hopper), 61, 138
Porter, Edwin S., 15, 25–26
Portis, Charles, 113
Power, Tyrone, 48, 145; *49, 144*
Presley, Elvis, 186; *187*
Preston, Robert, 65; *181, 214*
Price, Vincent, 48; *49*
Primus, Barry, *204*
Principal, Victoria, 107
Professional Gun, A (1968; Corbucci), 229
Professionals, The (1966; Brooks), 240; *12–13, 239, 241*
Pursued (1947; Walsh), 73, 221

Q

Quaid, Dennis, 147; *149*
Quaid, Randy, 147; *149*
Qualen, John, 239
Quinn, Anthony, 101, 102; *103*

R

Race for the Millions, A (1906), 26
Rachel and the Stranger (1948; Foster), 219; *220*
racism, 77–78, 180, 225–26, 227. *See also* bigotry;

genocide
railroad building, 37, 62–68; *36, 65, 66–67*
Rainbow Trail, The (1925; Reynolds), 177
"Raindrops Keep Fallin' on My Head" (Bacharach, David), 154
Ramona (1936; King), 178–80; (novel; Jackson), 178
Ramrod (1947; de Toth), 207
Rancho Notorious (1952; Lang), 207–9; *208*
Rashomon (1951; Kurosawa), 223; *224*
Ravetch, Irving, 258
Ray, Aldo, 103
Ray, Charles, 28
Ray, Nicholas, 147, 167, 212; *146, 167, 212*
Raymond, Paula, 182
Reagan, Ronald, *209*
Rebel without a Cause (1955; Ray), 147; *146*
Redford, Robert, 127–28, 150, 193, 249; *128, 129, 151, 152, 153, 194, 249*
Redman and the Child, The (1908; Griffith), 27
Red Raiders, The (1927; Rogell), 34
Red River (1948; Hawks), 59, 68–70, 166; *68, 69*
Redskin (1929; Schertzinger), 178; *178*
Reed, Pamela, 150
Reed, Tom, 92
Reid, Wallace, 35
Remington, Frederic, 24
Renegades (1946; Sherman), 110–11
Rescued from an Eagle's Nest (1907; Edison), 26
Return of a Man Called Horse, The (1976; Kershner), 198
Return of Draw Egan, The (1916; Hart), 28
Return of Frank James, The (1940; Lang), 145; *142, 145*
Return of Jesse James, The (1950; Hilton), 146
Return of Sabata (1972; Kramer), 229
revenge theme, 61, 101, 113–14, 120–28, 233
Revolutionary War, 43
Reynolds, Burt, 229
Reynolds, Debbie, 55; *55*
Richards, Dick, 117; *119*
Riddle Gawne (1918; Hart), 121
Ride Lonesome (1959; Boetticher), 136; *136*
Riders of the Purple Sage (1925; Reynolds), 33; (novel; Grey), 24
Ride the High Country (1962; Peckinpah), 174, 239–40; *238*
Rio Bravo (1959; Hawks), 159–62, 163; *159, 162, 163*
Rio Grande (1950; Ford), 83–84, 204; *84–85*
Rio Lobo (1970; Hawks), 163; *163*
Rios, Elvira, *62*
Ritt, Martin, 193, 223, 258; *192, 224, 260*
Rivero, Jorge, 163
Robards, Jason, 97, 233, 254; *215, 254, 256*
Rober, Richard, 185
Roberts, Kenneth, 39
Robertson, Dale, 184
Robinson, Edward G., 143, 209, 223
Rogers, Major Robert, 40; *38, 40*
Rogers, Roy, 91, 116, 128
Rogers Rangers, 40; *38, 40*
Roland, Gilbert, 73, 114
Rolfe, Sam, 134
Romero, Cesar, 92; *109*
Rooster Cogburn (1975; Millar), 113, 215; *114*
Rose, Reginald, 134
Rosenburg, Stuart, 249
Ross, Katharine, 151, 193, 206; *194*
Rossen, Arthur, 68
Roughing It (Twain), 24
Rounders, The (1965; Kennedy), 247–49; *247, 248–49*
Rowlands, Gena, 246; *246*
Rudd, Lydia Allen, 201
Rudolph, Alan, 139

Ruggles, Wesley, 30, 48, 207; *49, 207*
Run for Cover (1955; Ray), 166–67; *166, 167*
Rush, Barbara, 193
Russell, Charles, 24
Russell, Jane, 150, 170, 218; *172*
Ryan, Mitch, 240
Ryan, Robert, 134, 155, 240
Rydell, Mark, 118, 169

S

Sabata (1969; Kramer), 229; *229*
Saddle Tramp (1950; Fregonese), 117
Saga of Billy the Kid, The (Burns), 170
Saint Joseph, Missouri, 45, 60
Salkow, Sidney, 184
Salmi, Albert, *123*
Sampson, Will, 138
Samuel, Mrs. Zerelda, *146*
Sand Creek Massacre (1864), 197
Sandoz, Mari, 192
Santa Fe Trail, 39
Santee Sioux, 177
Satan Town (1926; Mortimer), 35
Saul, Oscar, 87
Savage, The (1952; Marshall), 184–86; *186*
Sawdust Trail, The (1924; Sedgwick), 34
Schaeffer, Jack, 240
Schell, Maria, 128
Schepisi, Fred, 114; *115*
Schertzinger, Victor, 178
Schnee, Charles, *68, 73*
Scott, Randolph, 61, 68, 91, 92, 98, 110, 135–36, 145, 148, 239, 240; *61, 90, 135, 136, 150, 238*
Scouts of the Prairie, The (Hickok), 138
Sea of Grass (1947; Kazan), 203
Searchers, The (1956; Ford), 78, 82, 87, 123–24, 186, 188; *16–17, 124, 125, 126*; (novel; LeMay), 123
Seastrom, Victor, 202
Seiler, Lewis, 92
Seiter, William A., 43
Seitz, George B., 178
Selfish Yates (1918; Hart), 30
Sellers, William, 235
Selznick, David O., 71–72; *70*
Sennett, Mack, 28
Señor Daredevil (1926; Rogell), 34
Sergeant Rutledge (1960; Ford), 225–26; *226*
settlement of the West, 39, 59–89
Seven Brides for Seven Brothers (1954; Donen), 205
Seven Samurai (1954; Kurosawa), 155; *157*
Shane (1953; Stevens), 129–31, 132, 133, 168, 219, 240, 260; *129, 130, 131, 243*
Shaw, Robert, 141; *141*
Sheridan, Ann, 214–15
sheriffs, 91, 97. *See also* lawmen
Sheriff's Streak of Yellow, The (1915; Hart), 28
Sherin, Edwin, 226
Sherman, George, 110, 111, 184
She Wore a Yellow Ribbon (1949; Ford), 82–83, 204, 233; *20–21, 83, 84, 126*
Shiloh, Battle of, 56
Shoot First, Laugh Last (1967; Lewis), 229
Shootist, The (1976; Siegel), 205, 235, 242–43; *243, 261*
Shoshone Indians, 182; *181, 184*
Siegel, Don, 103, 186, 243; *260*
silent films, 24–37, 108, 177
Silva, Henry, 122; *123*
Silver, 34
Silverado (1985; Kasdan), 59, 164–66, 260; *2–3, 165*

Silver King, 33, 144
Silverstein, Elliot, 198, 215
Simmons, Jean, 75, 214; *75*
Simpson, Russell, *51*
Sinatra, Frank, 157
Sinclair, Andrew, *51*
Siodmak, Robert, 140–41
Sioux Indian Ghost Dance (Edison), 15
Sioux Indians, 177, 180, 184, 185–86, 198; *184, 185, 186, 198*
Sirk, Douglas, 184, 214
Sitting Bull, 24, 138, 140, 184
Sitting Bull (1954; Salkow), 184
Skala, Lilia, *204*
Slade, Jack, 150
Sloane, Paul H., 180
Smith, Charlie Martin, 158
Smith, Clifford, 29
Smith, Joseph, 48; *49*
Smith, Steven Philip, 147
Smithee, Allen (Robert Totten and Don Seigel), 103
Snake Pit, The (1948; Litvak), 180
Soldier Blue (1970; Nelson), 197
Sollima, Sergio, 229
songs, 34, 54, 56, 84, 100, 124, 154
Son of the Morning Star (Connell), 140
"spaghetti" Westerns. *See* Italian Westerns
Spaulding, Eliza, 201
Spencer, Bud. *See* Pedersoli, Carlo
Spencer, Dorothy, 95
Spikes Gang, The (1974; Fleischer), 158
Spoilers, The (1914; Campbell), 27; (novel; Beach), 27
Spoilers of the West (1927; Van Dyke), 34
Squaw Man, The (1914; DeMille, Apfel), 27
Stagecoach (1939; Ford), 37, 48, 61–62, 97–98, 193, 233; *62, 63, 64–65*; (1966; Douglas), 62
stagecoaches, 61–62
Stallings, Laurence, 82
Stamp, Terence, 174
Standing, Jack, 29
Stanwyck, Barbara, 65, 73, 140, 206, 209–12; *73, 209, 210, 211*
Starr, Belle, 150; *150*
Starr, Ronald, 239
Steiger, Rod, 219
Sternberg, Josef von, 72
Stevens, George, 129, 260; *129, 130*
Stevens, Leslie, 173
Stevens, Stella, 254; *254*
Stewart, Elinore, *204*
Stewart, James, 54, 56, 92, 103, 113, 121–22, 134, 181, 182–84, 192, 205, 207, 221, 238, 242; *54, 105, 121, 122, 134, 180, 183, 188, 200, 218, 219, 237*
Stone, N. B., Jr., 240
Stout, Archie, 81
Straight Shootin' (1927; Wyler), 37
Straight Shooting (1917; Ford), 35
Strange Lady in Town (1955; LeRoy), 214; *215*
Strode, Woody, 226, 240; *226*
Sturges, John, 87, 95–97, 101, 155; *157*
Sullivan, Barry, 209; *210*
Sundance Kid (Harry Longabaugh), 150–55, 209; *151, 153, 210*
Support Your Local Gunfighter (1971; Kennedy), 164
Support Your Local Sheriff (1969; Kennedy), 164
surrogate father-son relationships, 166–74
Surtees, Bruce, 243
Sutherland, Kiefer, 174
Sutter, John Augustus, 59
Swarthout, Miles Hood, 242
Sweet, Blanche, 27
Swerling, Jo, 105

T

Take Me to Town (1953; Sirk), 214–15
Tall T, The (1957; Boetticher), 135–36; *135*
Taming of the West, The (1925; Rosson), 34
Tarzan, 34
Taylor, Joan, 185; *186*
Taylor, Robert, 98, 170, 182, 214; *170, 171, 181, 212*
Taza, Son of Cochise (1954; Sirk), 184
Technicolor process, 40, 83, 97, 145
Tehuan Indians, 178
telegraph, 61
Tell Them Willie Boy Is Here (1969; Polonsky), 193–95, 206; *193, 194*
Temple, Shirley, 81
Terror of Tiny Town (1938; Newfield), 223
They Died with Their Boots On (1941; Walsh), 140, 180, 203–4; *141*
They Live by Night (1948; Ray), 147
Thompson, J. Lee, 138
Thomson, Fred, 33, 144
Thorpe, Richard, 37
Threatt, Elizabeth, 43
Three Bad Men (1926; Ford), 37
Three Godfathers (1936; Boleslawski), *110*; (1948; Ford), 35, 111, 157, 203; *110*
Three Hours to Kill (1954; Werker), 121
3:10 to Yuma (1957; Daves), 101; *102*
Thundercloud, Chief, 180; *179*
Thundering Hoofs (1924; Rogell), 33
Thunder Riders (1927; Wyler), 37
Tierney, Gene, 145, 150; *150*
Tin Star, The (1957; Mann), 166, 167–68; *168*
Tiomkin, Dimitri, 72, 100
Toland, Gregg, 106; *106*
Toll Gate, The (1920; Hillyer), 30
Tomahawk (1951; Sherman), 184
Tombstone, Arizona, 92; *92, 93*
Tonka (1958; Foster), 140
Tony the Wonder Horse, 31; *33, 34*
Torn, Rip, 203; *204*
Toth. *See* de Toth
Totten, Robert, 103
Towers, Constance, 87; *88, 226*
Track of the Cat (1954; Wellman), 221
Tracy, Spencer, 40, 55, 73–75, 203; *38, 40, 74*
transcontinental railroad, 37. *See also* railroad building
Trevor, Claire, 62, 98, 207; *62*
Triangle Company, 28, 29
Triumphs of a Man Called Horse (1983; Hough), 198
Troell, Jan, 203; *203*
Trosper, Guy, 127
Trotti, Lamar, 48, 224
True Grit (1969; Hathaway), 113; *14, 112, 113, 114*; (novel; Portis), 113
True Story of Jesse James, The (1957; Ray), 147; *146*
Trumbo, Dalton, 247
Tumbleweeds (1925; Baggot), 23, 30, 48; *22, 31*
Tumbling Tumbleweeds (1935; Kane), 120
Tunstall, John H., 169–70, 173, 174
Turner, Lana, 204; *205*
Twain, Mark (Samuel L. Clemens), 24
20th Century–Fox, 31, 145, 154, 223; *92*
Two Flags West (1950; Wise), 87, 89
Two Rode Together (1961; Ford), 78, 186, 188; *188*

U

Ullmann, Liv, 203; *203*
Ulzana's Raid (1972; Aldrich), 198–99; *199*
Unconquered (1947; DeMille), 180

Unforgiven, The (1960; Huston), 77–78, 186–88; *78*
Union Pacific (1939; DeMille), 65–68, 206; *66–67*
Union Pacific Railroad, 37, 65, 68; *65, 259*
United Artists, 30
United States Cavalry, 78–87
Universal, 37, 148
Untamed, The (1920; Flynn), *32*

V

Valdez Is Coming (1971; Sherin), 226
Valerii, Tonino, 229
Van Cleef, Lee, 229; *123, 229, 237*
Van Fleet, Jo, *212*
Vanishing American, The (1925; Seitz), 178–79; *176*
Vanzi, Luigi (Vance Lewis), 229
Vidal, Gore, 173
Vidor, Charles, 110
Vidor, King, 39, 71, 170, 218; *38, 40, 70, 169*
Vietnam War, 174, 195, 197
Violent Men, The (1955; Maté), 209
Virginian, The (1914; DeMille), 27; (novel; Wister), 24, 27
Volonte, Gian Maria, 229

W

Wagner, Robert, 73, 147; *146*
Wagonmaster (1950; Ford), 30, 43, 50–54, 221; *51*
Wagon Tracks (1919; Hart), 178
wagon trains, 35–37, 39, 45–56; *35, 47, 51*
Waite, Ric, 147
Walken, Christopher, 258
Walker, Robert, 169
Wallace, Lew, 170, 214
Wallach, Eli, 229; *244*
Walsh, Raoul, 47, 109, 111–12, 140, 203, 214; *46, 141*
Wanderer, The (c. 1912; Griffith), 27
Warlock (1959; Dmytryk), 102; *103*
Warner, David, 254; *254*
War Paint (1926; Van Dyke), 34
Warpath (1951; Haskin), 140
Warren, Charles Marquis, 184
Washington, Ned, 100
Waterhole No. 3 (1967; Graham), 164
Waterston, Sam, 258
Wayne, John, 21, 43, 48, 59, 62, 69, 70, 79, 82, 83, 87, 91, 98, 100, 111, 113, 118, 120, 123, 124–25, 128, 159, 162, 163, 166, 169, 204, 205, 235, 238, 242, 243; *2–3, 8, 46, 62, 63, 68, 79, 82, 83, 84, 85, 86, 88, 112, 113, 114, 119, 124, 125, 126, 128, 159, 162, 163, 237, 243, 260, 261*
Weaver, Dennis, 226
Webb, James R., 55–56, 186, 192, 223
Welcome to Hard Times (1967; Kennedy), 103
Welles, Halsted, 101; *102*
Welles, Orson, 72
"We'll Gather at the River," 124
Wellman, William, 37, 41, 111, 139, 140, 214, 221, 224; *21, 111, 212, 225*
Wells, Henry, 60
Wells Fargo, 60
Wells Fargo (1937; Lloyd), 60; *60*
Werker, Alfred, 100, 121
West, Jessamyn, 75
West, Mae, 206; *206*
Westcott, Nebraska, 258
Westerner, The (1940; Wyler), 105–6, 107; *105, 106*

Western heroes, 128–31; aging and decline of, 235, 239–42; code of behavior of, 62; Indians as, 184–86
Western Union (1941; Lang), 61, 145, 180; *58*
Westward the Women (1952; Wellman), 214; *212*
When the Daltons Rode (1940; Marshall), 148
White Buffalo, The (1977; Thompson), 138
Whitehead, O. Z., 239
White Oak (1921; Hart), 178; *30*
Widmark, Richard, 75, 89, 102, 111, 192; *103, 188, 190*
Wild Bill Hickok (1923; Smith), 137
Wild Bill Hickok Rides (1941; Enright), 138
Wild Bunch, The (1969; Peckinpah), 143, 147, 155–57, 158, 163, 239, 255; *89, 154, 155, 156*
Wilde. *See* de Wilde
Wilder, Gene, 164; *164*
Wilder, Robert, 223
Wild Rovers (1971; Edwards), 158; *160–61*
Wild West shows, 24, 27, 34, 138–39; *27, 138, 139, 140*
Willamette Valley, Oregon, 39
Williams, Clara, *29*
Williams, Elmo, 100
Willingham, Calder, 127, 196
Will Penny (1968; Gries), 174, 240, 255; *242*

Wilson, Lois, 178
Winchester '73 (1950; Mann), 121; *121*
Wind, The (1928; Seastrom), 202
Winners of the Wilderness (1926; Van Dyke), 34
Winning of Barbara Worth, The (1926; King), 37
Winninger, Charles, 97
Winters, Shelley, 207
Wise, Robert, 87
Wiseman, Joseph, 78
Wister, Owen, 24, 27
Wittliff, William D., 116
Wolf Lowry (1916; Hart), 28
women, 16, 21, 70, 201–21
Wonderful Country, The (1959; Parrish), 128
Wood, Natalie, 123; *125*
Woodward, Joanne, 215; *215, 216*
Wurlitzer, Rudolph, 174
Wyatt Earp, Frontier Marshal (Lake), 92
Wyler, William, 37, 75, 223; *75, 77*

Y

Yellow Sky (1948; Wellman), 111, 206; *111*

Yojimbo (1961; Kurosawa), 227
Yordan, Philip, 121
Young, Brigham, 48; *49, 51*
Young, Carleton, 238
Young, Loretta, 178, 214, 219; *214, 220*
Young, Robert, 61
Young Billy Young (1969; Kennedy), 169
Young Deer, James, 177
Younger brothers, 147, 148; *149*
Younger Brothers (1949; Marin), 148
Young Guns (1988; Cain), 174
Young Guns II (1990; Murphy), 174
Young Strangers, The (1957; Frankenheimer), 147
You Only Live Once (1937; Lang), 61, 145
Yulin, Harris, 97
Yurka, Blanche, 73

Z

Zandy's Bride (1974; Troell), 203; *203*
Zinnemann, Fred, 98
Zsigmond, Vilmos, 254, 255; *253, 257*
Z. T. Ranch (Wyoming), *74*

Credits